On Your Feet
Magistrates' Court

First published in 2012 by CrimeLine Training Limited
Registered office: 1st and 2nd Floor, 7–9 Mesnes St, Wigan WN1 1QP
Tel: 01942 40 52 61
Email: admin@crimeline.info

Website: http://www.crimeline.info

For further information on our products please visit:
www.crimeline.info
© Rossano Scamardella and Kirsty Craghill
Authors have asserted their right under the Copyright, Designs and
Patents Act 1988, to be identified as the authors of this work.

Crown copyright material is reproduced with the permission of the
Controller of HMSO and the Queen's Printer for Scotland

All rights reserved.
ISBN 978-1-4716-6510-3
Typeset by Hope Services, Abingdon

Contents

CHAPTER 5: ADVISING ON THE EVIDENCE. 33

CHAPTER 6: THE CASE MANAGEMENT FORM – SUMMARY TRIAL. 47

CHAPTER 7: ADVISING AND TAKING INSTRUCTIONS FOR SENTENCE 51

Foreword

As a young graduate trainee court clerk in the late 1970's studying for my Bar Finals I was blessed with the opportunity of sitting in court on an almost daily basis alongside a Clerk to the Justices endowed with a wealth of experience gained at the Criminal Bar. That as well as an encyclopaedic knowledge of law and procedure he understood precisely how magistrates, judges, and those who worked with them and appeared before them functioned was my good fortune, for there was then no text the like of "On your feet".

In those days young lawyers enjoyed the benefit (although it was not always appreciated as such) of sitting in court for hours on end waiting for their cases to be called, all the time witnessing the advocacy skills of those more senior to them whose cases would be called on first. For those who watched and listened attentively what they learned during that waiting time, paid for by the public purse in those halcyon days, would stand them, like me, in good stead in future years. For before they took the plunge they saw what to do, what not to do, and they became familiar with the idiosyncrasies of particular tribunals. Not so nowadays when the newly qualified may find themselves at the top of the list, having to dive in unaided and be prepared to sink or swim.

That Kirsty Craghill and Rossano Scamardella did not sink is a testament to their skill and ability. I had the pleasure of witnessing their early days on their feet appearing as they did in front of me in the Brighton Magistrates' Court. They very quickly learned that "preparation is the key", they always dressed appropriately, arrived in good time, established a professional relationship with the client they had never previously set eyes on and above all they got to know the usher; for, as they observe "if you make friends with the usher then he can make your life in the Magistrates' Court so much easier for the entirety of your career".

Whilst the newly qualified lawyer may not enjoy today some of the benefits of my bygone era, Kirsty and Rossano rightly point out that "in this age of smartphones and iPads" advocates can have almost instant access to all the legal information they require. But the law has never provided all the answers. "On your feet" though does just that; it deals with all the questions the young advocate may be "too embarrassed to ask". I commend this small volume as essential reading for the newly qualified advocate; there are others too who might learn much from its comprehensive content.

District Judge (Magistrates' Court) Anne Arnold

Preface

As a criminal defence lawyer you are guaranteed to experience a wide range of emotions. Excitement and elation, dread and utter disappointment are just a few that may be career-long companions. However, in the early days the overriding emotion will be fear. Fear that is usually irrational and easily banished if only you knew the answer to that obvious question: this is where the idea behind 'On Your Feet' comes in.

The mainstream texts deal so well with statutes, case-law, sentencing and procedure such that there is nothing left to be said. However, there is a gap within those texts that it is hoped this book will fill. If like me, your first experience of a Magistrates' Court is the first time you will appear as a lawyer in it, you will have no idea where to stand, when to sit, who everyone is and how to address them, let alone how to advise and represent someone.

The first few months at court will probably leave you with one overriding feeling: everybody knows more than me. As a result you will feel reluctant; probably unwilling to ask any question that exposes your inexperience. 'On Your Feet' will answer those questions for you and will help you prepare a bail application, prepare a plea in mitigation, know when to submit a written basis of plea or manage the minefield that is the criminal procedure rules.

For most of us, representing people in the early days in the Magistrates' Court was trial and error, lots of errors and usually caused by a combination of anxiety and bewilderment. I am so pleased to have co-written this book that will help you enjoy (from a much earlier stage than I did) this rewarding and exciting profession.

I would like to thank the following people for making this book possible: my co-author Rossano Scamardella for coming up with the great idea in the first place; Andrew Keogh for having faith in the concept, for his ongoing advice, editorial support and for agreeing to publish it; Claire Mullarkey (Deputy Justices' Clerk – Sussex Central) for her invaluable advice on Magistrates' Court procedure; my business partner Teresa Mulrooney for giving me the time to write; Emma Wilson for her patience and assistance in proof reading.

The law and procedure stated is accurate as at the time of writing 2nd April 2012.

This book is dedicated to Ava and Enzo Scamardella and to Margaret Smart.

Kirsty Craghill
April 2012

Introduction

'Nothing in life is to be feared, it is only to be understood. Now is the time to understand more so that we may fear less'
                                      Marie Curie 1867–1934

Let me set the scene: February, 1999, Horsham Magistrates' Court. It was my second ever court appearance and at this rather quiet Sussex Court, I had been instructed to represent a man on his first appearance for a variety of offences of dishonesty. The court was relatively full of defence solicitors and barristers, a probation officer, a member of the press, court staff and the odd vaguely interested member of the public.

I was convinced that the hearing would be straightforward and I was also sure that my client, having seen me in all my glory, would contact my instructing solicitors and request that I conduct his trial in a few months' time.

I had been told by members of Chambers that at these first hearings, the prosecution would supply to the defence the advance information, which consisted of the witness statements, summary of the defendant's interview and a list of his previous convictions and then the Crown would not object when defence counsel asked for an adjournment of seven or fourteen days to consider the twelve pages of material that had just been disclosed. The justices would grant the adjournment and the court would convene at a later date when the defendant had been advised.

As simple as this process sounds I was still terrified. Nothing can properly prepare you for the cold fear you feel in those early days and I was no different. However, this particular hearing couldn't be any simpler and maybe I would not have to say a single word and the clerk and the friendly-looking justices would conduct the hearing as if I was not there.

So when the Clerk to the Horsham Justices looked at me and said:

'Can we deal with 'plea before venue', Mr Scamardella?'

I froze. This was not part of the script. I had absolutely no idea what the words meant on their own, let alone when put together as a question. I had not a clue what she was talking about. I got up slowly, stalling for time, desperately trying to think of what to say to give everyone the impression that I had expected this question. In the end I said something like:

'Well, to put my client in this terrible position is grossly unfair. For the court to adopt this course of action against such a young man is unusual to say the least. However, I can sense that the court's mind is made up and any submissions I may make will be futile. In those circumstances, I will not make any formal objection to this proposal, perhaps the less said about this regrettable suggestion the better.'

I sat down shaking my head, looking at the reporter of the Mid-Sussex Times as if the court was about to preside over one of history's worst injustices.

I genuinely did not know what was about to happen and I sat down and opened up my notebook and began writing in it. There was nothing for me to write and I wrote nothing of any consequence but it helped to hide my shame and I prayed that I had not just allowed something awful to happen to my client. When the Clerk, sensing that I was struggling, in fact recommended to the justices that we adjourn 'plea before venue' to another date, I felt an immeasurable sense of relief.

In suggesting the adjournment the Clerk of the court had told the justices that it was to allow the defence time to consider the advanced information. I have always felt deep down that this very kind clerk, (who I saw from time to time over the next few years, which never failed to make me run for cover) was just ensuring that when the defendant did have to deal with 'plea before venue', whatever that was, he did so represented by a more experienced lawyer or himself or, in fact, anyone but me.

Looking back it is hard to believe that I had no comprehension of what she was talking about, but I truly did not. Absolutely none. I have never forgotten this example and to this day, after thirteen interesting years, it still provides the best reason for writing this series of books.

My first hearing in the Crown Court had been little more successful. I had been instructed to apply to break a fixture in front of the resident judge at Lewes Crown Court, HHJ Brown. To have your first appearance in a Crown Court was frightening but to have it in front of such a glamorous audience was almost unbearable. HHJ Brown's murder trial awaited the conclusion of my feeble application and the three silks, (Rebecca Poulet QC, Rock Tansey QC and Camden Pratt QC, all of whom I am sure still remember the day like it was yesterday) in that case sat in silk's row waiting to begin. They muttered, shuffled, laughed and sneered, none of which related to me I am sure, but that is not how it felt at the time. The application was hopeless, as was I and I returned to Chambers feeling glad it was over but decidedly worried.

I was worried with good reason. I had felt ready to get started at the end of my 'first six' and nothing had prepared me for the things that would make me feel so out of my depth. I had anticipated struggling at times with the law, being told off by judges and magistrates, being sacked by unreasonable clients and heaven forbid, even losing trials, but I had not been worried about how to do the job itself.

I had seen enough cases to know my way around a brief and had been emboldened by that limited but priceless experience. Having had a chance to see cases from a more informed position than the public gallery made me feel ready. In reality I knew nothing; nothing about procedure, etiquette, protocol and the administration of justice and only being exposed to the coal-face highlighted this to me.

I am not sure anything can be done to make you feel completely at ease but I have always felt that some sort of basic guide to get you through the terrifying early weeks and months would be invaluable. Not a guide to the law or sentencing guidelines but a guide that tells you how to do it. Anyone who has been in this position will know precisely what I mean.

It is all very well telling pupils and newly qualified solicitors to look at Archbold, Blackstone's or Banks on Sentence but they can be equally frightening in their own way. With respect to the authors and editors of those very important books, they do not tell you how to deal with that very difficult client on a Saturday morning who has the most appalling record for violence and yet still wants you to apply for bail back to the same address he is said to have beaten someone half to death at or how to actually make your bail application for him.

This series of books, like any other, will not be able to cover every scenario but we hope to be able to deal with as many of the obvious and blindingly obvious situations, that we have all faced and not known how to cope with. It is not always possible or appropriate to speak to the friendly but unemployed senior tenant in Chambers, nor is it always possible to ring your professional body for advice. Sometimes you need to know what to do and you need to know immediately and we hope that these books can provide some help and relief when you feel, as we all have done, like you are drowning.

Being 'on your feet', whether that is in a police station, Magistrates' Court or Crown Court, can provide for moments of drama, exhilaration, surprise and enjoyment but in those early days, feelings of fear and trepidation are far more likely companions. Whilst those fears are natural they can be debilitating and the sooner they are banished the better.

Rossano Scamardella
April 2012

CHAPTER 1
THE BASICS – 3 PRINCIPLES

Being punctual is absolutely essential. The old adage that you should aim to get the train before the train you need to get remains sound advice. To be early to court is to give yourself as much control over the situation as possible and in those first few weeks and months anything that helps you to feel in control is crucial to your survival. To be able to speak to the defendant, the court staff, the prosecutor, the defendant's family, probation etc without fearing that you are likely to be rushed into court is the best way to allay your fears about the hearing.

There is no excuse for being late or rushed and planning your journey to court should be one of the first things that you do. Clients and client's families do not want to see their lawyer rushing up the court steps three minutes before the hearing is about to begin, files and papers all over the place, talking on their mobile phone seemingly unbothered about, what to the client, maybe the most important day of his life.

The importance of these first impressions to your client and his family cannot be overstated. You are the person that he is trusting to represent him in what maybe a life-changing day at court. The least you can do is be at court on-time. To help with this take some time the night before to find out where the court is, whether there is any car parking or how far it is from the train station. All this may seem inconsequential and boring but they are anything but.

You should always dress appropriately. A court is a solemn and serious place to be and there is a dress code that applies and that dress code should be complied with – each and every time you appear at court. Dressing 'down' for a quick mention or pre-trial review is not acceptable. Not only are you obliged to dress in a certain way, your client, quite rightly, has certain expectations about how you should look and dress. Novelty ties, flowery patterned skirts, training shoes and brown suits are sadly, real examples of what I have seen in visits to the Magistrates' Court just in the time whilst researching for this book. Do not do it. You will look ridiculous, it is completely unprofessional and your client will notice. The time for novelty ties is? There is in fact no time for novelty ties.

Clients, court staff, magistrates and judges, notice when an advocate is dressed properly but are even more likely to notice when one is not. However, District judges and magistrates should be doing more to ensure that dress codes are complied with, as some of what is worn by advocates at the lower courts is an embarrassment to the profession. Do not let the acquiescence of the court staff and the magistrates' mean that you lower your standards. Dress properly from your first day in court as you will then never get out of the habit and remember that you can expect to be told off in the higher courts if you adopt such sloppy standards. When I recently asked a Crown Advocate at court why he was wearing grey and white training shoes, he said 'well, it is not as if they can see my feet is it?' In which case you might as well wear roller boots.

Being prepared is also a very easy way to make you feel better about the day ahead. It is a very reassuring feeling to know that no matter what you are asked about the facts and circumstances of the case, you will know the answer. Magistrates, prosecutors, clients and their families can at times ask difficult questions to which you should know the answer (the defendant's date of birth was a regular question that a certain stipendiary magistrate used to ask, catching nine out of ten people out), if you have read the case thoroughly and prepared yourself properly for the hearing, your confidence soars.

Not knowing the papers does nothing for your performance in court or ability to deal with the defendant, who will want to discuss the finer points of the case even if the matter is listed for mention or a pre-trial review. Clients can be very perceptive, especially those entrenched in the system and they will have no trouble working out when their lawyer is not prepared.

In addition to the facts and the circumstances of the case, you must familiarise yourself with the relevant law and sentencing guidelines (even if the case is only listed for plea trial review). Clients will bombard you with questions, usually focusing on whether the crown can prove the case against them and if they are convicted what the likely sentence will be. Even if you do not have the relevant books to hand, in this age of smartphones and ipads, the relevant information is easily obtainable, even if only on the way to court on the train or in the advocates room before you meet the client. Not knowing the answers to these basic questions will undermine the defendant's confidence in you, sometimes to such an extent that you can never recover it. Remember, first impressions.

Being punctual, presentable and prepared helps in three very important ways; firstly, your client and his family and friends will be reassured, secondly, your opponent(s) and the magistrates will very quickly realise that you are no fool and thirdly, and perhaps in the context of this book most importantly, your confidence will grow.

Once you are in the habit of dressing properly, getting the early train and reading your papers the night before, to do anything else will seem wrong. There will be times when through no fault of your own you are late or you have to conduct a hearing without papers or preparation and providing your standards in this regard are usually high, nobody will hold it against you.

At this stage of your career it is often about calming your nerves and not letting the fear paralyse your performance, to follow these simple steps will not eradicate the fear altogether but it will go some way to ensuring that even if it doesn't feel like it, you are doing a pretty good job.

CHAPTER 2
INITIAL STEPS ON ARRIVAL AT COURT

Some of these things will sound self-explanatory but it is amazing how quickly the fundamentals can be forgotten. The first thing you should do without fail is to find your case on the court list. This will tell you what time your case is listed and which courtroom it is in. If you cannot find the list, do not be afraid to ask. Once you have found your case on the list the next thing to do is to locate the actual court room. Remember with clients, first impressions really do count and if you do not know something as basic as where the court room is it will make you look inexperienced and undermine your client's confidence in you.

Once you have found your court room the next step is to find the court usher and sign in with him. Do not under estimate the court usher, if you upset a court usher you are very likely to find your case at the bottom of the list. One of the biggest mistakes advocates make is to be rude to the usher or to mislead him about how long their case is going to take in an attempt to get their case on quicker. For obvious reasons they do not like this and it will do you or your client, no favours. Conversely if you make friends with the usher then he can make your life in the Magistrates' Court so much easier. You should also ask the usher whether your client has checked in yet. If you do not know your client, ask the usher to point him out to you. This can be a good way of identifying him without making it obvious that you have no idea who he is.

The usher will also be able to tell you where the advocates' room is within the court building and tell you the door security code, as with any consultation rooms. These basics are important as they give you the air of confidence and put you in control of the situation. It is also gives the client the impression that you have been to the court many times when in truth it could be your first ever time in court.

ADVANCE INFORMATION
(INITIAL DETAILS OF THE PROSECUTION CASE)

Advanced information usually contains: the charge sheet, some of the prosecution witness statements, your client's previous convictions and a summary of the interview.

If you do not know where to get the advance information from, ask the court usher. It can vary from court to court. Sometimes it is in court with the prosecutor, sometimes with security. It is crucial that you obtain your advanced information as early as possible so that you give yourself plenty of time to read it. The more time you allow yourself to prepare the more confidence you will have and appear to your client to have.

PREPARING FOR YOUR FIRST MEETING WITH THE CLIENT

If possible find somewhere quiet where you can read through the papers. Your client will expect you to know what the evidence is and will expect you to have a firm view about the strength of it. This is very important.

The four main things a client will want to know in that initial meeting are:

1) What have I been charged with?
2) Can they prove it?
3) What sentence will I receive?
4) Will I be going home today?

You need to have your mind addressed to these key issues throughout your preparation.

Crucially, if you are not familiar with the charge, look it up.

Then:

- Check what the elements of the offence/s are
- What the available defences are
- Whether it is a summary only, either way or indictable only offence
- Whether it is a specified offence (i.e. dangerousness)
- What the maximum sentence is for that offence
- What ancillary orders are possible; for example – a football banning order

Next, you need to consider:

THE INTERVIEW SUMMARY

Read this with caution. Often the summary will say for example that the defendant admits assaulting the victim but may sometimes omit to say that the defendant said that he did this in self defence. Remind yourself to check with your client what he said in interview and if at all possible, check it with the solicitor or representative who attended at the police station.

YOUR CLIENT'S PREVIOUS CONVICTIONS

Do not forget to look at these and consider:

- If they have no previous convictions or cautions or have not had any for many years *and* admitted the offence in interview whether a caution or a community resolution could be available as an alternative disposal
- What convictions/cautions they have, specifically any relevant previous convictions and the facts of any relevant previous if available
- Their compliance with previous court orders; i.e. previous breaches of community orders or conditional discharge.
- Whether a guilty plea will put them in breach of a conditional discharge or a suspended sentence order. If so, do not to forget to advise your client about this or forget to prepare for re-sentence for the original offences, if relevant.
- Whether they are subject to any period of unexpired license
- What if any history they have of committing offences whilst on bail
- Whether this offence was committed whilst on bail for another offence.
- Whether your client is likely to fall within the dangerousness provisions.
- Whether a guilty plea in this case by virtue of their relevant previous convictions would make an either way offence indictable only; i.e. three strikes for domestic burglary or specified drug offences *or* put them in a minimum sentence category.

CONSIDERING BAIL

One of the first questions your client will have is 'will I get bail?' This will be an obvious consideration for you if your client has been remanded by the police, and you are attending him in the cells, less obvious is the situation where the client appears on bail but is at risk of being remanded. In my early days I had a client who had been on police bail for months for a rape, had answered police bail on four separate occasions and had attended court as bailed. Embarrassingly at no point had I considered the risk of remand at the first hearing. During that first hearing the District Judge told me she was considering remanding him in custody and asked me to address her on bail, a question I had not even considered. Fortunately the client got bail but it is a lesson I will never forget. Do not make this mistake, particularly if it is a serious offence you must always consider the question of bail.

Make sure you establish what conditions of bail if any the client is already subject to. The bail sheet is usually contained within advanced information but if not you can check this either by contacting the person who attended the police station or by remembering to raise it with the prosecutor. If you do not know the bail position it makes you look unprepared in front of the client and if you still do not know it by the time you get into court, in some cases incompetent.

The important things to keep in your mind at this point when considering bail are:

- The strength of the evidence
- The seriousness of the offence and likely sentence
- Your clients' previous convictions in terms of the likelihood of the commission of further offences, particularly their history or not of committing offences whilst on bail
- Your clients' previous history of failing to answer bail if applicable

These are all the things you will need to consider when advising your client on the prospects of success of any bail application or an application to vary any existing bail conditions.

Finally, familiarise yourself with the relevant provisions of the Bail Act so that you are able to advise the defendant authoritatively.

SENTENCE GUIDELINES

Make sure you have an up-to-date copy of the relevant guidelines with you and that you have not only read them but have worked out in your mind where in the guidelines your clients' specific case falls. If you have forgotten them, get a copy. Look them up on your smart-phone, get your office or chambers to fax you a copy, ask to borrow the legal advisers copy or a fellow lawyers. Do not be too proud to ask for a copy, they are so important to the advice you will give that to not have considered them could cause real embarrassment in court.

Most common offences are now covered by the guidelines and your client will want to know what sentence he is likely to receive down to the day and in court when mitigating, the magistrates will expect you to refer to them. One of the best ways to help with your understandable nerves is to be prepared. Conversely nothing will make you feel more anxious than knowing that you have not got all the information you need to hand.

SPEAK TO THE PROSECUTOR

Do not leave this until the last minute, as the chances are you may miss your opportunity before the court session starts and will then have to wait until the magistrates retire before you have the opportunity. Often a District Judge will rarely leave court and then you are stuck. This will hinder your preparation and on a practical level may mean that you fall to the bottom of the court list because you are not ready. This wastes your time and the client's who will want to leave court as soon as possible. Most cases in the Magistrates' Court are paid by way of a fixed fee and therefore your instructing solicitor, senior partner or clerks will also want you in and out as quickly as you can so you can move onto the next billable matter.

Do not be intimidated by the prosecutor or their at times apparent lofty attitude. Many of them have been doing the job for years or are just pressured by the volume of their case load for the day and their lack of preparation time. Often they can be short with you but try not to take this personally.

Be sensitive to them and your fellow lawyers. If there is a queue of people waiting to speak to the prosecutor you will make no friends by pushing in. If it is clear the prosecutor is in the middle of speaking to someone else or doing something, wait your turn. There is no need at this stage to be overly adversarial with the prosecutor. You are unlikely to achieve favourable results for your client if your opening stance is confrontational. Remember, it is highly likely that at that court you will deal with the same prosecutors on a regular basis, do not fall out with them. You can be firm, even tough but do so courteously, sensibly and realistically throughout.

Things you may need to raise with the prosecutor at this stage are:

- What is their view on bail?
- If they seeking a remand, why and on what grounds?
- Whether you can agree bail conditions?
- Whether you can agree a variation of bail conditions?
- Whether they will consider an adjournment say for example, for you to make representations that your client should instead be cautioned?
- Whether they say the matter is suitable for summary trial?
- Whether in principle any deal can be done in terms of acceptable pleas/ basis of plea?
- Whether they agree with where you place your clients case in the sentence guidelines?
- Whether they will be seeking any ancillary orders on conviction?

Not all of these will apply to every case but these are matters that you should have in your mind in your initial discussions with the prosecutor

SPEAK TO PROBATION

It is important to discuss your client's case with probation, regardless of whether he has history with the probation service or not and try to do this before seeing your client.

Those subject to an order

Before the court hearing you should speak to the court liaison probation officer to establish how well your client is progressing on any current order he may be subject to and, whether for example, any breach proceedings are likely. It is amazing how often your client will tell you how brilliantly he is responding and yet when you check with probation you discover he has in fact completed three hours unpaid work in six months. If you forget to check this and then in court mitigate on the basis of your client's exemplary compliance with the existing order, remember that the court will always want to hear from probation and if the reverse is true it not only makes you look daft but it completely undermines your submissions. Do not just take the defendant's word for it. The advantage of doing this before you attend the client is that it enables you to advise more accurately and authoritatively. This will avoid wasting what little time you have by preparing the case on an inaccurate basis.

For all guilty pleas

If your client is likely to plead guilty then speak to the court liaison probation officer before seeing the client to establish whether in their view a pre-sentence report will be required and what type of report, i.e. a verbal/fast delivery report that can be done that day or whether an adjournment will be required for a full pre-sentence report. This enables you to advise the client more accurately and importantly gives your advice that added air of certainty.

In reality the court probation officer may not arrive in time for you to have these conversations prior to attending the client and if that happens do not worry but do ensure you speak to them before the hearing.

SPEAK TO THE LEGAL ADVISER/COURT CLERK

If after all this there is anything legally or procedurally you are not sure of, do not forget to use the legal adviser. Remember; do not be too proud or embarrassed to ask, it is better asked of the legal adviser in advance than to expose your lack of knowledge and experience in front of the client and the court. As long as you are not asking pointless questions or something that you have been too lazy to look up, the legal adviser will not mind helping you. Again, treat the legal adviser with respect. They are qualified lawyers with probably far more experience and knowledge than you at this stage. Making an enemy of the legal adviser is not a good idea as their assistance can be invaluable to you in the early stages, let alone their ability, when it suits them, to have your case called on quickest.

CHAPTER 3
THE FIRST MEETING WITH THE DEFENDANT

It is not possible to overstate the importance of the first meeting with your client. He may have been building up to this day for a long time and one of the matters foremost in his mind will be his representation, and quite rightly so.

It is highly likely that if you are reading this book then the defendant will not be expecting *you* at court to represent him. Most defendants or a member of their family will be expecting the partner of the firm to conduct every hearing and one of the first things you will often have to do is to win people over. If the defendant is expecting someone else then apologise to him, not because you are representing him but because he should have been told that there is a change in his representation. This is not something you should dwell on – you are conducting the hearing and he will have to live with it.

Start by trying to find somewhere private to conduct the conference. Most Magistrates' Courts have rooms but if not, find a quiet spot where the meeting can continue relatively uninterrupted. Formally introduce yourself, explain where you come from (I mean Chambers or firm rather than place of birth) and then a little detail about what will happen at court.

The manner in which you conduct this first meeting is bound to vary from case to case. Your approach to a 17 year old girl of good character charged with causing death by dangerous driving is bound to differ from your approach to a 40 year old football hooligan however, what you need to achieve in that first meeting is precisely the same. At the end of that first meeting your client needs to feel reassured that you are the best person to represent him on that day, it will not always be possible but that should be your aim.

In a serious case that is destined for the Crown Court, that you obviously have no hope of conducting yourself, do not be ashamed to tell your client this. Explain how straightforward the hearing is and that he can expect to meet his trial representation very soon but for the purposes of his first appearance, you are more than capable of representing him.

Some defendants could not care less about your experience and in those situations do not feel that you have to volunteer to him that he has probably been involved in more trials than you. Other clients may take a keener interest and when that situation arises be careful to strike a balance between not underselling yourself and not telling such huge fibs about your experience so as to potentially embarrass yourself and/or the instructing solicitors at a later stage.

Telling a client that you are more than capable of conducting a difficult bail application is one thing, but telling him that you can normally be found at the Old Bailey is a huge mistake. Most chambers and solicitors firms have websites and some clients take a very close look at them and even do so at court. I have experience of a client's father-in-law asking me at court how many cases of a certain type I had conducted and for once I told the whole truth, which was lucky as he used his iPhone to search for me on google, finding my chambers profile and checking that I was not misleading them.

Having got this matter out of the way, you will begin that all-important first conference with your client. Regardless of experience you need to be assertive, defendants and in particular their families have a habit of focusing on issues that are only marginally relevant to the case, which has a tendency to de-rail the meeting. You will be short on time and you need everyone to listen to you as you explain the procedure or the law or the guidelines. A defendant or his father banging on about how he was denied a hot drink at the police station and therefore his human rights have been breached is unhelpful and you need to find a way to shut him or them up by being polite but firm.

You need to identify the matters that need to be discussed for the purpose of that hearing and try to ensure that it is those matters and nothing else that occupies your time. You can always tell the defendant and his family that there will be plenty of time after the hearing to discuss all the very interesting matters that they want to raise.

There will however be times when a client has to be allowed to let off steam. The case may involve a complaint by his neighbour arising from a long running boundary dispute or an allegation by his ex-wife that he has beaten her up and these are the types of topics that will be bound to stir emotions in defendants. As such you must be prepared to listen – not endlessly but for long enough to make him feel that you care. Much of what he says maybe irrelevant or unhelpful but that should not stop you appearing to be interested in, what to him, is the single most important issue in his life. A huge part of representing people is making them feel that you understand and sympathise with their plight, even if it is at times for some of the vilest people in society. So, let him have his say, preferably at the end of the conference after you have dealt with the necessary matters, and you will find his confidence and faith in you soars. Letting someone vent their anger or emotions is not to allow the conference to drift out of control, far from it, it can be a very useful tactic to gain the defendant's trust. However, be sure not to let this to detract from the advice that must be given, letting a client have his say about the injustice of it all is one thing but letting him take over is something else altogether.

If you do control the conference and deal with everything in a professional manner and with clarity and courtesy, the defendant and his family will be encouraged to overlook any reservations they may have had about your inexperience, making this first meeting so vitally important.

Having met your client you must now consider the issue of getting paid and in most cases that will mean applying for legal aid.

CHAPTER 4
APPLYING FOR LEGAL AID

PRELIMINARIES

How to apply for legal aid is one of the most important things that you need to learn, and learn quickly. Without it – unless you are lucky enough to be paid privately – you will not get paid. Applying for legal aid and actually getting it granted are two increasingly different things and it can be a minefield. Often legal aid will have been granted in advance of your first hearing but for the purpose of this book we will assume that it is not yet in place.

This book deals only with Magistrates' Court legal aid applications and for all references to legal aid, please assume that they relate to Magistrates' Court legal aid.

Legal aid for adults is subject to a means and merits (interests of justice, or IOJ) test. Legal aid for youths is subject to the merits test alone.

In some courts the legal aid forms will be available from the court but more usually you will be expected to bring your own. If your client is in custody remember to take the forms to the cells with you as often there will not be any in the cells and you will waste valuable time by having to go back and get them. The forms that you need can be downloaded from the Legal Services Commission website.

Make sure that you know your firms legal aid supplier number (or the supplier number of the firm that you have been instructed by) because you will need to put it on the CDS14.

Under the court duty solicitor scheme if legal aid is applied for but refused, the client may not then be entitled to free representation by the court duty solicitor as the duty solicitor may deem it not in the interests of justice that representation be provided. The question of whether your client is likely to qualify for legal aid is therefore something that you need to consider carefully before submitting the application. If you put in an application that you think it is unlikely to be granted you may not be acting in the client's best interests as the effect of this could be to deprive him of free legal representation at court. If you think the application is borderline then you should advise the client of this and the implications of a legal aid refusal with regards to their right to see the court duty solicitor. Some clients may be happy to proceed with the application on the basis that if you do not ask you do not get and in the event of a refusal, pay you privately or represent themselves.

Magistrates' Court legal aid is not contribution based; i.e. the client does not have to pay towards his legal costs. Either he qualifies for legal aid or he does not. This differs to Crown Court legal aid which is available to everyone regardless of means *but* depending on means, may be contribution based.

If granted, legal aid is effective from the date the (properly completed) application is received by the court. If you are at court for the first hearing make sure that you submit it prior to the hearing. If you submit it after the hearing and it is refused, then you will not get paid for the work you have just done. If there is a problem with the application and the client needs to get further information or for example, take it home so his partner can sign it, ask the legal aid department at court to date stamp it so that when it is eventually granted it will be back-dated to cover the first hearing. If the client is taking the original date stamped copy away with him it is a good idea to take a copy of it for your file so that if he loses it, you can evidence to the court the date the original application was received. This is an example learnt to my cost, I had a client who pleaded guilty at the first hearing and his case was committed to the Crown Court for sentence. His application was date stamped at the first hearing but required further information so he took the original form away with him and promptly lost it. Whilst we were able to submit a fresh application to cover the Crown Court sentence we were unable to back date it to cover the Magistrates' Court proceedings and did not get paid for them.

The legal aid forms should be submitted to the legal aid administrative department at the Magistrates' Court dealing with the case.

Finally make sure that you give an answer to every question on the form, do not ignore an answer or cross through it because it does not apply. If you do, the application will be rejected, for example, if your client is homeless do not just ignore the address section, state that he is of no fixed abode.

CDS14/15/15C

There are three legal aid forms for the purposes of a legal aid application – CDS14, CDS 15 and CDS15C. CDS 14 must be fully completed for every client. CDS15 (and in some cases CDS15C) must be completed for those who:

- Are not 'passported' (see below for explanation), or
- Do not know their national insurance or application registration card (ARC) number or do not have one, or
- Earn a gross income of more than £12,475 (including their partner's income if applicable).

If your client is married or living with his partner then the partner/spouse must also sign the form/s and provide details of their means unless the partner/spouse is the alleged victim, a co-defendant (with a conflict) or a prosecution witness.

If there is a genuine reason that your client's partner is unable to sign the form for example, she is in hospital then you must explain this on the CDS14 on page 10. Generally speaking however legal aid will not be granted unless and until the partner has signed the form.

If your client does not know his national insurance number but can evidence his benefit i.e. by a letter confirming it from the benefits agency, then this will be sufficient for the CDS14 as long as it is a 'passported' benefit.

PASSPORTED APPLICATIONS

Magistrates' Court criminal legal aid is means tested unless the client is:

- Under 18
- In receipt of income support
- In receipt of job seekers allowance
- In receipt of a guaranteed state pension credit
- In receipt of income-related employment and support allowance

Such clients are referred to as 'passported' for the purposes of legal aid and the means assessment does not apply which means your client does not need to complete the CDS15.

SUMMARY OF CDS14

Common errors in completing the form will be highlighted where applicable. Always assume that every question must be answered unless the form specifically refers you to a later section

The applicant's details

- If the client has a national insurance number or ARC number, you must insert this at Q1. If he does not know his national insurance number or ARC number or does not have one and cannot prove his benefit otherwise, he will have to complete CDS15 too.
- If the client is of no fixed abode then this must be stated at Q3, do not just leave it blank.

Partner's details

- If the client has a partner, he must provide details of his partner at Qs 8–12 unless he/she is involved in the case as specified in Q12 in which case you must tick the relevant box.
- If the client's partner is genuinely unable to sign the form, give reasons at page 10.

Income details – client and partner if applicable

- If the client's benefit is not recognised on the court's system, he will have to complete a CDS15 giving full details of his benefit.
- If the client ticks yes to one of the benefits stated in Q14, he will not need to complete the CDS15 unless the court's means check does not recognise his benefit.
- Complete all income questions for both the client and his partner if applicable. If the combined family income does not exceed £12,475 then the client need only complete the CDS14.
- Remember that unless it is a Magistrates' Court case *AND* he is in custody *OR* on a passported benefit, the client will need to provide evidence of his income.

Further income questions and details of charges

- Make sure you list all charges against your client.
- If your client is not on benefits and not in receipt of any income you must complete Q22, tick the 'yes' box and explain how your client is supporting himself.

Co-defendant details

- *Unless* there is a potential conflict, if there are multiple co-defendants in the case for the purposes of legal aid only one solicitor should act for all of them. If there is a potential conflict, you will need to spell it out in order to get a separate representation order.

Reasons for wanting legal aid. The interests of justice (IOJ) criteria

- You must apply at least one of the criteria listed. You may answer and apply more than one to your case.

Details of the applicant's legal representative (including their LSC account number)

- The legal representative must sign the form. If you are the solicitor, tick Q31.1. If you are a barrister instructed by a solicitor's firm, tick Q31.2. In all cases you must insert the firms' LSC account number.
- The gender question must be answered but the client can opt to tick the 'prefer not to say' boxes.

Disability/ethnic monitoring and evidence

- These sections must be answered but the client can tick the 'prefer not to say' box. Do not leave it blank.

Legal declarations for the applicant, their partner (if applicable) and their solicitor

- Do not forget, if the client has a partner, they also need to sign.

SUMMARY OF CDS 15/CDS15C

The CDS15C is basically an overflow form and the client must only complete it if additional financial information is required, see below.

Again, common errors will be highlighted. Every question must be completed unless as a result of the answer given the form directs you to the next section.

Details of the applicant and his partner (if applicable) and employment details

- Unless one of the exceptions applies, if the client is living with his partner then the partner's details must also be completed.

Self-employed/company director/partnership

- If the client or partner has more than one business/directorship etc then details of the additional business etc must be given on the CDS15C page 2.

Other benefits received and other sources of income

- Ensure that each question is answered by ticking the yes or no box. If yes, provide the relevant details.

Details of outgoings and 'other questions'

Details of additional outgoings and property.
- If the client and/or his partner owns more than one property he must complete CDS15C

Property and capital.
- As above

Bank accounts and savings.
- If the client/partner has one or more bank accounts then this section must be completed giving as much detail as possible. If the client does not know the account number or the sort-code, the branch name must be provided along with an approximate balance.
- If the client and/or partner's bank account/savings details exceed the space available on the CDS15 then he must complete CDS15C also with the additional details.

Payment details, legal declarations and evidence checklist.

THE MERITS TEST (INTERESTS OF JUSTICE)

This is the interests of justice test (IOJ). In order to get this part right you should use as much detail as possible. The IOJ is dealt with on the CDS14.

The CDS14 on page 6 contains the following list that you will need to consider and apply specifically to your client's case.

- *It is likely that I will lose my liberty* – Include in this section, the charge, his previous convictions and his response to previous orders and/or quote the relevant sentencing guidelines that demonstrate that your client is at risk of receiving a custodial sentence including any aggravating features. Loss of liberty includes a likelihood of being remanded into custody and disposal by way of a hospital order. If the starting point on the sentence guidelines is not a custodial sentence you will need to demonstrate why your client is at risk.
- *I have been given a sentence that is suspended or non-custodial. If I breach this, the court may be able to deal with me for the original offence* – for example; a breach of suspended sentence order by virtue of this new offence. In order to demonstrate this you should give details of the relevant sentence, the requirements of it and whether either this sentence has been breached before or other similar community orders/conditional discharges have previously been breached.
- *It is likely that I will lose my livelihood* – for example; loss of employment if convicted. If your client is likely to plead guilty you will need to demonstrate how having legal representation could help to avoid losing his job. An example of this would be where your client's employer has indicated that if he receives a community order then he will lose his job but if he receives a conditional discharge or a fine, he will not. You will need to say this on the form and also that a lawyer is required to argue why the magistrates should or could deviate from their guidelines.
- *It is likely that I will suffer serious damage to my reputation* – for example, a man of good character. Another example of serious damage to reputation may arise if the client holds a position of trust within the community. If your client is considering pleading guilty you then it may be that negotiation with a prosecutor is required perhaps in an effort to persuade them to proceed with a lesser charge. This lesser charge may mean less damage to the defendant's reputation underlining the need for a lawyer.
- *A substantial question of law may be involved* – for example; whether the defendant was acting in self-defence. This applies to any likely point of law within the proceedings which your client cannot be expected to deal with unaided. A recent application of mine was initially refused by the legal aid officer where the point of law I had mentioned was 'intention to permanently deprive'. The legal aid officer told me that the client did not

need a lawyer to advise him on that so I asked her what she understood it to mean within the definition of the Theft Act, at which point she quickly changed her mind and granted my application. Do not rely on questions of fact so if your client is simply denying that the alleged offence happened then this section does not apply. If you are aware of any relevant case law or statute then include it in the application.

- *I may not be able to understand court proceedings or present my own case* – for example; the defendant has a mental health condition or requires an interpreter. This also includes age, vulnerability and physical health. If for example, your client required an appropriate adult at the police station, put this on the form. The more complicated the case the more likely you are to succeed on this. If your client's case is likely to be dealt with in one court sitting you may be asked by a more savvy legal aid officer why the duty solicitor cannot assist instead of you. An answer to this could be that now you have submitted your application for a representation order, if it is refused, under the regulations, your client will not be entitled to representation by the duty solicitor.
- *I may need witnesses to be traced or interviewed on my behalf* – this applies to both a not guilty plea and also to witnesses required for mitigation or a basis of plea. You will need to demonstrate why the client is unable to trace them himself.
- *The proceedings may involve expert cross examination of a prosecution witness* – for example; the prosecution rely on the live evidence of 5 police officers or a forensic scientist. Essentially this is arguable where the Crown intends to rely on disputed evidence from a witness whose expertise is over and above that expected of an ordinary witness of fact.
- *It is in the interests of another person that I am represented* – for example; the prosecution witness is known to the defendant or the witness is a child or he has been charged with a sexual or violent offence.
- *Any other reasons* – for example; he intends to plead not guilty. This is a catch-all section and you should put any information here that you have not already put on the form that you think will assist in demonstrating why legal representation is in the interests of justice.

At least one or more of the criteria must apply. If more than one applies, spell it out on the form under the relevant section. The IOJ has become increasingly difficult to satisfy so you can never put too much information on the form about why legal aid should be granted. On a practical note, the legal aid application should be completed in the first person.

Do not assume that the person who is considering your legal aid application will automatically know the law and the relevant guidelines. Legal aid is now granted by non-qualified court administration staff and if there is insufficient detail on the form to persuade them that legal aid is in the IOJ, it will be refused.

THE MEANS TEST

If your client is not passported and earns a gross annual income of more than £12,475 (including the income of his partner if applicable) then he will have to complete form CDS15 to determine whether he is eligible for legal aid.

1 The initial means test:

This takes into account the client's gross annual income and family circumstances for example; how many dependent children they have.

Unless the client is on a basic low level income then working out financial eligibility is complicated and you should use the online eligibility calculator on the Legal Services Commission website to establish if your client is likely to qualify.

In short if the applicant's –

- Adjusted income is £12,475 or less he will pass the initial means test and assuming he has passed the merits test, qualify for free legal aid.
- Adjusted annual income is more than £12,475 but less than £22,325 he may be entitled to free legal aid but will have to be assessed under the full means test
- Adjusted annual income is more than £22,325 he will not qualify for free legal aid in the Magistrates' Court.

Calculating the adjusted income

To work out the adjusted income you need to consider the following:

1. Gross annual income:

Applicant's gross annual income + partner's gross annual income = gross household income.

For example; client's gross annual of income £12,500 + partner's gross annual income of £7,000 = £19,500.

2. Weighting:

The gross annual income is then weighted depending on their family circumstances. If the client is single with no dependent children then the gross annual income remains unchanged. If he has a partner and/or children then the gross annual income is weighted (or in practical terms reduced) depending on the relevant multiplier.

Relevant multiplier –

Applicant	1
Partner	0.64
Child aged 0–1	0.15

Child aged 2–4	0.30
Child aged 5–7	0.34
Child aged 8–10	0.38
Child aged 11–12	0.41
Child aged 13–15	0.44
Child aged 16–18	0.59

The relevant age for the child is the age the child will be at their next birthday from the date of the application. If there is more than one child in the same age category you multiply the weighting per child.

You then need to calculate the total weighting.

For example; your client has a partner and three dependent children aged 2, 7 and 13.

Client	1
Partner	0.64
Child aged 2	0.30
Child aged 7	0.34
Child aged 13	0.44
TOTAL	2.72

3. Calculate the adjusted income:

Gross annual income ÷ weighting = adjusted income.

For example; £19,500 ÷ 2.72 = £7,169.12 and therefore the client passes initial means test and qualifies for legal aid.

If you took the same client's income but this time he is single with no dependent children his application would have to go to the full means test; i.e.. £12,500 ÷ 1 = £12,500.

2 The full means test

The full means assessment calculates the client's disposable income. If your client has a disposable income of under £3,398 then he will qualify for Magistrates' Court legal aid. If he has a disposable income of £3,398 or above, he will not.

Calculating the disposable income

Applicant's gross household income – their allowable outgoings + the weighted annual living allowance = disposable income.

1. Gross household income

Applicant's gross annual income + partner's gross annual income = gross household income.

For example; the client's gross annual income is now £15,000 + partner's gross annual income of £7,000 = £22,000.

2 Allowable outgoings

- Tax and national insurance
- Annual housing costs
- Annual childcare costs
- Annual maintenance to former partner/children

Using again the same client as an example;

Allowable outgoings:

- Tax and national insurance = £2,000
- Annual housing costs = £4,500
- Total allowable outgoings = £6,500

3 Annual living allowance

The annual living allowance if £5,676. This represents a figure that includes the following expenses:

- Food and non-alcoholic drinks
- Clothing and footwear
- Housing (net of mortgage payments, rent and council tax), fuel and power
- Household goods and service
- Health
- Transport
- Communication
- Education (excluding school fees)
- Water rates
- Insurance premiums
- Miscellaneous goods and services

4 Weighted living allowance

This is calculated using exactly the same multipliers as for the initial means test.

Relevant multiplier –

Applicant	1
Partner	0.64
Child aged 0–1	0.15
Child aged 2–4	0.30
Child aged 5–7	0.34
Child aged 8–10	0.38
Child aged 11–12	0.41
Child aged 13–15	0.44
Child aged 16–18	0.59

The relevant age for the child is their age at their next birthday from the date of the application. If there is more than one child in the same age category you multiply the weighting per child.

You then need to calculate the total weighting.

Using the same example as above with the client who has a partner and three dependent children aged 2, 7 and 13, his weighting will be 2.72.

In order to work out the adjusted living allowance you then need to multiply the annual living allowance by the weighted multiplier.

Continuing with the same client example; £5,676 × 2.72 = £15,438.72

5 Calculate the disposable income

Gross income – allowable outgoings – weighted living allowance = disposable income.

Following through with the same client:

Gross income £22,000 – allowable outgoings £6,500 – weighted living allowance £15,438.72 = disposable income of £61.28 = qualifies for legal aid.

COMPLEX MEANS

The following applicants are described as having complex means:

- Those who are self-employed
- Those in a business partnership
- Company directors
- Those in the armed forces
- People subject to a restraint or freezing order.

Procedurally, such applications are still submitted to the Magistrates' Court but are then sent by the court to the LSC's National Courts Team who will then assess the application. If your client has complex means then it is not possible to get an instantaneous decision from the court as to whether it has been granted.

DOCUMENTS REQUIRED IN SUPPORT OF THE CDS15

Original documentary evidence of your client's means is essential. Without it the application will be rejected. If for example your client says he is not in receipt of state benefits but also not working, he will need to provide evidence of how he is supporting himself. If as often happens the client says he is working cash in hand and he puts this on the form, he will need to evidence it. If the client says he is supported by his mum and dad, he will need to provide a letter from his parents to this effect.

Occasionally the completion of a legal aid application will put your representation of the client in jeopardy. For example, if the client has told you for that he is working cash-in-hand but does not want to put this on the form for fear that it will cross-checked with other government agencies i.e. the Inland Revenue, then you must advise him that if he knowingly applies for legal aid without putting full information on the form, he could be guilty of a fraud offence. If he persists in doing so and you know that he is doing so, you should withdraw. If he does not want his means scrutinised then he may be better off not submitting an application for legal aid and either seeing the court duty solicitor, paying you privately or representing himself.

Generally speaking the following original documents are required in support of the application:

- Most recent wage slip (or wage slips if the client has more than one job), this must be dated within the last three months. If the client is unable to provide a wage slip he will need to explain why and instead provide a letter from his employer confirming how much he has earned within the last twelve months.
- Evidence of housing costs if over £500 either by way of a tenancy agreement or mortgage statement.
- Evidence of maintenance costs if over £500.
- Last 3 months bank/building society statements
- Evidence of childcare costs if over £500
- Partner's most recent wage slip
- Partner's last 3 months bank/building society statements

If the client is self-employed then in addition to this he will need to supply:

- Most recent tax return
- Most recent set of accounts

DOCUMENTS REQUIRED FOR CLIENTS IN CUSTODY

Applicants who have been remanded in custody by the Court can self-certify as to their income (for the purposes of Magistrates' Court legal aid) on page 8 of the form and must tick the box at Qs 34–35. If the client is not in receipt of income or benefit then he can still self-certify but must provide a full explanation on the CDS15 as to how he manages to live; i.e. he is supported by his parents. If the client has self-certified you should warn him that the LSC can verify the details given with a third party, most obviously his employer.

If the client has been remanded in custody by the police he cannot self-certify and unless he is subsequently remanded by the court will have to provide evidence of his means exactly as described above before the application is processed. If the client is not passported *and* has been remanded by the police *and* is likely to be further remanded by the court then tactically on this occasion, it is better to submit the application after he has been remanded by the court so that he can self-certify his means. If your client has been remanded by the police and is either likely to get bail by the court *or the* hearing conclude that same day then the decision about whether to represent him for that initial hearing is a difficult one and largely based upon whether you trust that he will provide you with evidence of his means retrospectively. If he provides satisfactory evidence of his means following the hearing then as long as the original application is date stamped for the day of the first hearing, you will be covered for that hearing. If he does not then legal aid will be refused and you will not get paid.

If in doubt, the safest course is to ask the custody duty solicitor to represent the client for that first hearing and for you to submit your application once the client has provided you with the correct evidence of means. In real terms this is something that a lot of solicitors are reluctant to do for fear that they will ultimately lose the client to the duty solicitor. If you are unsure what to do in this situation you should contact your instructing solicitor or the senior partner in the firm to see what they want you to do.

WHAT DO I DO IF MY CLIENT'S LEGAL AID IS REFUSED ON THE MERITS TEST?

If your client is refused on the merits test you can ask for the IOJ test to be reconsidered by a legal adviser. If the legal adviser refuses the application on the IOJ you can then make an oral application directly to the Magistrates.

If the legal aid officer refuses your application on the IOJ it is worth querying it with them in the first instant and sometimes it may just be that you have not put sufficient information on the form. If so, then recomplete the IOJ test on the CDS14 in more detail and re-submit it to him/her.

WHAT HAPPENS IF THE CLIENT IS REFUSED ON THE MEANS TEST?

If the client has failed on the means test you will receive a printout (known as a MAAT printout). You should check this with your client and ensure that there are no errors. If there is an error in the calculation then resubmit it to the legal aid officer and ask for it to be recalculated. If as a result of this legal aid is subsequently granted make sure that the representation order is back-dated to the date the application was originally received by the court.

If your client was initially refused legal aid but now has a change of circumstances meaning that he is now likely to qualify for legal aid then he will need to complete a new CDS15 (with evidence as before) and the application will be re-considered. If it is granted as a result of the change of circumstances it will be dated as at the date the fresh application was received by the court.

HARDSHIP APPLICATIONS/EXCEPTIONAL CIRCUMSTANCES

A full review of hardship is outside of the scope of this book and full guidance can be found on the LSC website.

In summary for the sake of completeness, applicants who have failed the means test but who have genuine reasons for not being able to fund their own case can apply for a hardship review using form CDS16. The review takes into account other expenditure for example, loan and credit cards repayments and re-assesses the client's means eligibility. If taking into account the additional expenditure his disposable income then falls below £3,398 then he will then be eligible for legal aid.

Procedurally the original CDS16 should be submitted with supporting evidence of the additional expenses *and* a copy of the CDS14 and 15 initially submitted to the Magistrates' Court, who will then send it the NCT for a decision. Again, this is not something that the legal aid officer at a court will be able to make an instantaneous decision on at court.

TRANSFER OF LEGAL AID

Legal aid can be transferred from one firm to another BUT only in very limited circumstances. Courts are very reluctant to transfer legal aid and will only do so if you can establish a good cause to do so. The reason for this is to avoid unnecessary cost to the public purse in duplication of work and costs.

The following will always amount to good cause:

- The solicitor who currently holds the representation order is under a duty to withdraw in accordance with their professional codes of conduct. For example; the solicitor subsequently discovers that their firm has previously represented the alleged victim or, having admitted the offence to the solicitor, the client now wants to run a positive defence.
- A genuine breakdown in the solicitor/client relationship to the extent that effective representation is no longer possible. For example; the client has been unacceptably abusive/violent to the solicitor (members of staff) or the solicitor has done no work on the client's behalf to properly prepare his case. If the client is alleging a breakdown in the solicitor/client relationship in support of an application to transfer legal aid, the full facts of the breakdown must be specified. It is not sufficient to simply say 'I have lost confidence in my solicitor' or that the solicitor does not have enough expertise. The court will infer from the fact that the solicitors firm has a legal aid contract that they are of sufficient quality and experience; the applicant will need to demonstrate otherwise. The fact that the client doesn't like the advice he's been given will not justify a transfer.

- Through circumstances outside of the solicitors' control, he is no longer able to represent the client. For example; the firm has been declared bankrupt.

The following *may* amount to a good reason:

- Some other substantial and compelling reason. For example; the client applied for legal aid with the duty solicitor in respect of the instant matter but has legal aid with his own solicitors on a number of other on-going matters and it is therefore in the interests of justice that one solicitor has conduct of all of his cases.

MAKING THE APPLICATION TO TRANSFER
AS THE EXISTING SOLICITOR

Procedurally you can either make an application in writing or an oral application to the Magistrates. If you are making the application in advance of an actual hearing then you should do it in writing. If you are making a responsive application to a situation that has arisen at court then you should make an oral application.

If you make the application in writing and the client has already identified a new solicitor then you should write to the court and set out the reason why the transfer is required and out of courtesy send a copy of that letter to the proposed new solicitors. The court will then write to the new solicitors to ascertain whether they are prepared to take over conduct of the case. In cases where there is for example, a professional conflict this will almost always be done administratively.

If the client has not already identified a new solicitor but you are professionally unable to continue acting then you should write to the court setting out the nature of your application (remember you cannot waive privilege, it is enough to say there is a professional conflict, you are not required to say what it is, nor should you.) and ask for the representation order to be discharged.

If a professional conflict arises whilst you are at court then you will need to make an oral application to the Magistrates. You should advise the client that you can no longer act for him because of a professional conflict and that he will need a new solicitor from a different firm. If he has a solicitor in mind then as a matter of assistance to the client you should contact that solicitor and ask if they are willing to take over the case. Remember again that you should not spell out the nature of the conflict as you will not only waive privilege but could end up embarrassing them too. If they are willing to take over conduct you should ask them or a representative on their behalf to come to court so that the application can be dealt with. If the client does not have a solicitor in mind then you should liaise with the court duty solicitor to see if he is happy to take over conduct. You will then need to make the verbal application to the magistrates. The crown has no input into an application to transfer legal aid except for occasions when a defendant is applying to transfer legal aid in an attempt to frustrate the process. In these circumstances the crown would be entitled to remind the court of previous examples of a defendant to transfer legal aid and of the effect that the delay is having on the proceedings.

If legal aid is transferred, you should ask the usher to copy a set of the prosecution papers for the new solicitor. Depending on the reason for the transfer, be careful what other documents you provide them with, for example; your police station notes. You can only give the new solicitor documents and correspondence prepared between you and the client, if the client authorises you to do so. As soon as the magistrates have transferred legal aid you can leave the courtroom and leave the new advocate to conduct the remainder of the hearing.

APPLICATION TO TRANSFER AS THE NEW SOLICITOR

You can only make the application on the basis that there has been a breakdown in the existing solicitor/client relationship or for some other substantial and compelling reason. If it is your application for these reasons then in reality this will usually be an application made in writing in advance of a pending hearing. Your written application must contain in detail the reason for the request and contain a signed authority for the client specifying the nature of the breakdown or other reason. You will then need to send the application to the Magistrates' Court dealing with the case and as a matter of courtesy, send a copy of your letter to the existing solicitors. The court will then contact the existing solicitors asking whether they consent to the transfer and for their response. Even if the existing solicitor agrees to the transfer, ultimately it is a matter for the court.

If the existing solicitor opposes the transfer then the court will list the matter for an oral hearing. Set out the reasons for the transfer in depth and demonstrate to the justices why it is in the interests of justice to transfer and that the client has good cause. The existing solicitor will then respond (remembering to be careful not to waive privilege). The magistrates will then decide whether legal aid should be transferred. If the application is successful, then you as the new solicitor will take over conduct of the remainder of any proceedings before the court. If the application fails you should leave and the current solicitor will continue.

HOW TO DEAL WITH CLIENTS WHO WANT TO TRANSFER

It is a depressing reality that there are defence lawyers who are willing to cut the throat of another firm. Within your first few months of practice you will attend a prison or a courtroom to find your client in conference with another solicitor who has instructions to apply to transfer legal aid. Make contact with your instructing solicitor or senior partner to find out if there is a background to this and if so, what? If this comes as news to everyone ask the solicitor to leave the room in order to speak to your client. These awkward and sometimes intimidating situations often involve more experienced lawyers claiming to have the new instructions. Until you have spoken to your client do not discuss representation with the new lawyer and certainly do not concede that legal aid will be transferred.

In your meeting with your client ask him if indeed he wants to transfer to the new firm and if so, the reasons why? Do not have this meeting in the company of the new solicitor. Be alive to defendants being told how much better their situation will or could be if represented by another firm. An example of this is where a solicitors firm lays claim to having expertise in a certain area of criminal law. Sometimes you can reassure the defendant that there is no need for him to apply to transfer and where you think the application is spurious you should make every attempt to do so. You may find that the presence of the new solicitor is due to a recommendation from the defendant's cellmate or another on his wing and defendants are understandably anxious about their representation particularly when told by a trusted friend inside that their solicitor has the best reputation for representing defendants in a given field. You can understand why the defendant will want to explore this. Ultimately It is a matter for your judgment and if you think that the defendant has good reason and you think that your relationship will break down at some point due to his desire to be represented by another then it may be that you take the pragmatic early decision to allow him transfer. Remember however that it is a matter for the court. For counsel this is an even trickier area and any decision must be made by your instructing solicitor.

As a matter of client care you should always re-assure the client that if the transfer is refused, it will not affect your representation of them or compromise their case.

APPLYING FOR AN ADJOURNMENT
FOR LEGAL AID TO BE GRANTED

The courts are extremely reluctant to allow adjournments for any reason and will only do so if it is in the interests of justice to do so. An application to adjourn for the client to obtain legal aid must be made to the Magistrates and their guidance/training in accordance with the Criminal Procedure Rules (CPR) is that a plea should be taken at the first hearing and so you or the client (if making the application unrepresented) will have to persuade the Magistrates that they should exercise their discretion and depart from the CPR.

Unless it has been done already, the court must take the defendant's plea [Crim PR 3.8(2)(b)]. This obligation does not depend on the extent of advance information, service of evidence, disclosure of unused material, or the grant of legal aid. [Lord Chief Justice, Essential case management: applying the Criminal procedure rules. December 2009]

The overriding duty of the court is to ensure that criminal cases are dealt with justly and this will be your strongest argument, i.e. that your client faces a serious charge and through no fault of his own has been unable to secure legal aid in time for the hearing and to proceed today without legal representation would be contrary the court's overriding duty.

Whether the application will be granted very much depends on how long the client has had to obtain legal aid in advance of the hearing and when he first made his application. If the client was charged ten days prior to the hearing but then attends court on the day of his first hearing without having previously submitted an application for legal aid, if it is not possible for the court administration to process his application that day, it is unlikely that the magistrates will grant the adjournment. Conversely if the client is a person of complex means who submitted his application in good time but because of the complexity of his means the NCT have not yet processed it, then it is more likely that the magistrates will grant the adjournment. Essentially in deciding whether to grant the adjournment, the justices will bear in mind that they have a responsibility for ensuring, so far as possible, that summary justice is speedy justice.

If the legal aid application is a simple one, for example; the client is on a passported benefit, the court will not adjourn the case for consideration of legal aid but will instead put the case back in the court list to enable the legal aid officer to process the application.

CHAPTER 5
ADVISING ON THE EVIDENCE

ADVICE ON THE EVIDENCE WHEN
THE EVIDENCE IS COMPLETE

How to give your advice – introduction

Advising your client is a vitally important aspect of your job. The advice that you give at this initial meeting will have ongoing implications for the rest of his case and it is crucial you get it right. In the early days it can be hard to do this with authority since you will naturally question your own opinion but if you have done all the necessary preparation, you will almost certainly have got it right. One of the most essential skills that you need to learn is to take control of the meeting from the outset. Throughout your career you will continue to encounter difficult clients who whether through fear, mental health or just plain arrogance will try to dominate the meeting. Your time with the client pre-court is precious and you do not have time to get side tracked. Experience will teach you how to do this but essentially, just be firm. You are the lawyer and the client will expect you to take control, do not apologise for doing so.

Be blunt in your advice to the client so, if the situation is bad then tell him so. It is your duty to give him accurate and realistic advice and not to give a client false hope. If the evidence is overwhelming, tell him and if he is likely to go to prison, tell him. Remember, one of the best ways of getting new work is either by repeat clients or by recommendation. If you are straight with your client they will thank you for it and they will re-instruct you, notwithstanding the robust advice you have given him.

It is important to structure that meeting. For example:

- Explain what he has been charged with
- Tell him what the law relating to that charge is
- Tell him what the possible defences are
- Tell him what the evidence against him is and whether it is strong, i.e.., can the Crown prove the offence on the face of it
- Run through what if anything, he has said in interview
- Take his instructions
- Give robust advice on what you think his prospects of success are on those instructions
- Advise him in the event of conviction, what sentence you think he will get

33

- Advise him about bail and take instructions for your bail application if necessary

Clients often want to launch into their instructions immediately but there is a very important reason to delay this until you have gone through your checklist, you do not want to become professionally embarrassed. There is nothing improper about giving the client the options before he gives you his instructions. It is your job to advise on the facts and the law, including the available defences. However, clients will often assume that part of your job is to invent their defence for them. It does not take this book to tell you that you should never succumb to what at times will be pretty fierce pressure from a client who asks you repeatedly what the best thing is for him to say about a certain aspect of the case. You have to leave your client in no doubt that you will never assist him in that way and your career and reputation means more than him and his case. To be investigated for perverting the course of justice by inventing your client's instructions would be an unwelcome entry on your website profile.

At the heart of your relationship with the client is the lawyer/client confidentiality and it is important that you make it clear to him that anything he tells you is confidential and (save in exceptional circumstances) you cannot tell anyone what he has said to you without his permission, as it is subject to legal privilege. Whilst this of course depends on the client, their experience of the criminal justice system and to some extent what they have been charged with, some clients will not automatically trust this and particularly when they see you writing things down, will clam up thinking that you are going to show your notes to the prosecutor or the court. It may sound obvious but is important to explain to him that the notes that you are taking are for you and his legal team alone.

You must make your professional duties clear to every client. Whilst in accordance with your relevant code of conduct you must act in his best interests you have an overriding duty not to mislead the court so tell him for example, that if he admits the offence to you but then wants to put forward a positive defence at trial, you will not be able to represent him as you cannot mislead the court.

Last but not least, when giving your advice, speak in plain English so that he can follow you.

Advice on the law and evidence

Explain to the client what he has been charged with, what the Crown has to prove and what his defences are. Take him through the evidence and rather than just reading the statements to him tell him what you think about them bearing in mind that the only thing he will want to know is whether the case against him can be proved. Where possible give robust advice and avoid ambiguous or uncertain advice that leaves him no clearer about what your view of the strength of the case against him. Make sure you know in your own mind what advice you will give, hesitancy is bound to unsettle a defendant and undermine his confidence in you.

Read through the interview summary with him and check that he maintains the account (if any) given in interview. Go through his previous convictions with him firstly, to confirm that he agrees with them and secondly, to explain the implications of them; for example, a bad character application.

In all cases you are duty bound to advise your client that if he pleads guilty at the first opportunity he will receive credit for his plea and make it clear that his credit and any consequent reduction in sentence diminishes as each day goes by in the lead-up to the trial itself.

On a practical note it is important that you take a clear note of your advice to the client in relation to all of the above to ensure that your file note is contract compliant with the Legal Services Commission but also so that you have clear record of the advice you have given in the event of a complaint at a later date. If your firm/instructing solicitor does not already use a *pro forma* court attendance note then it is a good idea to create one for yourself so that it can act as a prompt for you.

When taking notes or a record of a meeting with client, try to do so contemporaneously as to try to remember all that has been said on the way home on the train will be an almost impossible task.

Taking the clients instructions on the offence/evidence

Now you have gone through the evidence with the client you need to take his instructions about the offence and what he says about the prosecution statements.

If your client is pleading not guilty you must complete a case management form and on that form set out the nature of his defence, what is agreed, what is disputed, which witnesses are required and why. To do this properly, you need to take your client's full instructions. Time constraints will probably mean that you will not have an opportunity to take a full proof but you do need to take sufficient detail so that you can advise him properly and in the event of a not guilty plea, properly complete the form.

You then need to go through the prosecution statements with him and ascertain what he agrees with and disagrees with. You should do this whether the client is pleading guilty or not guilty. The purpose of doing this in the event of a guilty plea is to check with the client whether he is pleading guilty on the full facts or whether he is pleading guilty but disputes some of the facts (see below for basis of plea). The purpose of doing this for a not guilty plea at this stage is to assist with your completion of the case management form.

If your client is denying the offence, do not feel obliged to nod politely and write down his instructions unchallenged. If you are not convinced you should challenge what he says, cross-examine him in a gentle way to make clear to him how implausible his account is. Whether you believe him matters not but if you find his story incredible, his chances at trial do not bode well and experience teaches you how to do this in such a way as not to offend him. This exercise, although it may not appear at first, is in the best interests of the defendant you are duty-bound to highlight weaknesses in his case to ensure that he does not appreciate the difficulties for the first time when he is in the witness box being cross-examined

Some defendants will dislike this approach and will not like their lawyer appearing to be hostile and dismissive of their story and chances of success. This is understandable and you should pitch this challenge of the defendant at a level suitable for him to understand and in language that he can follow.

Alternatively if you have a client who has a strong defence but is wavering on plea because for example; he just wants his case over with today; you should be equally robust about his prospects of success.

Advice on plea

Be prepared to advise a client what you think he *should* do in the circumstances, ensuring he understands that his plea is always a matter for him. This includes telling him he should plead guilty, when as far as you are concerned he has no defence and he will be convicted in record time. There will be times that, notwithstanding your sound advice, he opts to take a different course and that is entirely normal. Do not worry about it just ensure that you have a good note of what your advice was and how the defendant decided to ignore it.

In terms of telling a client what to do, you cannot and should not make them do anything. You must simply advise them. Often what will influence them is what sentence they will receive if they plead guilty or whether it will impact on bail etc and this is why it is important that you know the options so that you can give that advice. Clients want to know the bigger picture, not just what they should do today but what effect this will have in the long run. So, for example, if given his previous convictions and non-compliance with previous community orders it is your view on sentence that a guilty plea to this matter today could be the difference between a custodial or non-custodial sentence, tell him. Or, if he is in custody and the Crown are opposing bail and your view is that he's likely to be remanded until his trial date but a guilty plea today could mean his release today with a community order, tell him.

If your client is pleading not guilty you are duty bound to advise him of two things:

1 If he pleads guilty at the first opportunity he will be entitled to credit for his guilty plea, *and*

2 If he doesn't attend for his trial, the likelihood is that it will proceed in his absence.

When you complete the trial management form you will be asked to tick the relevant boxes to confirm that you have advised the client of both and you will also be asked this in open court. It is therefore essential that you do and embarrassing if you have not.

Professional embarrassment

What this means is that to continue acting for the client would put you in breach of your professional code of conduct. The prime example in this situation is where the client has admitted the offence to you either at court or to you or a colleague at the police station but then wants to put forward a positive defence, i.e. to deny it.

Clients will often start by saying 'between you and me'. If they do, alarm bells should start ringing and you should shut down the conversation and remind the client of your professional duties.

If the client admits the offence to you but wants to plead not guilty on the basis that he will strictly put the Crown to proof, then you can continue to act for him. A good example of this is a client who has been charged with assaulting his partner and admits to assaulting his partner but does not think she will attend court to give evidence. He has indicated to you that if she does turn up to give evidence at trial then he will plead guilty. Subject to you giving him the proper advice about credit for a guilty plea etc it is perfectly proper for you to continue representing him. However if that same client instructs you that if he she turns up to court to give evidence against him he will deny the offence and take his chances then you can no longer represent him. If your advice to the client is that the Crown cannot prove an essential element of their case for example; an essential piece of continuity evidence is missing then despite his admission to you, again it is perfectly proper for you to put the Crown to strict proof on his behalf, subject to you having given him the proper advice about receiving credit for his guilty plea.

If the client has admitted the offence to you but wants to give positive evidence in his defence at trial or for you to put a positive defence forward in cross examination on his behalf, you cannot continue to represent him. You must tell him the reasons why and unless he reverts back to his original instructions you must tell him that he needs a new representative. If you are have legal aid for this client (or are acting as an agent for a firm who does) you must then make an application to transfer/discharge the representation order.

In all of these examples you should get a signed endorsement from the client setting out the nature of your advice. Remember that defendants will often look for someone to blame when things do not go according to plan and you leave yourself worryingly exposed to this when your advice and the defendant's decisions based on this advice are not recorded in writing.

If your client has instructed you that he wishes to plead guilty but on a basis of plea you must now consider a written basis of plea.

Basis of plea

The use of a 'basis of plea' document has become increasingly popular even in the short time that I have been at the Bar. It used to be that the odd case would require one, but now it seems that almost every other guilty plea is accompanied by a basis of plea.

The increase in their popularity is largely due to them being used wrongly. Most of those that come before the courts are a combination of mitigation and an absolute defence to the allegation. Their over-use is to be discouraged.

The idea of submitting such a document is that it reduces the culpability of your client in relation to the facts of the offence in order to achieve a lesser sentence. If the document you have drafted does not do that it is not worth submitting. Pleading at paragraph 1 of the document (which happened in a case I prosecuted many years ago) that the defendant committed the knife-point robberies because he had got drunk due to the death of his mother, is inappropriate. This is a matter for mitigation only and has no bearing on whether he is not guilty, guilty or very guilty.

The effect of a proper basis of plea (for example in the above case, he did rob the victims but did not have a knife) is that it is likely to make a material difference to the sentence and if the crown has some evidence that contradicts the defendant's version, then they will suggest a Newton Hearing. If they do not, the judge or magistrates will. Newton Hearings are to be avoided if possible – defendants tend not to win them and the resultant evaporation of any credit he had for pleading guilty can make such a difference.

You will have to use your judgment to decide whether it is all worth it and prior to submitting a basis of plea you will want to consider the strength of the Crown's case on the contentious issue, the evidence they can call to support their case, whether it is worth risking losing your entire credit for plea to dispute one issue, how convincing your client will be in the witness box, what supporting evidence you can call and of course the overall prospects of success.

Before you launch into drafting a basis of plea, speak to the prosecutor. The last thing you want is a document with your client's signature on it that admits that he stole £2,000 from the church repair fund that he set up, only to find that the crown have decided that due to the accounts being in such a state they can only prove that he took £200.

Engaging in polite but firm negotiation can be a very good way of reaching some sort of compromise between you and this way it may then be possible to present to the court a joint position, which, is infinitely more likely to persuade the court not to hold a Newton hearing than if there is disagreement between you. On the issue of whether your client kicked the victim whilst on the floor or if he was carrying a hammer during an affray, there may be very little room for any agreement but in so many cases there will be some furtile areas for discussion. There may be all sorts of reasons why the Crown want to avoid a trial and the prospect of a plea can be such a welcome indication to the prosecutor that there may be a real opportunity to gain an advantage for your client. A good example of this is cases of domestic violence where, as is often the case, the victim is unwilling to attend.

There are times when you will be confident that to submit a basis of plea will not result in a Newton because the crown's evidence is ambiguous. The classic example is an affray where one prosecution witness says that the defendant had a knife and two witnesses who say that he definitely did not. The defendant instructs you that he did not have a knife and although it will certainly make a difference to sentence, you know that the crown will be on shaky ground positively asserting that he did have the blade. In such circumstances to submit a written basis of plea is entirely appropriate.

Be prepared to give your client robust advice if the opposite situation arises. All three of the witnesses mentioned above do see him carrying a blade during the affray yet he still denies having it. Tell him straight, that unless something spectacular and unexpected happens at the hearing it is likely he will lose the trial of issue and any credit he could have expected for his plea. An advocate is not doing his job properly if he is not prepared to tell a client that the situation is bleak. Too often in robing rooms you hear advocates saying 'well if those are his instructions, who am I to stand in his way?' Sometimes, that is a proper approach but more often than not, clients will listen to you, their lawyer, about the prospects of success in the case. So, if his chances of winning a Newton hearing are hopeless do not be timid, tell him. He'll thank you in the long run.

If there is to be a basis of plea it must be in writing and copies must be supplied to the court, the prosecution and the probation service if appropriate. Agreeing something verbally with a prosecutor over morning coffee is all very well but when that same prosecutor is not available for the sentence and you are faced with an opponent who says 'there's nothing on the file' and the court clerk can find no mention of it either, you will be in an embarrassing and difficult position.

Write the basis of plea, preferably typed rather than handwritten, it should carry the defendant's signature and date and your brief should be fully endorsed with the advice you have given the defendant about the implications of losing a Newton hearing. You must ensure that your position is protected when the time comes that the trial of the issue is lost and the defendant gets the maximum sentence available to the court and he is looking for someone to blame.

Example basis of plea:

IN THE BRIGHTON MAGISTRATES' COURT

REGINA

-V-

JOHN SMITH

BASIS OF PLEA

The defendant will plead guilty to the charge of Affray on the following basis;

1. He accepts threatening the nightclub door staff

2. He accepts that after uttering the threat he punched one of the doormen in the face

3. In the ensuing fight he accepts that he punched the doorman approximately four times as they rolled around on the floor.

4. At no stage did he kick anyone

5. At no stage was he holding a knife

Signed   _____

Dated   _____

ADVISING A CLIENT WHEN THE EVIDENCE IS INCOMPLETE

It is likely that in your first few weeks or months you will need to advise a client(s) in situations where the prosecution evidence at that stage is either weak, incomplete or as in some circumstances, non-existent. It is in these situations you are most likely to be asked questions such as 'what would *you* do?' or 'will they get more evidence against me?' or 'Can I wait to see what they get before entering my plea?' and these understandable questions must be answered.

You will find that this situation arises in cases that are triable either way and summary only, the principles are the same but there is the important distinction with offences that are triable either way that the defendant must be advised of his right to enter 'no plea' – affording him an opportunity to wait and see what the Crown's case really does entail. However, despite what some lawyers would suggest, this tactic is not without its risks.

Matters triable either way

There will be occasions when you read the material served at court and perhaps with the exception of highly relevant bad character, you cannot identify any evidence against your client. The defendant should be advised of this in no uncertain terms. Be brave enough to tell him that as things stand the crown cannot prove one or more or all of the essential elements of the offence and that if tried on this evidence he would be acquitted.

However, this is not the end of your advice in this situation; he must be advised that today is the first chance he has to plead guilty and the only chance he has of being afforded maximum credit for his guilty plea. It is unlikely that any sentencing tribunal, particularly a District Judge, will be attracted by a submission at a later date that the defendant should still receive full credit because at the first hearing the crown's evidence was weak or non-existent. We have all heard judges barking at advocates who make such a submission 'the criminal justice system is not a game and the defendant knew as well then, as he does now, that he was guilty'

So, advise the defendant that there is always the prospect of the crown's case against him becoming stronger and if he intends at some stage to plead guilty then the time to do it is at that first hearing.

A situation that you are more likely to be faced with is where the prosecution evidence is incomplete and therefore not particularly strong at that early hearing.

The classic example of this is burglary where the prosecution awaits the evidence of the fingerprint expert. Your client now aged 38 was a prolific burglar in his teens is found in the area of a burglary in the early hours of the morning, upon arrest inside the shorts he is wearing (It is the middle of summer by the way) the police recover a pair of gloves. He answers no comment in interview and at the identification parade the owner of the burgled premises, who had a face-to-face confrontation with the burglar in his kitchen, fails to identify your client. Scenes of crimes officers have recovered a number of fingerprints from the point of entry and the police await the comparison results between those marks and your client's prints.

This is precisely the type of situation where a defendant will want your help. He will know that there is circumstantial evidence against him (his presence in the area, the gloves and his record) but that alone may be insufficient to convict him. However, he also knows that if the crown can place him at the scene by virtue of his prints, he has had it.

You must advise the defendant that, notwithstanding the missing scientific material, there is a case for him to answer and that there is a risk that he will be convicted in light of the circumstantial evidence alone. The court will still consider that first hearing to be the first opportunity he could have taken to enter his guilty plea regardless of any further evidence served later. A plea of guilty at any later stage will attract only limited credit. Therefore if he is the burglar, he should plead guilty and get as much credit as he can for doing so. If they are his fingerprints at the scene then more often than not the evidence will show that.

The defendant may not be convinced by this advice having been given the unexpected boost of the homeowner failing to identify him and he may instruct you that he wants to take his chances and you must not forget to advise him of something very important. If he pleads not guilty or enters no plea, the court will consider plea before venue and his case will be committed to the Crown Court for a plea and case management hearing (PCMH), by which time it is highly likely that the crown will have all their evidence – including his grubby print at the scene.

I am aware that some lawyers will argue at this stage that Crown Court judges will always give a defendant full credit for pleading guilty at the PCMH so why not just take the chance. I disagree for two very important reasons; firstly, judges in the Crown Court are keeping an increasingly beady eye on how either-way matters are getting to the Crown Court and in cases where a defendant has elected Crown Court trial or entered no plea and then entered a guilty plea at the PCMH, if a non-custodial sentence is passed hitting the defendant hard with costs orders. Secondly, I have always believed that judges, when faced with a defendant who has been committed for sentence following a plea of guilty, do give that extra bit of credit, especially in circumstances where the prosecution case was weak or incomplete when he entered his plea. These are two compelling reasons to give proper advice about the strength of the case, credit for pleading guilty and possible financial implications at a stage when the crown's case may not be particularly strong.

There will be occasions when the defendant has no intention of pleading guilty in circumstances such as these but wants you to confirm that the case against him is weak, giving his decision a degree of legitimacy. Be careful to still give complete advice even if you know it is falling on deaf ears and to make a note of the advice that you have given him. You can rest assured that when you are instructed to represent him at the PCMH and he pleads guilty (the case against him by then is overwhelming) and the sentencing hearing is adjourned for the preparation of pre-sentence reports, he will tell the probation officer that he only pleaded not guilty at the Magistrates' Court because his lawyer told him that the crown's case was pathetically thin.

Summary only

The principles are exactly the same but defendants do not have the 'safety net' of the 'no plea' option that they have with either way offences. Therefore, your advice, as ever, needs to be robust.

Take the example of an offence contrary to section 2 of the Protection from Harassment Act 1997. The defendant's ex-partner has made a lengthy statement detailing how she has been harassed by text message by your client. In interview the defendant denied sending any messages whatsoever. He is a man of good character.

As things stand, the crown's case does not include any telephone interrogation evidence but the prosecutor tells you that the complainant's telephone was seized. If the defendant pleads not guilty then they will consider going to the expense of having the phone examined for the presence of text messages from your client that are said to be not only unpleasant but also, due to their content, capable of identifying your client as the sender of them.

Without the telephone evidence it appears to be a straight fight between the defendant and the complainant who in light of his good character, may feel that his credibility surpasses that of his ex-partner who has a two convictions for benefit fraud.

The defendant is reluctant to lose his good character but asks if he can hold off from entering his plea until the crown have decided whether they will interrogate her telephone. The crown and the court are not willing to countenance such a course of action so he must make a decision on the spot.

You must advise him that if the phone is examined and the report appears to show that he was sending her hundreds of texts a day then he will almost certainly have committed the offence alleged. If that is not enough he will be forced, should he maintain his not guilty plea, to explain why he lied to the police when he said he had not been in contact with his ex-partner since their split.

If the defendant instructs you that he wants to take the chance on the prosecution not interrogating the telephone then make a note of the advice you have given him and ask him to sign an endorsement on your brief that he has received the advice. You must at all times protect yourself from the client who when convicted will tell anyone who is prepared to listen that you said that the crown do not intend to get the phone interrogated and therefore their case is weak and in any event she probably will not turn up to give evidence.

When the prosecution advises you that they have yet to decide whether they are going to seek further, potentially more damning, evidence against your client there will be a decision to be made by the defendant at that stage that could have serious ramifications for the future of the case. It is a decision he must make having been fully advised by you about the consequences of a late guilty plea should the evidence against him become so strong.

THE CLIENT THAT WANTS TO PLEAD GUILTY DESPITE INSTRUCTIONS THAT AMOUNT TO A DEFENCE

You will spend a lot of your career advising defendants that they do not have a defence known to law, however there will be occasions when you are faced with a client who insists on pleading guilty despite the instructions he has given you amounting to a perfectly sound defence to the charge.

It is important to remember that a defendant can plead guilty to any charge that he wants to for absolutely any reason that he wants to. It usually follows that a defendant pleads guilty because he is guilty but this is not always the case. A wish not to have an ex-partner cross examined, an attempt to bring an end to the police investigations, to take the blame for someone else higher up the chain are all reasons cited to me for pleading guilty when a perfectly sound defence has been advanced in conference.

Once you are satisfied that you have taken the defendant fully through the evidence and taken his instructions, which you consider amount to a defence, but he makes clear his intention to plead guilty you must give him some very careful advice.

Firstly, the defendant should be advised that if he is not guilty then he should plead not guilty but the decision is his. Secondly, explore with the defendant why he wishes to plead guilty if he is not guilty and see whether there is any way in which he would feel able to plead not guilty in accordance with his instructions.

If after this advice the defendant insists that he will plead guilty you must advise him of the consequences of that plea, namely that despite his claims of innocence the matter will appear on his list of previous convictions or worse still be the offence that gives him a criminal record and he must also be advised that the prospect of a successful appeal against that conviction, in light of a plea of guilty is extremely remote. There is a also a practical effect that the defendant must be warned of; if he enters a guilty plea to a crime he says he did not commit he must be told that there will be restrictions on the mitigation that can be advanced, and what is advanced can only be on the basis that the defendant is guilty and will otherwise be strictly limited, for example you will not be able to advance in mitigation that the defendant has shown remorse as demonstrated by his guilty plea.

If the defendant is still certain that he want to plead guilty then you should make a clear note of the advice you have given and then make a call to your instructing solicitor or if you are a solicitor, the partner of the firm. Even if it is just to leave a message, a contemporaneous record of your instructions and the advice you have given is a very good idea.

Once this advice has been given and you are satisfied that the defendant has understood it, if he still maintains his wish to plead guilty, you must ask him to sign an endorsement that reflects the advice he has received. This is one of the most important times for you to ensure that you do get written confirmation of the defendant's intention. Without it you know that when the defendant receives an unexpectedly severe sentence and he regrets his decision to plead guilty, he will contact new lawyers to investigate the possibility of appealing against his conviction. That lawyer will look at every aspect of the case including the defendant's instructions to you and the advice he was given. There is no better way to safeguard your position from any criticism by newly instructed lawyers than a signed endorsement from the defendant showing that he pleaded guilty following entirely appropriate advice.

The defendant should be invited to endorse a declaration that he has given unequivocal instructions of his own free will that he intends to plead guilty despite his instructions that he did not commit the offence and that he understands the advice given by his lawyer and in particular how this will hinder the mitigation that can be advanced on his behalf and his future prospects of a successful appeal against his conviction. The defendant should be told that he does not have to endorse the declaration and if he is not willing to, make a clear note to this effect and telephone the partner or your solicitor again to ensure another contemporaneous note is made of the tricky situation that you are in.

ADVICE TO CLIENT ON VENUE

If your client is charged with one or more either way offences you will need to advise him about the venue for his trial. It is surprising how few clients understand the difference between the Magistrates' Court and the Crown Court and particularly for those more inexperienced clients, you need to make sure that they understand the distinction between the two courts and their options in relation to both.

In deciding whether they will accept jurisdiction of the case the test for the magistrates is whether their sentencing powers are sufficient in the event of conviction. For the purpose of this decision, the prosecution's case is taken at its highest. They do not take into account the defendant's previous convictions, personal circumstances or mitigation.

In giving your advice to the client you should begin by telling him whether the magistrates are likely to accept jurisdiction of the case. In most cases this should be easy as the likely sentence is clearly set out in the sentencing guidelines. If your advice is that the magistrates are likely to decline jurisdiction then explain to the client why. This will include showing him the aggravating and mitigating features of the offence. If there are not guidelines then consider relevant cases and text book commentary.

If you think the magistrates are likely to accept jurisdiction you must advise the client of his right to elect Crown Court trial in any event and the pros and cons of having his trial in either court. Even if the case is one where summary trial is inevitable you must still remember to do this. Very early on when dealing with, a low value theft case I had forgotten to advise my client about his right to elect Crown Court trial. It was not until the legal adviser dealt plea before venue that I realised my mistake. I then had the embarrassing experience of having to give this advice at the back of the court with everyone aware of my error. As anticipated he wanted his trial in the Magistrates' Court so in reality no damage was in fact done but it is unlikely he was impressed at the way I conducted the hearing.

There are times when your advice to your client about the venue for his trial will be straightforward but most examples of this advice are arguable either way. You will have to consider a number of factors including the defendant's ability to give evidence, the nature of the charge, his history, the speed at which he wants the case dealt with, the cost implications and other factors that will be particular to each case. It is not possible to list which cases are appropriate for the justices to try and which cases are better heard in the Crown Court but you will get a feel very quickly for what the defendant should do and advising defendants on this issue will become easier as you become more experienced. Remember it is the defendant's choice and although you must advise him, there is no question of you making the decision for him.

If your client is pleading not guilty and will be having a trial in the Magistrates' Court, you must complete the case management form.

CHAPTER 6
THE CASE MANAGEMENT FORM –
SUMMARY TRIAL

If your client is pleading not guilty and will be having a trial in the Magistrates' Court you *must* complete a case management form and advise the client that you are required to do so. The completion of the form is made mandatory by paragraph v 56.2 of the Consolidated Criminal Practice Direction. In completing the case management form you *must* comply with the CPR [R3.2(2)(a) and R3.3(a)]. The court can require that the issues are identified by the parties in writing.

You are required to complete the form on behalf of your client and to identify all issues in the case including which witnesses are required to attend court to give live evidence at trial. You are not required to waive privilege and/or disclose the content of any confidential discussions with your client. If the real issues in the case are not spelt out on the case management form your client may be prevented from relying on that issue at trial and it is your duty to warn him of this (*Writtle v DPP* [2009] EWHC 236).

The case of *Firth v Epping Magistrates' Court* [2011] EWHC 388 (Admin) suggests that there are occasions when the information added by the advocate on the case management form may be admissible as evidence at his trial. In that case the defendant was charged with a common assault and his counsel completed the case management form, identifying the trial issue as self defence. The charge was later substituted with a charge of assault occasioning actual bodily harm. At the committal hearing the defence asserted that there was no case to answer on the basis that there was no evidence that the defendant was the assailant. The magistrates rejected the application of no case to answer and relied upon the 'admission' of self defence in the case management form as sufficient identification evidence to establish a prima facie case. The court in this case distinguished the case of *Hutchinson* (1986) 82 Cr App R 51. *Hutchinson* however remains good law and it would appear that the crucial difference as to whether admissions made by agents are admissible is what the consequences of it are for the defendant, i.e. conviction or, as in Firth, the lesser consequence of committal to the Crown Court for trial (see: *Newell* [2012] EWCA Crim 650). Post Newell it would appear that only in the most exceptional cases would such evidence be admitted at trial.

Notwithstanding the above, you cannot advise your client to disobey a statutory obligation i.e. the completion of the case management form or to omit information from it.

> 'The lawyer's duty is not to give the defendant advice on what to do. The lawyer's duty is to explain the statutory obligation that he has and to explain the consequences which follow from disobedience of it.' (Rochford [2010] EWCA Crim 1928).

This seems to contradict everything that you have been taught but *Rochford* is very clear on the point; your job in this situation is not to advise the client about what to do but instead advise him on what he needs to do and that if he does not, not only will he gain no advantage from it, but that the case is likely to be adjourned and any increased costs as a consequence are likely to be borne by him.

PUTTING THE PROSECUTION TO PROOF

If your client is raising a defence then the completion of the form is easy and presents no real problems. Difficulties arise where your client has no positive defence to raise and the issue is 'putting the crown to strict proof'. Whilst the CPR does not purport to undermine the fundamental principle that the prosecution is required to prove the case against your client it does make the mechanics of doing so difficult. All you can properly identify as the trial issue is that 'he is putting the prosecution to proof'. If pushed on this by the court you cannot say that in your view there is no defence – this is bound by privilege.

If your client is putting the prosecution to proof on the basis that he does not think the victim is going to attend court to give evidence then you will need to mark on the form that you require that witness to come to court to give live evidence. There is nothing wrong with doing this and he is entitled to put the crown to proof. In terms of the reason you cite for requiring that witness – you can only put 'the crown is put to proof'. You cannot advance any other positive reason for requiring that witness to attend court, for example; his evidence is disputed. In the course of the hearing you will be questioned rigorously by either the legal adviser or District Judge as to what you mean by 'putting to proof' and pressure will be put on you to expand on it. You cannot and must not. Your answer is 'the defendant puts that witness to proof'.

If, on the other hand, the defendant is pleading not guilty, for example, to buy himself more time and you agree all of the evidence then you can mark the form that all witnesses are agreed. Again, this is perfectly proper however you must be warned that increasingly in such cases, the court will look for either an immediate trial or one in the very near future. You will need to advise your client of this.

If your client refuses to allow you to complete the case management form then you must advise the court that your client refuses to allow you to disclose the nature of his defence to the court. It is then a matter for the court as to how they wish to proceed. As long as you have given the client the proper advice about his statutory duty to disclose the nature of his defence then you cannot be criticised and you do not need to withdraw. You are not professionally embarrassed. Remember in this case to give the client absolute advice about the consequences of later advancing a positive defence at trial and ensure that you get a signed endorsement from your client, setting out your advice and the consequences of him not following it. The reason for doing this is to cover you in the event of a complaint at a later stage when either he is prevented from advancing his defence at trial or faces increased costs for an unnecessary adjournment of trial.

In all cases where issues about your client's defence are not straightforward, take time to reiterate to your client, your advice about receiving credit for an early guilty plea. Playing games with case management rarely works in the defendants favour.

A Law Society guidance note on this issue can be found on its website.

CHAPTER 7
ADVISING AND TAKING INSTRUCTIONS FOR SENTENCE

Advice on sentence must be clear and realistic as overly optimistic advice helps no-one. If you think your client is going to get an immediate custodial sentence then tell him so as he will need to prepare for this.

When you are advising about sentence make sure you explain every aspect of the likely sentencing options to the client. Many first time offenders do not understand what a conditional discharge or a community order is. Most clients understand what a custodial sentence is but a surprising number do not understand that that means they will be taken to the court cells immediately sentence is passed. Clients will want to know what the maximum length of a curfew is or what the maximum amount of hours of unpaid work they could be ordered to complete are so make sure that you have the answers. If you do not it will make you look unprepared and undermine the client's confidence in you.

Do not shy away from asking a lot of questions about both the offence and your client's personal details. Some clients will not like being asked but that is something he will get over once he realises that the more you ask him the better your mitigation will be. If you encounter a client who is reticent in giving you the information that you need, make sure that you explain to him what you are doing and why. Your mitigation will only ever be as good as the information you are able to glean from your client.

SENTENCE GUIDELINES AND ANCILLARY ORDERS

Make sure that you remember to tell the client about any ancillary orders that the court could make, for example; if the offence relates to a football match – a football banning order.

Most offences are covered by the sentence guidelines. Take your client through the guidelines and tell him where his case falls within them. Take him through the mitigating features of his case and the aggravating features. Based on those guidelines and any other relevant information advise him of the likely sentence and do so with clarity. Suggesting that he might receive a prison sentence is not particularly helpful, tell him what sentence you think he is likely to receive and for approximately how long.

Explain to your client how you will approach the plea in mitigation explaining at all times why you will and why you will not include certain submissions. Advising the client at this stage about your reasons will avoid a confrontation at a later stage about why you have left out of your submissions something that he thinks is important when the result does not go his way. Clients are often keen for you to tell the court their life history including a number of things that do not actually help in mitigation. Your job is to properly advise them what helps and to be frank about what does not.

ANTECEDENT HISTORY

Take your client through his list of previous convictions including cautions and reprimands etc. If he has previous convictions for similar offending, check the details of those convictions with him so if possible you can distinguish those offences from this one.

Where there is a pattern of offending emerging it may be that there is a reason why this is so which could help with your submissions in mitigation. A common example is the drug addict who is accumulating multiple convictions for theft by stealing from shops. In this case you would hope to persuade the magistrates that a community order directed at drug rehabilitation would be appropriate.

If your client has a long list of previous convictions but there has been a significant gap in his offending, find out why. Using the example of the drug addict he informs you that he has been drug free for five years which coincides precisely with his last court appearance. Again this can be powerful mitigation when seeking to persuade the magistrates towards one type of order or another.

BREACH OF A CONDITIONAL DISCHARGE

If his guilty plea and conviction will place him in breach of an earlier conditional discharge then you must be fully instructed on the circumstances of the original offence. Advise your client that he is now at risk of being re-sentenced for that original offence together with sentence for the current offence.

BREACH OF SUSPENDED SENTENCE ORDER (SSO)

If his guilty plea and conviction will put him in breach of a suspended sentence order then you must advise your client that the overwhelming prospect is that the justices will activate the custodial element of that sentence in full or part *unless* it would be unjust to do so. Take instructions from him about how well he has complied with the requirements of his SSO. If he was ordered to complete two hundred and forty hours unpaid work and he has in fact done two in six months find out why. Is it because he just could not be bothered or, does he have a genuine reason? These are all matters that you will need to address the magistrates on. The reason behind any non-compliance (if applicable) will help you tailor your advice to your client about the likelihood of activation of the custodial element of the sentence and if so, for how long.

RESPONSE TO PREVIOUS COMMUNITY ORDERS

If your client has a history of breaching previous community orders then ask him about this and be prepared to tailor your advice accordingly. If he has received five previous community orders and has breached every single one of them then you will face an uphill struggle attempting to convince the justices that on this occasion he will comply. It may be that there was a reason for that non-compliance which could assist with your mitigation, for example his history on non-compliance took place during a period of homelessness and alcohol dependence but since that time he has now found stable accommodation and is addressing his alcohol addiction.

If your client is currently subject to an order, take instructions about how well he is complying with that order. Hopefully by this time you will have had an opportunity to verify this with the court liaison probation officer and if so, tell the client what the probation officer has said. If you have not yet had that opportunity, remind the client that this information will be verified with probation. This sounds obvious but so many clients will tell you they are doing well on their order when in fact, the opposite is true. Newly qualified lawyers are prone to taking what client's say at face value. I have mitigated on the basis that my client's positive response to his existing order was his best submission. As soon as I sat down the court's probation officer could not wait to tell the court that in fact he was in breach of every element of his order and that in fact breach proceedings were pending. This was an embarrassing lesson but one which I have never forgotten.

If your client is not responding well, find out why. It may be that there are genuine reasons or difficulties that are complicating his order that could be useful in your submissions in mitigation on his behalf.

CHECK SUITABILITY AND WILLINGNESS
TO ENGAGE WITH YOUR PROPOSED SENTENCE

If you are proposing to mitigate towards a community based sentence check that the client is willing to comply with it and able to comply with it.

If your client tells you he is not willing to perform unpaid work or comply with whatever sentence you are proposing, be blunt with him about the implications of this; i.e. custody. Faced with a direct choice between custody and unpaid work, he will probably change his mind. Alternatively, avoid setting your client up to fail and if the reality is that he will never comply with a community based order you may be better advising him towards a short custodial sentence which at least has the merits of getting it over and done with.

If your client is unwell, physically, mentally or by virtue of a drink or drug addiction then check with him whether he is fit to do what you are proposing. Remember to check this too with the probation officer. Do not set your client up to fail.

ADVICE ON WHEN THE CLIENT WILL BE SENTENCED

You will need to advise your client whether he is likely to be sentenced today or whether an adjournment for a pre-sentence report will be required. If the guideline sentence for your client's offence is a fine or conditional discharge then in most cases, sentence will take place immediately. If the guideline is a community order but for reasons specific to your client's case, you will be asking for a fine or conditional discharge and the magistrates agree, sentence will take place immediately.

If the guideline is a community order or a custodial sentence and realistically that is the likely sentence to be imposed then the magistrates will order a pre-sentence report (PSR). Whether that report will require an adjournment in most cases depends on the following:

1. Whether the case is complex and requires additional assessments for example; suitability for an alcohol treatment requirement or a psychiatric assessment.
2. Whether your client is vulnerable due to serious mental health issues or other such serious issues.
3. Whether the case involves serious sexual or violent offending (including high-risk domestic violence cases).
4. Whether the case involves complex and serious child safeguarding issues.
5. Any other issues that make the case unusual for example; whether there are outstanding breach proceedings that ought to be dealt with at the same time.

Approximately 70% of cases in the Magistrates' Court are sentenced either on the same day or within 5 days. You should advise the client of this. Some client's might not appreciate that by pleading guilty at the first opportunity they may in fact be at risk of going to prison that very same day. Unless your client's case is complex then assuming there is sufficient court time, most cases are put back in the court list for a verbal PSR and his sentence will therefore take place later that day. If there is not sufficient court time then the case will be adjourned for a maximum period of five days but will generally be listed for the following day.

If you are asking the magistrates to deal with your client by way of a custodial sentence the court is under a duty to consider whether a pre-sentence report is required. Whether a report is ordered is a matter for the justices and you should advise your client accordingly.

If your client is in custody and his case is adjourned for a full PSR the sentence hearing will take place within two weeks of the guilty plea, three if he is on bail.

If your client is entering mixed pleas then if the offences are linked, he will be sentenced for the guilty pleas at the outcome of the not guilty matters. If the guilty plea matters are unrelated, for example a Bail Act offence within the proceedings, he will be sentenced for that matter either immediately or following the preparation of a PSR if one is required.

ADVICE ON PRE-SENTENCE REPORT

If your client's case is likely to merit a pre-sentence report you should advise the client how to deal with the probation officer. Whilst you cannot tell him what to say it is entirely proper that you advise him what the purpose of the report is and how he should conduct himself in the interview.

The purpose of a pre-sentence report is to assist the court in assessing the most appropriate way of dealing with the offender. The report will look at the offence, the offender, his attitudes to the offence, including evidence of genuine remorse. It will also assess risk of further offending and danger to the public and will discuss previous convictions and compliance if any with previous orders. The author of the report (whether oral or written) will then make proposals for sentence.

It is important to advise your client that although the probation officer is writing a report ostensibly for his benefit they are independent of any party and that anything he says good or bad, if deemed relevant will appear in the report. This will include bad manners, rudeness, unwillingness to discuss the offences and worse still, abuse. Whilst you will quite properly tailor your mitigation around the more helpful aspects of your client's case and (as long as you are not misleading the court) repeat only those instructions that are helpful to it, the probation officer will have no such filter.

The defendant should be reminded that if he is genuinely sorry for his behaviour and ashamed of what he has done, he should impress this upon the probation service. One of the most important features of the report is whether the defendant has insight into his offending and linked to this whether his plea indicates a genuine remorse for his crime. He must make this clear to the author of the report.

ADVICE ON COMMITTAL TO THE CROWN COURT FOR SENTENCE

If your client is at risk of being committed to the Crown Court for sentence, do not forget to tell him so. This is something commonly forgotten but very important and if you have not advised him of this and his case is committed for sentence he will be understandably unimpressed.

TAKING INSTRUCTIONS

The following is a checklist that you should use when taking instructions for mitigation:

1. Details about the offence and why he committed it, i.e. background to the offence
2. Age
3. Employment
4. Qualifications/education
5. Family history
6. Family circumstances; for example – dependent children/elderly parents he looks after etc
7. Mental health; including any treatment/medication
8. Physical health; including any treatment/medication
9. Alcohol history; including what if any steps he has taken to address it/ whether he is willing to
10. Drug history; including what if any steps he has taken to address it/ whether he is will to
11. Any other information you think is relevant depending on the individual circumstances of the case.

COMPLETING THE MEANS FORM

Finally do not forget to give your client a means form to complete or direct him to the usher who will provide him with one. It is worth reminding him that the magistrates are not overly sympathetic to a weekly expenditure on cigarettes, alcohol and gambling and that if the client includes this in his listed expenses, it is in fact likely that the Magistrates will include this figure as part his assessed disposable income for the purposes of paying court fines/compensation.

CHAPTER 8
TAKING INSTRUCTIONS FOR BAIL
AND ADVICE ON BAIL

BAIL – CLIENTS IN CUSTODY

Advising on bail can be one of the most difficult parts of your job. When you see the client, the chances are that he will already have been in police custody for at least 24 hours, dying for a cigarette and withdrawing from drink or drugs. All he is interested in is whether he will be released on bail. Sadly, all you will be thinking about is 'what an earth can I possibly say for this man who has 25 previous offences committed whilst on bail and 10 Bail Act offences?'

This can make your job very difficult as not only are you trying to take instructions about the offence, plea, sentence or whatever it may be but you may also have to deal with a truculent client who is interested in one thing only, and that is getting out.

I recall in my early days, a client who was in custody upon an allegation of the eighth breach of his ASBO. He had been arrested on the Friday night, interviewed, charged and remanded by the police on the Saturday afternoon and I represented him at the Magistrates' Court on the Monday morning. He was found by the police drunk and having soiled his clothing and unhappily for me, he was produced at Court still wearing the clothes in which he had been arrested in. Not only was he withdrawing from alcohol and desperate to get out for his next drink but the smell was intolerable. His chances of getting bail were hopeless and it was tempting to dissuade him from making a bail application allowing me to make a very swift exit. However, he had the right to bail and he wanted me to make a bail application and it was my job to sit and listen and take instructions in order to properly prepare an application for bail. Personal inconvenience should not stand in the way of making submissions on bail for a defendant no matter how hopeless his predicament seems. Not all clients will be philosophical about their chance of being admitted to bail and you must be prepared to make a bail application should you be instructed so to do.

Taking instructions from a client in the cells is a pressured task. The court prioritises custody cases which means the court wants to get your case on, your client wants to get his case on and often you just want more time leaving you stressed, rushed and flustered. Sometimes there will be perfectly legitimate reasons as to why you are not ready promptly in which case do not be pressured into agreeing to your case being called on. Common examples of this are; the legal aid officer has not yet assessed your client's legal aid application *or* the prosecutor has only just given you the papers *or* you are waiting to speak to someone who can provide details and confirmation of a residence address. In those cases it is perfectly proper for you to speak to the legal adviser and explain why you are not ready and to ask for more time and if necessary make that application to the Magistrates. Some District Judges will simply call your case on irrespective of whether you are actually ready and if that happens, you should make an application for more time explaining to the court why you are not ready, apologising for the delay but making the firm submission that it would not be appropriate to call the case on at this stage and without all the information before the court. The court may be sympathetic to an application for more time if through no fault of your own the case is not ready. It is incumbent upon you to be ready and available when the case is listed if it is ready to be heard and the court will take a dim view upon an application for more time if it arises out of you not being ready because you were enjoying a leisurely breakfast. A reputation for being a time waster is not an easy one to shift.

When bail is agreed in principle with the prosecutor in advance of seeing the client, subject to his ability and willingness to comply with the suggested conditions, it can be a relatively easy application to make. However more often than not bail will be opposed and you will need to address the issue of bail with your client and the reasons for the Crown's objections.

Remember however that just because the prosecutor agrees bail conditions, it is ultimately a matter for the court and you must still be ready to address the Magistrates or District Judge should the need arise.

TAKING INSTRUCTIONS FOR THE PURPOSE OF MAKING A BAIL APPLICATION:

In order to make a properly argued bail application you will need to take full instructions from your client on the following key areas:

1. The offence
2. His personal circumstances
3. His previous convictions (if applicable).
4. Proposed bail conditions

The offence

In most cases the first bail application will also be the first hearing before the court, in which case you will be taking instructions about the offence.

For the purposes of a bail application however you need to address the following:

- What does the client say about the alleged offence?
- What did he say in his police interview?
- If the client is there having breached his existing bail conditions – does he accept the breach and if so, why did he breach?

His personal circumstances

In general, you should obtain details about the following:

1. His address:

- Who owns the property?
- In what capacity does he live there?
- How long has he lived there?
- Who else lives there?

2. His community ties:

- His date of birth/age?
- His place of birth?
- Where was he brought up?
- By whom?
- His education/qualifications (if any)?
- His relationship status?
- Does he have any dependent children or children with whom he has regular contact?
- Where does his friends/family live?
- Is he employed and in what capacity?
- How long has he been employed?
- What are the contact details for his employer?
- If he's not working, how long been unemployed?
- Does he have any trade or profession?
- What benefit is he on if any?
- How often does he sign on (if applicable)?

3. Physical/mental health:

- What if any mental or physical health condition he suffers from?
- His GP details?
- What prescription if any is he on?
- Details of any help agencies he is engaging with? For example, AA.

His previous convictions:

In particular –

- Details of any relevant offences
- Details about any previous Bail Act offences

- Details about any previous breaches of court orders and/or his successful completion of previous court orders.

Proposed bail conditions:

Obtain details of the following where applicable to your case –

- What is his proposed residence address including the contact details of anyone who can confirm that he either lives there or can live there? If the alleged victim is someone he lives with, does he have an alternative address or if necessary, an address out of the area?
- What is his local police station for the purposes of a reporting condition including what times/days of the week that he can report there?
- Does he have anyone who is willing to act as a surety and if so, their contact details?
- Does he have anyone who is willing to act as a security and if so, their contact details?
- Can/will he comply with a curfew and if so what times?
- Would there be any difficulties in complying with a condition of non-contact with the victim/prosecution witnesses? For example; a neighbour or a work colleague.
- Would he have any difficulties in complying with an area restriction/exclusion zone? i.e. would it prevent him from accessing his place of employment/home address/children's school etc.

YOUR ADVICE TO THE CLIENT ON BAIL

It is important to be realistic with your client about the prospects of success of their bail application but unless he is charged with murder and subject to the statutory exceptions to bail, he has the right to make two bail applications in the Magistrates' Court. No matter how soul destroying it may seem, you cannot and must not refuse to make a bail application on his behalf. Whilst of course you can advise him that it is likely that bail will be refused, ultimately the choice is his and most clients take the view that if you do not ask, you do not get and they have a point. I recall a seven handed sophisticated cultivation of cannabis case where all defendants were Vietnamese nationals, all in this country illegally. The evidence against them all was overwhelming but nonetheless, all advocates in the case were instructed to make a bail application. No-one was more surprised than us when the magistrates granted bail. The prosecution appealed the decision and they were all safely remanded into custody by the Crown Court Judge by 4pm the same day, but it underlines the point.

A seeming reluctance on your part to make a bail application is a sure fire way of upsetting the client if for no other reason than it shows a lack of willingness to fight on his behalf, particularly if there are co-defendants making bail applications. What may appear to be a hopeless bail application may well end up being the piece of advocacy that persuades your client of your abilities.

On occasions, your client will instruct you not to make a bail application for him and if he does so, you should advise him that if he chooses not to make a bail application at that first hearing then that will count as one of his bail applications and likewise the second. The defendant does not in fact have the right to two bail applications he has the opportunity to make two bail applications.

If the client consents to being remanded in custody or is unlikely to be admitted to bail you should ask him whether he wants to be produced for any future re-remand hearings or whether he consents to being re-remanded in his absence. This is something that you will be asked in court so you need to know the answer. Often clients do not want to be troubled by any further remand hearings and just want to settle into their time in custody untroubled by unnecessary court appearances.

Clients and their families will be anxious to know which prison he will be taken to in the event of his remand in custody. Try to find this out as early as possible as it often a welcome relief to terrified clients, in particular those who have never been remanded in custody before. Anything you can do (excluding at this point the obvious of getting them bail) to ease the process is all part of the job and more cynically, a good way of keeping your client happy.

Often your client will either have asked to or have been put down to see the court community psychiatric nurse (CPN). If your client has not already seen him or her by the time you get to the cells you should advise him firstly, that he does not have to see the CPN and secondly, that whatever he says to the CPN will go in their report and will be read by the magistrates and the prosecution. As an example of this I had a client who was withdrawing from drugs and thought that if he saw the CPN he would get some medication and for that reason alone, asked to see him. In fact what he did was tell the CPN precisely how bad his habit was and that he was routinely shoplifting in order to fund it. In doing so, he secured his own remand into custody.

ADVICE TO CLIENT WHEN BAIL IS REFUSED:

If bail is refused on the first occasion you should tell the client that he will have the opportunity to make a second bail application within a maximum of eight clear days (unless the matter is sent to the Crown Court for trial in which case, his next bail application will be to the Crown Court judge in chambers). This hearing will usually take place by way of the video link from the prison. If there was any information lacking in your first bail application you should ensure that you take details of anyone you can contact who could bolster your chances on the next occasion, for example; a surety.

If he is remanded following the second bail application you should advise him that unless there is a change of circumstances he cannot make any further bail applications to the magistrates but he does have the right to a judge in chambers bail application in the Crown Court.

If you have not already found out then if possible, you should tell him which prison he is going to.

Lastly, but importantly, do not forget to ask him whether he consents to you discussing his case with any family members, friends or his partner and get specific names of those people and how much he is happy for you to tell them. As a practical point you should get his written authority on this in case of any complaints of breaching client confidentiality at a later stage. If any family or friends are at court they will inevitably want to speak to you about the case and without authority from the client, you cannot do this. On the other hand, keeping the family happy can be an important way of keeping the client happy so you do not want to keep them in the dark unnecessarily. A happy family is generally a happy client.

ADVICE AND INSTRUCTIONS ABOUT BAIL

Advice on bail generally

If, having considered the papers and your client's antecedent history you think that there is a chance that the court will consider a remand in custody despite the fact that he has appeared on bail, you must advise the client of this and take full instructions for a bail application as above so that you are prepared in the event of being asked to make a bail application for him at short notice.

If your client is granted bail or is on bail to attend court on a future date you should advise him that if he fails to attend court without a reasonable excuse then he may be committing a separate offence under the Bail Act, the maximum sentence for which in the Magistrates' Court is a three month custodial sentence and in the Crown Court, a twelve month custodial sentence. In practical terms you should also tell him that if he is unfit to attend court then he will need a doctor's certificate specifically saying that he is unfit to attend *court*, why he is unfit and for how long he will remain unfit. A medical certificate simply signing him off work will not be sufficient.

He should also be advised that if he fails to attend court without a reasonable excuse it is likely that a warrant without bail will be issued meaning the he is at risk of being arrested at some unearthly hour and kept in custody to be brought before the first available court where the question of bail will be re-considered and he will be at risk of being remanded in custody until the next court date.

Advice where the client is subject to bail conditions:

Firstly you need to consider whether the bail conditions are necessary under the Bail Act. Since the introduction of fixed fees at the police station, fewer solicitors or legal representatives are present for the charging decision. This means that the defendants may be charged and bailed by the police subject to often unnecessary and unworkable bail conditions. A good example is a condition not to be on any licensed premises. This includes shops, supermarkets and garages which are licensed to sell alcohol although they may have no relevance to the reasons for the imposition of the condition which usually relates to pubs. If your client has been made the subject of any such bail conditions then make an application should be made to vary or lift those conditions.

There will be times when you will be required to apply to vary your client's bail conditions. You will have advised your client about the prospect of success of any such application warning him about making spurious applications. However, if there is merit in his application do not be afraid to apply to the court to vary his conditions. A common example of a case in which this arises is offences of domestic violence. Reconciliation between partners leads to the defendant instructing you to apply to be allowed back to the matrimonial home and he will often come to court with the complainant in support of his application. Courts can be unimpressed with the victim of such an assault then appearing at court in support of their assailant and their wishes to have him return to the home address will certainly not always be granted. When faced with the complainant in a case of this nature refer him or her to the prosecutor so as not to appear to be in any way influencing his or her decision.

If your client is released by the court subject to bail conditions then he should be informed that any suspected breach will result in his arrest and he will be kept in custody to be brought before the first available court within twenty four hours. Always remember to check that the police and prosecution have complied with this time frame and if they have not your client's alleged breach will go unpunished. If the breach is proven, the question of bail will be re-opened and he will be at risk of being remanded in custody until the next court date. Again using an offence of domestic violence as the example, if conditions of non-contact apply, the defendant should be reminded that responding to contact initiated by the complainant is still contact. It is not a defence to say, 'she texted me first'. We have all conducted cases where we suspect that the complainant is responsible for instigating contact between the pair and have sympathy in those circumstances with our client. However, it is not the complainant who has court or police imposed bail conditions. If your client instructs you that this is happening then you should speak to the prosecutor at court and ask for him to convey to the victim or whoever it is that contact should cease and on a practical note to the client, tell him to keep a log of the contact and report any contact to the police but not to respond.

BAIL APPLICATION CHECKLIST

NAME:

CURRENT ADDRESS:

PROSECUTION OBJECTIONS:

STRENGTH OF EVIDENCE?

PROPOSED BAIL ADDRESS

—WHO OWNS PROPERTY

—IN WHAT CAPACITY DOES CLIENT RESIDE THERE?

—HOW LONG HAS CLIENT BEEN RESIDENT?

—OWN ROOM/SHARED

—WHO ELSE RESIDES THERE?

—RENT PAID BY WHOM? HOW MUCH?

COMMUNITY TIES

—DOB

—PLACE OF BIRTH?

—WHERE BROUGHT UP?

—BY WHOM?

—EDUCATION?/LEARNING DIFFICULTIES?

—MARRIED/SINGLE/DIVORCED/COHABITING?

—CHILDREN?

—WHERE PARENT/PARTNER/FRIENDS/RELATIVES LIVE?

—EMPLOYED?/BY WHOM?

—LENGTH OF EMPLOYMENT?

—CONTACT DETAILS?

—TELEPHONE NO?

—IF NOT WORKING HOW LONG U/E?

—ANY TRADE OR PROFESSION?

—WHAT JOB PROSPECTS?

—DAY/HOW OFTEN/AMOUNT OF SIGNING ON?

—WHICH BENEFIT?

—GP DETAILS?

—PRESCRIPTIONS?

—OTHER HELP AGENCIES?

—SURETY/SECURITY? AND DETAILS?

IS ANYBODY ATTENDING COURT ON DEF BEHALF? AND DETAILS?

OFFENDING HISTORY:

—DETAILS AND RELEVANCE OF PREVIOUS CONV

—RECORD OF OFFENDING WHILST ON BAIL

—PREVIOUS RECORD OF ANSWERING BAIL

HAVE YOU DISCUSSED THE CHANCES OF BAIL WITH THE CLIENT?

WHAT CONDITIONS ARE ACCEPTABLE TO CLIENT AND THE COURT?

AND HAVE YOU EXPLAINED WHAT CONDITIONS ENTAIL AND THE CONSEQUENCES OF FAILING TO SURRENDER AND/OR BREACH

CONTACT WITH CPS:

—CAN BAIL CONDITIONS BE AGREED?

PROPOSED CONDITIONS:

—RESIDENCE

—REPORTING

—SURETY

—SECURITY

—CURFEW

—PASSPORT SURRENDER

—NO CONTACT

—AREA RESTRICTION

—OTHER

IF BAIL REFUSED LIKELY PLACE OF DETENTION:

FURTHER BAIL APPS/M CT/C CT?

HAVE YOU TOLD THE CLIENT THE PROSPECTS OF SUCCESS

FURTHER INFORMATION TO BE OBTAINED PRIOR TO NEXT BAIL APPLICATION

CHAPTER 9
PRE-COURT MISCELLANEOUS

FINAL PRE-COURT DEALINGS WITH THE PROBATION OFFICER – GUILTY PLEA

If your client is going to plead guilty, prior to your case being called on, you should speak to the court liaison probation officer if:

1. **You think the case is going to be dealt with by way of a community penalty or above.** (If your client is obviously going to get a conditional discharge or a financial penalty you do not need to speak to probation.)

   The reason for doing this is to discuss with the probation officer the level of pre-sentence report, if any, they think is necessary in your case. If your client is pleading guilty on an agreed basis then tell the probation officer this. You should also give the probation officer a brief summary of your proposed mitigation and any issues that your client has, i.e. drink, drugs or mental health as this may affect the level of report required.

   Check with the probation officer the timings of their proposed report, i.e. can it be done today or will an adjournment be required for the preparation of it, and if so, how long?

   If your client has recently been sentenced for an offence and in respect of that offence a pre-sentence report was before the court it is likely the probation officer will have a copy of it and if so, you should ask for a copy of that report. If there is a relatively recent report in existence it is likely that the probation officer will be able to deal with this case by way of a brief verbal update to the court.

2. **Your client is already subject to an order.**

   This is to establish how well he is complying with his order and what if any recommendations the probation service has in mind for this sentence.

   If the probation officer tells you that your client is responding badly to their existing order then I'm afraid you cannot ignore it and you must deal with it head on in your mitigation. You cannot mislead the court and furthermore, the Magistrates will hear it from the probation officer in any event.

   If this happens to you then you will obviously need to go back to the client and take his instructions on and the reasons for it.

DEALING WITH FAMILY AND FRIENDS OF THE DEFENDANT

Dealing with family and friends can be very difficult particularly when emotions are running high and your client is in custody or likely to receive an immediate custodial sentence. Whilst it can seem like the very last thing you have time to do when you are running about the courtroom, worrying about your bail application, it is actually a very important aspect of the job. Most families will want to ensure the best representation for their loved ones and will not take kindly to you appearing to have little time to discuss matters with them. Remember that defendants in custody have prison visits usually in between court appearances and a disgruntled father telling his son that his lawyer was rude and dismissive of the family concerns, is likely to cause irrevocable damage to your relationship with the defendant.

Before speaking to the family, obtain your client's authority to do so. Impress upon him how useful it will be to have a point of contact on the outside if he is remanded into custody. Do not begin discussions with a client's family no matter how much they hassle you until you have the requisite authority.

Once you have the authority of your client to discuss matters with his family then make sure that you are as realistic with them in terms of what is likely to happen to the defendant as you have been with the defendant himself. No matter how experienced the defendant is with the criminal justice system, families can find the process bewildering and frightening so remember to be tactful with your advice ensuring that they understand what is likely to happen and the reasons why.

Taking some time to discuss with family and friends the process and the likely outcomes is reassuring for them, particularly with young or vulnerable defendants is important for two reasons. Firstly, it is part of representing your client and is acting in his best interests but also it may assist with repeat instructions and this motivation if nothing else should spur you on to spend a little time with a defendant's family.

To give this some life, in my early days I was asked to represent a 13 year old at the police station. He had been arrested for a robbery. His mother was the appropriate adult and was quite possibly the most irritating woman I had ever come across. Dealing with a young and quite difficult client for a serious offence was quite problematic enough and I had better things to worry about than placating his overbearing mother. However, by spending some time with her, talking to her, reassuring her about the process, I won her over. She went on to ask for me every time her son was arrested. Ten years later, I am now on file 54 for that same client.

If a client asks you to call his girlfriend after the hearing to let her know what happened, then take the time to do it. These things do count. No matter how good your bail application or mitigation was, if you forget to do these seemingly small things afterwards, your client will forget all about your good work and remember that one important thing that you have not done. Never forget that if a client is in custody, he is unable to communicate with his family and will trust you to do it for him.

DEALING WITH THE PRESS

In the Magistrates' Courts, you are unlikely to have to deal with the press particularly often. However, there will be times when you will be approached by members of the press, usually the written press, asking for some information about the case.

The most you will usually be asked for is your name (avoid the temptation if things haven't gone well to give one of your roommates' names) as the case has attracted some level of public interest and they want to report one of your more catchy submissions, you should always be willing to provide them with this. However, there will be occasions when what they ask for is a little more detailed: Where does the defendant work? What's his home address? How long had he been in a relationship with the victim? In these circumstances you must always have your client's interests and wishes in mind. If the question and therefore the answer has not formed part of the evidence and is not a matter of public record under no circumstances should you give the press the information. However, it maybe that what is being asked for has been mentioned in open court and technically there is no reason for you not to tell the press the answer. However, if your client would not want you to, then do not; you are under no obligation to tell the press anything. You can refuse their request politely explaining to them that your client would prefer it if you did not disclose anything to them and all journalists should be used to this and take no offence at your stance.

If you are conducting a trial that is being reported in the local paper on a daily basis, your client may have a dim view of the way the case is being reported. It will usually be a complaint that the paper is only reporting one side of the story and although his worries are understandable, there is nothing that you can do about it. However, do keep an eye on the way the case is being reported and be sure to take action if something is reported inaccurately, by raising it with the clerk of the court and then the justices. This has the obvious effect of potentially drawing something to the attention of the court that they had been unaware but you must not take a risk if the inaccuracy has the potential for real prejudice to your client. Whether you do take action will of course be a matter for your judgment in the circumstances but try not to be over sensitive, very often a quiet word with the journalist can see the error rectified or at least not repeated.

There will be occasions, usually following an acquittal, when a journalist will ask if your client would like to be interviewed for the local paper. I have always thought that defendants giving interviews is a really bad idea, especially on the steps of the court when emotions are still running high.

The defendant may be determined to give the interview but try to stop him, it is hard to see how gloating about the result, threatening to sue everyone, criticizing the police and or the CPS or making accusations about witnesses, can in any way help your client's position. There may even be times when the defendant does have a potentially legitimate civil claim of some sort and in those circumstances to give an interview to the local hack about his intention to sue everyone from the Attorney General to the CPS typist, is hardly likely to help his position.

If possible, dissuade the defendant from talking to the press, if he ignores you, so be it, you will have done as much as you can.

CHAPTER 10
PRE-COURT HEARING PREPARATION

HOW TO PREPARE AND MAKE A BAIL APPLICATION

Whilst the content of your bail application will vary depending entirely on the circumstances of the case, the way you approach your preparation should always be the same.

On a practical note there is nothing wrong with writing your application word for word as long as when you are on your feet you are not so constrained by sticking to your script that you forget to respond to the points made by the prosecutor in their remand application.

There is an art to making an effective bail application and it is a skill well worth learning properly. A well-argued bail application that changes the minds of the magistrates is a very good way of scoring early points with your client. It is one of the first opportunities that you have to demonstrate your skills as an advocate to the client and no matter how hopeless the application is in reality, as long as the client has seen that you have made a genuine attempt for him, he will be happy. If despite the odds you actually succeed in your application you will have a happy client, out on bail singing your praises.

As with most aspects of advocacy, the real skill in making a bail application is refining what you say to the absolute minimum. There seems to be a sense with so many advocates that the more you say the more likely you are to succeed and I believe that the reality is the complete opposite. From the Magistrates' Court to the Court of Appeal, brevity is a welcome trait and this includes bail applications. If you have three good points to deal with the Crown's objections, just use those three points, a fourth, less powerful submission may have the effect of diluting the strength of the good points as the magistrates' thoughts drift to thinking what they will have for their lunch. I have seen in recent months an advocate, faced with a near impossible task of applying for bail in a nasty harassment case, persuade the room that his client deserved bail only to prolong his submissions by so much so as to lose the interest of the court. When he resorted to laughing in response to a question from the justices, one sensed it was a lost cause. Do not laugh in court when making submissions, to your client there is very little that he will consider humorous about the day's events.

Your bail application must address the objections to bail raised by the crown. If the crown are objecting to bail on the basis that your client is likely to commit

71

further offences whilst on bail there is no point basing your entire submission around the fact that your client has no previous bail act offences and is therefore likely to attend court if bailed.

If the crown's objections to bail are legitimate then you must meet them head on, do not ignore them but instead counter them with realistic submissions and properly considered suggested bail conditions that will address those objections and the concerns that the court will have in relation to them. It is often a powerful tool to concede that the court will have understandable concerns but to submit that those fears can be allayed by the imposition of certain of conditions.

In terms of style always refer to the client by his name which personalises the application. Do not refer to him as 'the defendant'. A common habit amongst advocates when making a hopeless bail application is to say 'I am instructed to make a bail application'. Do not do this. By saying this what you are actually saying to everyone in the courtroom is 'I know my application is hopeless and I am awfully embarrassed to be making it but my very annoying client insists'. The more experienced defendants will also know that this is what you are saying. Do not be embarrassed about making a well-argued bail application despite the seemingly hopeless merits of it. It is your job and everyone in the court room knows that.

In terms of how you should approach your application you should focus your mind on:

1. The strength of the evidence (although a recital of the arguments for and against will not be appropriate)
2. Your client's personal circumstances and community ties
3. Their antecedent history
4. The Crown's objections to bail
5. Realistic counter arguments
6. Your proposed bail conditions

You must also read the relevant sections of the Bail Act (make sure that it is up-to-date) and other related legislation so that you are live to the relevant law that applies in your case.

Strength of the evidence

Proper preparation for a bail application begins with consideration of the strength of the evidence against the defendant. It is the offence itself that the magistrates will principally have in their minds when considering bail and as a rough rule of thumb, the more serious the offence, the more likely they are to consider a remand in custody. If the evidence is strong then try not to pretend otherwise. For the purposes of a bail application the crown's case is taken at its highest and if taken at its highest the evidence is overwhelming there is no point droning on trying to convince the magistrates otherwise.

Conversely if the crown's case taken at its highest looks unlikely to succeed, then identify the apparent weaknesses but do so succinctly, this is not a closing speech in a trial. This is particularly important in cases where a principle crown witness has retracted their statement and the trial is two months away.

If your client is before the court on a serious charge the prosecutor will make the most of it, particularly if they are relying on the fact that your client is unlikely to surrender to bail. If the charge is serious but the evidence is weak then to emphasise this can be a powerful way of countering this. Assuming they help, refer to the sentence guidelines to demonstrate that actually your client is not necessarily facing a lengthy custodial sentence such that is likely to make him fail to surrender.

Alternatively if the evidence is strong but it is a relatively minor charge that will attract a short custodial sentence or a community penalty then it is perfectly valid to make the point that were the client to be remanded in relation to this offence he is likely to serve longer on remand than the likely sentence if convicted. Although this is not a consideration under the Bail Act it is a submission worth making.

Personal circumstances and community ties

This is particularly important where the crown suggest that your client is likely to fail to surrender. As part of their reasons for assessing whether this exception to bail applies, the magistrates will consider the personal circumstances of the defendant and assess whether he has significant community ties, including family and employment. As with any aspect of your bail application, this section should always be addressed towards the crown's objections. If for example the crown says he is likely to fail to surrender and your client is a working man with family commitments including his elderly mother who he takes to the hospital for her weekly check-up then be sure to tell the justices of this. Attendance at court of one or more of the defendant's family maybe something you should also consider informing the justices about.

If the crown says he is likely to commit further offences it maybe that certain submissions about his community ties will assist. If your client has been charged with a night time offence of non-dwelling burglary but has since gained night-shift work at the local supermarket, this maybe a submission regarding his community ties that helps to persuade the justices that the prospects of him having the opportunity to commit further offences is slim.

Antecedent history

If your client is a man of good character then your job is much easier. There is no demonstrable history of failing to surrender to bail, interfering with witnesses or indeed committing offences whilst on bail and you should use that in your submissions.

More often though your client does have convictions and whilst this can often make the job much harder, in some cases you can use those convictions to successfully demonstrate your point. Make sure you read them carefully as a bail application based on mis-information is bound to fail and will also make it look as if either you are deliberately trying to mislead the court or have not read the papers properly.

If the crown's case is that he is likely to fail to surrender and your client has ten previous convictions but no bail act offences then use that and turn it on its head to demonstrate that in fact it shows the court that he is a man who does attend court when required to do so.

If the crown's objection for the same client is that he is likely to commit further offences whilst on bail and whilst he does have ten previous convictions, none of them have been committed whilst on bail, then use that. If their objection is that he is likely to interfere with witnesses but he has no previous convictions for offences of that nature, then say so.

If your client has previously been subject to a conditional discharge, community order or a suspended sentence order and has no history of breaching such orders, this can be a useful way of demonstrating that he is in fact someone who can comply with court orders and is therefore capable of abiding by bail conditions.

Analyse the convictions for patterns and gaps. If the damaging convictions are a long time ago then make that point.

THE CROWN'S OBJECTIONS TO BAIL AND HOW CAN YOU REALISTICALLY COUNTER THOSE OBJECTIONS

1 Likely to commit further offences

- How long ago was the offence committed? Does the offence pre-date charge by a noteworthy length of time and have there been any offences since?
- Does the client have a history of committing offences whilst on bail and if so, how long ago?
- Is there any evidence that he is likely to commit further offences?

2 Likely to fail to surrender

- Does the client have previous bail act offences? If so, how long ago? In what circumstances? Are his circumstances more stable now? Has he faced further charges before the court since then for which he has attended?
- Does he have a fixed address?
- Does he have strong community ties?
- Does he have a full time job?
- Does he attend the benefits agency regularly to sign on?

- How many times did he attend the police station on bail prior to charge?
- Is the evidence so strong or the sentence so great that he will inevitably fail to attend?
- Has he been on bail for serious matters previously and attended?
- If he has previous convictions, has he previously pleaded guilty to them and is he contesting this matter?

3 Likely to interfere with witnesses or obstruct the course of justice

- Is the victim known to your client?
- Does he have any history of witness interference or perverting the course of justice?
- When did the alleged offence occur, if it was a few days, weeks, months ago has there been attempt to interfere or obstruct since?

Proposed bail conditions

The purpose of your proposed bail conditions is to address and counter the Crown's objections to bail. Conditions should only be attached where necessary. In your desperation to get bail, do not make the mistake of suggesting every bail condition possible in order to free your man. Think about what you are proposing and why.

Objections:

1 Likely to fail to surrender:

- Residence: So that the police know where he is, consider coupling this with a requirement of doorstep presentation. i.e. if the police attend to check his whereabouts he has to present himself to them.
- Reporting to the local police station: To remind him of his on-going responsibility to attend and so the police can keep tabs on him. If your client is homeless this can be particularly useful in the alternative of an address.
- A surety or security: To demonstrate that someone or many people have sufficient faith in him that he will attend that they are prepared to risk their money.

2 Likely to commit further offences:

- A curfew condition – (consider electronic monitoring only as direct alternative to custody): This is particular useful for night-time offending, less so if the offence was committed in the daytime. It can also be useful where for example the client is in full time work to reduce the amount of time that he has at large to offend.

3 Likely to interfere with witnesses/obstruct the course of justice:

- Non-contact with the prosecution witnesses: To prevent interference with them.

- Non-contact with co-defendants: To prevent collusion or destruction of evidence between them.
- Residence out of the area coupled with a condition not to enter the area (save to attend court and his solicitors – if necessary): To reduce the concern that he will have any contact with the victim/witnesses or interfere with them.
- An exclusion zone – make sure this is properly delineated on a map so that it is clear to the client: Again, to reduce the chance of interference with witnesses/contact with them.

The list above is by no means exhaustive but are examples of matters for you to consider when you are preparing your application. Do not just read the papers and give up. Analyse them and you will always find that there is at least something you can sensibly say.

MITIGATION

One of the most important skills to have as an advocate is to be able to advance a proper plea in mitigation. Whilst we would all like to think that we are so good that our clients are rarely convicted the reality is that you will spend far more time mitigating than you will doing almost any other discipline in the job, which makes the lack of thought and care that goes into this aspect of defending astonishing.

Most examples of the mitigation advanced by advocates in all courts, but particularly the Magistrates' Courts, is poorly prepared, lazy and without any sort of structure. To take the view, which far too many do, that the justices have made up their minds and therefore there is no point putting any effort or work into the plea in mitigation is a terrible abrogation of your duties as a defender. To be in court and see a magistrate, district judge or even Crown Court judge have his or her mind changed by the powerful, persuasive mitigation advance by a skilful advocate is one of the great spectacles of the profession and we should all strive to be that advocate.

It rarely happens that there is dramatic change in the type or length of the sentence but every time you get to your feet at this stage of the case, you should be aiming to make a difference of some sort, whether that be reducing the hours of the curfew, arguing for a custodial term to be suspended or trying to lower the level of a fine. There is always some sort of target and for that reason mitigation is almost always vitally important and to fail to prepare properly for it is unacceptable.

As part of my research for this book I spent quite a bit of time at local Magistrates' Courts observing, and the terrible standards of mitigation was one of the stand-out features of the process. I watched an advocate mitigating for a man who had assaulted a police officer, not it should be said, the first time an officer had been on the receiving end of his aggression. This chap had pleaded guilty and although that was undoubtedly one of the best points, to repeat it four times was completely unnecessary. The DJ had cause on more than one occasion to ask the advocate to stop repeating the same point. The defendant got cross with his solicitor as she seemed to irritate the judge every time she spoke and she then had the rather embarrassing experience of trying to placate him at the back of the court which, because of the glass that encases the dock, had to be done rather more loudly than anyone would want.

The mitigation continued but did not improve and it was clear to anyone watching and listening that absolutely no thought had gone into this crucial hearing and the DJ sentenced the defendant to 9 weeks imprisonment. Now, the likelihood is that the sentence imposed on this chap was beyond criticism and I doubt whether a higher court has interfered with it in anyway. However, I left court that morning utterly convinced that if the mitigation had been prepared and presented with care and skill, the defendant would have left court through the front door. Instead, his advocate bumbled her way through a submission which had no structure or direction and I know that if that had been me on the receiving end of the DJ's spiky remarks I would have left court feeling that I had not done my job properly and that the defendant missing a month or so of daytime television was down to me – and I would have been right.

I suppose it boils down to this; Probably 99% of sentences imposed by the justices are, on paper, beyond reproach but that does not mean that some of them could not have been improved upon with more skilful advocacy at the sentencing hearing. Almost every time you get to your feet to say a few words on the defendant's behalf there will be an aspect of the sentence that you can influence if you do it properly. If you adopt this approach to every plea in mitigation that you advance then, from time to time, you will achieve a result that nobody expects and one, which will bring professional reward in the form of further instructions and personal satisfaction knowing that it was you, and you alone that made the difference.

I have an approach to preparing a plea in mitigation that has not changed since pupilage. I was shown this by Jeremy Gold QC (now HHJ Gold QC) before he was a silk and when I was in his chambers. I am yet to find a case where the approach doesn't work and its simplicity seems to provide a natural structure for the submission. Before I detail the approach I want to say a few words about the preparatory work that must be done before you sit down to write your mitigation remarks.

Firstly, know the sentencing regime for the offences in detail. In order to advise your client about what prize he or she is likely to receive then you need not only to know the maximum sentence (as clients so often ask this question) but the types of sentences available and the sentencing guidelines. I will never forget confidently advising a 17 year old that although I felt the offences to which he had pleaded guilty were deserving of a custodial sentence, I was sure I could persuade the sentencing judge to suspend the custodial term.

It is that sort of mistake that shows a lack of preparation and completely undermines any faith your client may have had in you, especially if, as I did in that case, you do not realise the error and begin your bold address by telling the judge that you hope to have persuaded him by the end of the submission to do something which unbeknown to me was, and always had been, completely beyond his powers.

Since 2003 and the introduction of the Sentencing Guidelines Council (now the Sentencing Council), courts are more slavishly following their guidelines and why people do not make more use of them is a mystery. They are a pretty bulletproof way of advising your client as to the sentencing range and should avoid any awkward conversations after the hearing where your client accuses you of woefully understating the seriousness of the case as he climbs aboard the prison van.

Secondly, make sure have thoroughly read the pre-sentence report and any other reports that will be used by the sentencing tribunal. Some of the information contained within these reports can be weaved into your mitigation remarks adding an unbiased weight to your submissions. However, do not become overly reliant on the report, it is only the view of the probation service and do not, whatever you do, rehearse the report in a slightly different order as your plea in mitigation. Many a DJ opens a sentencing hearing by hearing the facts and then saying:

'Mr Bloggs, I have read the pre-sentence report on your client and I consider its conclusion to be wholly unrealistic, I'll take some persuading to follow it...'.

If you have not bothered to do anything other than re-jig the report you will be in serious trouble at this stage.

You must learn how to use the report to supplement and bolster your submissions where possible but not to form the basis of them. The conclusions in pre-sentence reports can range from very helpful to utterly unhelpful to hopelessly unrealistic and consequently their use to you as the defending advocate will vary and you must be prepared to be flexible with how much you use and rely upon them.

However, there are certain times when you will have to confront aspects of the report head-on with the justices, even if you do not want to. The most common example is when your client has met with a probation officer and said something like:

'I did hit the victim 45 times with a house brick but I only did it because I was defending myself and I only pleaded guilty because my barrister told me to'.

No matter how ludicrous it sounds you must speak to your client about it as the sentencing judge or magistrate will not be able to ignore it. The chances are that your client will deny making any such remark and in which case you need to find an appropriate form of words that can satisfy the court that it is all an unfortunate misunderstanding. Be careful not to overly criticise the probation officer, even if that's what your client's instructions amount to. DJs and magistrates do not take kindly to such criticism for two main reasons; firstly, the probation service perform a very important role and to have defendants routinely decrying their efforts through their advocate would not be a healthy situation and secondly and more importantly, it is unlikely that the probation officer has just attributed a remark to your client that has no foundation whatsoever and in the unlikely event that they have, the tribunal will not believe that to be the case. So, be careful to find a neutral form of words that satisfies the court that the defendant's plea is unequivocal, appeases your client's sense of being wronged whilst not being critical of the probation service. There will be occasions when your client leaves you with no choice but to criticise the author of the pre-sentence report and, when that situation arises you must be very careful not to just become a mouthpiece for your client's insulting and offensive views about the probation officer. Make the submission, without fear of course but do so politely and sensitively.

Thirdly, be realistic. When you are writing your mitigation remarks and you are thinking about what it is you want to persuade the justices to do, have an achievable target in mind and do not ever lose sight of it. If the target you set is realistic and justifiable then each of the individual points that you have within your plea will, on their own sound so much more convincing and overall the submission will be so much more persuasive. Far too many advocates misjudge this and set such high targets that they, and more importantly their clients, are destined to be disappointed.

Their reasoning for doing so is flawed. They are treating the submissions in mitigation as some sort of negotiation process with the sentencing tribunal, making an early, very low bid believing that the sentencer will be prepared to compromise from his/her original view of the appropriate sentence and meet the advocate half-way or thereabouts. Let me give this point some life. A man is charged with common assault on his partner. This is the fifth time he has been charged with assaulting this woman and he has ten other convictions for offences of violence of varying degrees. He drinks too much and when he does he becomes violent. The current offence was committed whilst he was still subject to a period of unexpired license relating to his last conviction for attacking the same woman. He pleaded not guilty and the justices convicted him in ten minutes flat. He has made it clear to the author of the PSR that he will not engage with the probation service for supervision as he thinks that they hate men, he will not do unpaid work as he will have to mix with criminals and will not abide by a curfew as that would interrupt valuable drinking time.

Everyone knows that this man is going to prison and your submissions should focused on keeping that inevitable prison term to the absolute minimum. The advocate I was describing above would know that the justices are considering 5–6 months imprisonment and therefore he would ask for a suspended sentence. His flawed logic being that the justices are likely to meet him half way if they give any credence at all to his submission for the custodial term to not be immediate.

This approach is wrong for two good reasons; firstly, being unrealistic is likely to irritate the sentencing tribunal into rejecting almost everything you have to say and secondly, you are filling your client with false hope at a time when he needs to be told precisely what is about to happen to him.

Magistrates will not become embroiled in a Dutch auction with an advocate whom they will know is chancing his arm. That advocate should know that the first thing that the magistrates will do is to seek guidance from the court clerk who, if experience is anything to go by, is unlikely to be sympathetic to this sort of bluffing. The legal adviser will tell the justices that the guidelines say that he should go to prison for almost the maximum period available and they will follow his/her advice.

A better approach would be to concede that custody is inevitable and to focus on two or three reasons why they might be able to reduce the sentence below what is to be expected. Concessions are amazingly powerful tools in mitigation and are much underused. Some advocates think that to concede anything at all is a sign of weakness – utter nonsense. To make a concession takes courage but so often it is the right thing to do.

My method, as I have already said is about as straightforward as it could be. I split the mitigation into three categories, offence, offender and proposal. There are no circumstances that I have encountered where this approach is unsuitable.

Offence

Within this section I start by making any concessions about the seriousness of the offence or the impact on the victim. Get the bad bits out of the way and then focus on what maybe more positive, in particular any mitigating features (always check the sentencing guidelines for what constitutes a mitigating feature but do not limit yourself to that list if there is another feature that you feel genuinely mitigates the seriousness of the offence).

I always end this section, where the case permits me, by mentioning the guilty plea. With a large range of offences it provides a defendant with his best mitigation and credit for a plea can be the difference between a custodial sentence or not or a suspended rather than immediate prison term.

Pleading guilty always spares the court the time and expense of a trial and for that there is credit to be afforded to the defendant, however, for offences of a violent or sexual nature giving evidence can be a miserable ordeal and an embarrassing experience. Reliving the crime in a room full of people can be degrading and upsetting and if a defendant spares a victim this by pleading guilty, especially in a timely fashion, be sure to make forceful submissions about it.

This is often an area where referring to the pre-sentence report is a good idea. If a defendant has persuaded the author of the report that he has shown genuine remorse and has real insight into the impact of his offending upon the victim then tie that into your mitigation regarding the guilty plea. A plea of guilty is one thing but one that is entered for all the right reasons is even better.

Offender

I always begin with age, domestic situation and employment as there is usually something to be said regarding one of these areas that amounts to mitigation and it does give the court some sort of background about your client.

I then deal with previous convictions. If they are numerous and relevant you have to confront the subject, this will be expected of you and you must try to find a way to grasp something positive from the position. If of course he has convictions but not relevant ones make that point and better still, if he has none, make a song and dance about it. Nothing is better for the defending advocate than being able to describe his client as having acted wholly out of character especially if the crime to which he has pleaded guilty is a one-off incident. Be careful about describing someone as acting wholly out of character when they have been stealing £50 a week from their elderly aunt for the last twelve months.

This is often a good time to introduce any references the defendant has provided but make sure you read them carefully. Referees are always well meaning but the contents of their testimonials can often sound unsympathetic to a victim and dismissive of the seriousness of the offence that has brought the defendant to court. No magistrate or judge wants to read in a character reference that the defendant is the real victim in the case as, if it was not for an appalling accounts system at work he would never have been tempted to steal £5,000 from his employer.

It is often quite a tricky decision to choose which to use, as even those that contain inappropriate remarks will often have some useful information within them. However, if a defendant has been convicted after a trial, you must never hand in a reference that questions the validity of the conviction; even if it goes on to make some very helpful comments. Even if this person has watched the trial and considers the conviction to be a travesty of justice, what this person thinks is utterly irrelevant and often very unhelpful. Remember, the justices that presided over this travesty will be the justices sentencing the defendant and criticising their decision is disrespectful to the court and unhelpful to the defendant's cause.

If it permits me to, I then deal with two areas contained within the pre-sentence report. An assessment that the defendant poses a low risk of re-offending and/ or future harm can be a powerful tool in mitigation and it should be drawn to the attention of the justices, in particular if you are trying to persuade them that the defendant has acted out of character.

Before I deal with the recommendation I focus on any issues relating to substance abuse whether drink or drugs which often ties in quite neatly with any suggested non-custodial options in the psr, as they often form the basis for the probation officer's reasoning.

The proposal

By proposal, I mean your proposal. Very often this will coincide with or be steered by, the suggestion in the report but it is not always the case. There may be occasions when an aspect of the probation proposal is too onerous or a little unfair and in those circumstances, do not be afraid to make an amended suggestion to the justices.

You should have your proposal well in mind when drafting your mitigation remarks. Every point you make should be geared towards persuading the justices that your suggestion makes sense, is fair to the defendant whilst being commensurate with the seriousness of the offence. If your submissions have been focused, succinctly put and supported by the PSR and other testimonials before the court then your suggestion is likely to be favourably received. If on the other hand your submissions lack clarity, structure or supporting documentation by the time you reach the part of your address where you are suggesting a particular disposal, the tribunal are likely to have stopped listening, and from what I have seen at some of our courts, quite rightly so.

Mitigation is a skill that advocates all too frequently ignore. Bad advocacy at this stage of the proceedings can be so costly that it makes no sense not to learn how to do it properly. I was lucky enough to be shown this idiot's guide to mitigation during my pupillage and I do not foresee many situations when I will depart from it. There will be times when the DJ wants to set the agenda for the presentation of the plea in mitigation and that will mean a departure from the usual format but do not think your preparation has then been pointless, quite the opposite. If you are well prepared no matter what order or format it takes, you will be able to advance the appropriate mitigation. It is when you have not prepared that in that situation it all very quickly goes wrong.

Finally, be prepared to be brief. Sometimes you read a case and think to yourself there are only really two points in mitigation; that is just fine. If there are only two points worth making do not kid yourself that you can turn an average point into a good one – you cannot. Genuine mitigating factors are finite and to know the limits is a skill worth learning. At a recent Magistrates' Court visit I heard an advocate mitigating and he was doing quite a good job 'my client has a job (shows responsibility), when he is not working he looks after his poorly mother (caring boy), he doesn't drink alcohol (will be able to do unpaid work hangover free) and is good at saving money (can pay the fine and compensation)'. Having made these three or four good submissions he hit the justices with his finest point ... 'and Sir, on top of all of that the defendant is a vegetarian.....'. I still have absolutely no idea what the point was and nor, by the look on their faces, did the magistrates'. It is a light-hearted, albeit true, example of a serious point. Do not make unnecessary submissions just for the sake of saying something. A punchy, well directed, ten minute submission, that makes only three points about the defendant or his case is worth so much more than making twenty dubious points in a forty five minute, sleep-inducing address.

Summary of sentences available in relation to adults in the Magistrates' Court

SENTENCE	DETAILS	MINIMUM/MAXIMUM LENGTH/AMOUNT
ABSOLUTE OR CONDITIONAL DISCHARGE	Test is: 'Having regard to the circumstances of the case, it would be inexpedient to impose any further punishment'.	Absolute: No minimum or maximum Conditional: No minimum. Maximum 3 years.

SENTENCE	DETAILS	MINIMUM/MAXIMUM LENGTH/AMOUNT
FINE	Note: If client remanded by the police and offence imprisonable, consider asking for 1 day's detention in lieu of fine. Note: If client unable to pay immediately, ask for magistrates to make a collection order. Note: In terms of amount of fine, if D on low income, ask magistrates to make it commensurate with means.	See statutory maximum available for offence. Level 1: Max £200 Level 2: Max £500 Level 3: Max £1000 Level 4: Max £2,500 Level 5: Max: £5000 Additionally court must impose victim's surcharge of £15.

SENTENCE	DETAILS	MINIMUM/MAXIMUM LENGTH/AMOUNT
COMPENSATION	Note: If D of limited means, compensation takes priority over fines and cost. Note: Can be imposed in addition to a custodial sentence. Note: Unless compensation is agreed, prosecution must evidence amount.	No minimum amount Maximum amount £5,000 per offence

SENTENCE	DETAILS	MINIMUM/MAXIMUM LENGTH/AMOUNT
BIND OVER	Test is: court must be satisfied that a breach of the peace involving violence or an imminent threat of violence has occurred, or there is real risk of violence in the future. Note: Court must be satisfied of above beyond all reasonable doubt. Note: Can only be made by consent. Note: Order must be clear and precise in terms of prohibited conduct.	No minimum or maximum amount of recognizance BUT if amount is 'less than trivial' – should be enquiry into means. No minimum length. Maximum length should not normally exceed 12 months

SENTENCE	DETAILS	MINIMUM/MAXIMUM LENGTH/AMOUNT
COMMUNITY ORDER	Test is: Offence or combination of offences is serious enough to warrant a community order. Note: Community order can only be imposed for imprisonable offences Note: Even if community threshold passed, court can impose a lesser sentence. Note: Court must obtain a PSR unless of the view that it is unnecessary.	No minimum length Maximum length: 3 years Requirements **Unpaid work:** Minimum hours: 40 Maximum hours: 300 Must be completed within 12 months If more than one offence, ct can impose consecutive hours but must not exceed 300 in total

84

SENTENCE	DETAILS	MINIMUM/MAXIMUM LENGTH/AMOUNT
	Note: D <u>can</u> be subject to more than one community order.	**Activity requirement:** No minimum Maximum aggregate 60 days.
	Note: Assess whether offence seriousness is low, medium or high and ensure that proposed requirements are proportionate to the level of seriousness.	**Programme requirement:** Length must be expressed as a number of sessions. No minimum or maximum sessions. Must be coupled with a supervision requirement.
	Note: Order must contain at least one requirement but contain a combination of requirements.	**Prohibited activity requirement:** No minimum period. Maximum: 3 years
		Curfew requirement: No minimum length of order. Maximum length of order: 6 months. Minimum hours of curfew period: 2 Maximum hours of curfew period: 12. Can specify different places or different periods for different days.
		Exclusion requirement: No minimum. Maximum: 2 years.
		Residence requirement: No minimum. Maximum: 3 years.
		Mental health requirement: No minimum. Maximum: 3 years. Court must have medical evidence from approved practitioner.
		Drug rehabilitation requirement: Minimum length: 6 months Maximum length: 3 years

SENTENCE	DETAILS	MINIMUM/MAXIMUM LENGTH/AMOUNT
		Alcohol treatment requirement: Minimum length: 6 months Maximum length: 3 years **Supervision requirement:** Supervision requirement length will be the overall length of the community order. **Attendance centre requirement:** Minimum: 12 hours Maximum: 36 hours. Maximum length of session: 3 hours

SENTENCE	DETAILS	MINIMUM/MAXIMUM LENGTH/AMOUNT
SUSPENDED SENTENCE ORDER NB CAN SUSPEND SENTENCE FOR ALL OFFENDERS 18+	Test is: Has the custody threshold been passed? Is the offence or combination of offences so serious that neither a fine or community penalty can be justified? Note: Magistrates must decide that custody is the only option and the length of it before making the decision to suspend it. Note: Court should consider a PSR unless it is of the opinion that it would be unnecessary.	Minimum custodial period: 14 days Minimum operation and supervision period: 6 months Maximum custodial period: 6 months Maximum operation and supervision period: 2 years. Court MUST impose at least one community requirement subject to the maximum available for the specific requirement

SENTENCE	DETAILS	MINIMUM/MAXIMUM LENGTH/AMOUNT
DETENTION IN YOUNG OFFENDERS INSTITUTION DEFENDANTS AGED 18–20	Test is: Has the custody threshold been passed? Is the offence or combination of offences so serious that neither a fine or community penalty can be justified? Note: The court can impose a custodial sentence when d refuses to co-operate with a community order. Note: Court should consider a PSR unless it is of the opinion that it would be unnecessary.	Minimum: 21 days Maximum: Dictated by statute BUT in any event, 6 months where one or more summary only offence. 12 months where two or more either way offences.

SENTENCE	DETAILS	MINIMUM/MAXIMUM LENGTH/AMOUNT
IMMEDIATE CUSTODY DEFENDANTS AGED 21+	Test is: Has the custody threshold been passed? Is the offence or combination of offences so serious that neither a fine or community penalty can be justified? Note: The court can impose a custodial sentence when d refuses to co-operate with a community order. Note: Court should consider a PSR unless it is of the opinion that it would be unnecessary.	Minimum: 5 days (unless 1 days detention in lieu of fine) Maximum: Dictated by statute BUT in any event, 6 months where one or more summary only offence. 12 months where two or more either way offences.

SENTENCE	DETAILS	MINIMUM/MAXIMUM LENGTH/AMOUNT
HOSPITAL ORDER	Note: Can only be made in respect of imprisonable offences. Note: Ct must have oral or written evidence from two registered Drs that the D suffers from: Mental illness Psychopathic disorder Severe mental impairment Mental impairment Of a nature and degree that makes it appropriate for him to be detained in a hospital	Date of release determined by the hospital NOT the court.

FINAL PRE-COURT STEPS

Now you are ready for your hearing the final thing you should do is to go and find the court usher and tell him that you are ready. The usher is very important in the Magistrates' Court as he basically controls the court list on the day and is not a person to upset. If you are courteous, polite and realistic about the timings of your case with the usher he will do his best to help you out, whether it to be to get your case on quickly or delay it for you if you are likely to be held up.

It is very easy in the beginning to think that you and your case are the most important feature of the court's business that day when the reality is that you are just a tiny piece of the system. Many pupils and newly qualified solicitors appearing in court in the early days fail to show sufficient respect to the court staff and in particular the usher. The usher is a vital part of the system with considerable power at his fingertips so be polite and courteous at all times, you never know when you will need a favour and you are unlikely to get one if you have been ordering people around as if they are your servant.

The usher will usually ask you how long you are going to be or what is happening in your case so try to be realistic with your estimate of the court time that you will need. Sometimes through no fault of your own you will get it wrong, no-one will criticise that but telling an usher at 1255pm that you will be five minutes is not on if you are still making submissions at 120pm, taking up the valuable lunch break of the court staff.

If your client is particularly vulnerable or has a genuine need to get on quickly for example, a doctor's appointment then tell the usher this and they will usually try and accommodate you.

FINAL PRE-COURT STEPS IF YOUR CLIENT IS PLEADING GUILTY

Once you have established that your client will be pleading not guilty you need to do the following:

1 Speak to the prosecutor

Not guilty plea – Magistrates' Court trial agreed.

- Tell the prosecutor that your client is pleading not guilty.
- Discuss with the prosecutor which witnesses can be agreed. If there is a witness whose evidence you could agree subject to editing then raise that with the prosecutor and see if he is able to agree the proposed edits. In reality it is unlikely that he will have the time or even the authority to make that decision in which case you should warn the witness to attend for trial until such time as your proposed edits can be agreed.

- Hand the prosecutor your fully completed case management form for him to complete his section if he has not already done so.
- Discuss/agree with the prosecutor the time estimate for the trial.
- If your client wants to apply to vary/lift his bail conditions – see if they can be agreed with the prosecutor. This will help you address your mind to those objections in your application.
- If the prosecutor is applying for a remand in custody, confirm on what basis and what his objections to bail are. Canvass with him your proposed bail conditions and see whether you can persuade him to agree them. Usually by this stage the prosecutor will have made up his mind but it is still worth a try *unless* a remand is so inevitable that the conversation would be futile. Remember here to be realistic with the prosecutor so as to maintain your credibility for any future, more sensible representations.

Not guilty plea – Venue not agreed.

- Now that most offences are covered by sentencing guidelines it is unlikely that there will be much dispute between you and the prosecutor as to whether the matter is suitable for summary trial as the likely sentence is clearly prescribed in the guidelines. However, if you disagree with the prosecutor's view of where your case falls within the relevant guidelines or case law make your representations to the prosecutor. Do not be afraid to show them the guidelines and be prepared to argue your point. If there is still no agreement between you, then you will need to make those representations to the magistrates.

Not guilty plea – Crown Court trial agreed.

- Tell the prosecutor that your client will be pleading not guilty and is either electing or conceding Crown Court trial; whichever is applicable.
- Discuss bail as above if applicable.

2 Liaise with any co-defending advocates (if applicable)

- If you have already completed the form, then hand them your copy to complete on behalf of their client or vice versa.

3 If summary trial – ascertain defence witnesses dates to avoid for trial where possible

- If your client has provided you with the contact details of his proposed defence witnesses then you should contact them to find out if they have any dates to avoid for trial, likewise if any potential witnesses are at court in support of your client.
- If your client does not have the relevant contact details with him or you are unable to contact the witness, make sure that when you are listing the matter for trial you make it clear to the court that you are setting the trial date without the benefit of your clients' witnesses dates to avoid for trial,

therefore putting them on notice that an application to vacate the trial date may become necessary in due course.

- With regards to expert witnesses, it is extremely unlikely that you will even have a particular expert in mind at this stage let alone his dates to avoid. Magistrates' Court trials are routinely set without the defence having yet instructed their own expert and as long as you have notified the court that a defence expert is a possibility, you will not be criticised, should an application to vacate the trial become necessary at a later date.

CHAPTER 11
THE FIRST COURT HEARING

THE COURT-ROOM LAYOUT

The following is a general guide to court room layout:

- The magistrates or district judge sits at the front of the court. If it is a lay bench, the chair of the bench sits in the middle of the three.
- The legal adviser sits in front of the magistrates.
- The prosecutor sits in the front row nearest the witness box.
- The defence advocate/s sits in the front row on the other side to the prosecutor – or if the dock is at the side of the court, nearest the dock.
- The court liaison probation officer sits [usually] at the side of the court-room.
- The defendant sits in the dock which is usually to the side or the rear of the court-room.
- The interpreter (if applicable) once sworn sits in the dock with the defendant.
- Members of the public sit in the public gallery which will either be at the side or the back of the court or upstairs in a public gallery overlooking the body of the court.

If in doubt about which side you should sit on, ask the court usher or the clerk or just look to which side the prosecutor is sat and sit on the opposite side to them.

COURT-ROOM ETIQUETTE

In the early days trying working out the many unspoken rules of courtroom etiquette can be difficult and embarrassing if you get it wrong. I remember spending my first few months in the Magistrates' Court never knowing when to get up or sit down, I had not been told and was too embarrassed to ask.

If you are in court prior to the magistrates you should stand up as they come in and stay standing until they have sat down. This applies irrespective of whether your case is the next to be dealt with as it applies to everyone who is present in the courtroom at that time. If the magistrates retire then as they stand up so should you and you should stay standing until they have left the courtroom. If you are leaving the courtroom whilst the magistrates are sitting then just before you exit, you should turn and bow in their direction.

When making submissions in your own case always stand to address the magistrates and stay standing until you have made your submission and it is clear that the magistrates expect or require no further response from you. If in doubt, you should ask them whether they require any further assistance from you. If your opponent is responding to your submission, sit down and stand again when he has finished in order to respond if necessary. If the magistrates or legal adviser direct a question at you, you should stand up to answer.

If you are addressing a District judge you call him/her – Sir/Madam.

If you are addressing the bench collectively you address your response to the chair and say 'Sir/Madam and your colleagues'. If you are addressing the chair alone, you call him/her –Sir/Madam

If you are referring to the prosecutor or a co-defending advocate, if he is a solicitor, you call him 'my friend', if he is a barrister, you call him 'my learned friend'.

If you are referring to the legal adviser you call him 'the learned clerk/legal adviser'.

If you are referring to the probation officer, if you know his or her surname, then use it, failing that you refer to him or her as the 'court liaison probation officer'.

This will all seem very strange to begin with but you will get used to it and it is important that you get it right.

WHO SPEAKS FIRST?

With most hearings it will be the prosecution who will make the first submission unless the matter is listed specifically for a defence application. In multi-defendant cases, defence advocates will make submissions in order of charge.

INTRODUCTION TO THE FIRST HEARING

When your case is called on you should move to the front row and take your place. If you are co-defending you sit in the order that your clients appear on the charge sheet (from left to right).

Generally speaking the usher will call your client into court and ask him to stand in the dock but if the usher is unavailable you should stand up and ask the magistrates for permission to leave the court to go and find your client. Once your client is in the dock then he should stay standing until asked to sit down by the magistrates or the legal adviser. If your client is in custody he will be brought up from the cells by the jailers.

The legal adviser will then tell the magistrates the client's name so they can locate the case on their court list. The legal adviser will then ask your client to give the court his full name, date of birth and address.

Next, the legal adviser will (normally) ask you whether your client is ready to enter his plea. You should stand up to answer this. If he is not then you will need to tell the court why and you will either need to make an application for more time that day or to adjourn the hearing for a future date. [see chapter chapter 16]. If the legal adviser proceeds straight to taking a plea then be prepared to stand up before this happens with your application to adjourn. If you have the chance before the case is called on it is a good idea to tell the legal adviser that you intend to make such an application.

CHAPTER 12
FIRST HEARING – GUILTY PLEA

ENTERING THE PLEA

Your client should stay standing until he has entered his plea. If it is a summary only matter then the legal adviser will read out the charge and your client is required only to say the word 'guilty'. If there are multiple summary only matters your client will respond by saying the word 'guilty' after each individual charge is put to him.

If your client has been charged with an either way matter then the legal adviser is likely to ask you to indicate whether your client is pleading guilty. If you indicate a guilty plea the legal adviser will then warn your client that if he pleads guilty he will be convicted of the offence and the court may have the power to commit his case to the Crown Court for sentence if the magistrates think their sentencing powers are insufficient. The charge will then be put to your client and he will respond with the word 'guilty'. If your client has been charged with a combination of summary only and either way offences – the either way matters will be dealt with first and following pleas to those matters – the summary only offences put and the plea/s taken. Your client will then be asked to sit down. It is perfectly acceptable for you to give an indication on your client's behalf (so long as you are sure that this will be his plea) – It simply speeds things up.

If your client is vulnerable or you think he needs prompting it is a good idea to look at him whilst the charges are being put so that you can remind him of his plea if necessary. Clients will often look to you for re-assurance in any event when they enter their plea so it is a good habit to get into.

If your client is entering pleas to some of the charges that he faces and those pleas are an acceptable disposal to the prosecution, the prosecution will then apply to the court to offer no evidence or withdraw the remaining charges.

THE PROSECUTION OPENING

The prosecutor will then open the facts of the case and will usually read their opening from the case summary prepared by the police. Make sure that you have read the case summary and are happy that it accurately reflects the facts of the case and the account, if any, given by your client in interview. If your client has made any comments on arrest or during the course of the incident the prosecutor will often read those out directly from the statements. If as part of the exhibits in the case there is any CCTV and/or photographs the prosecutor will invite the justices to consider it. Unless the photographs or CCTV offends an agreed basis of plea this course is unobjectionable. Incidentally, if there is CCTV of the incident *and* the Crown intend to show it to the magistrates – make sure that you have watched it prior to the hearing and so has the defendant. In more complex cases, the prosecutor will also refer the magistrates to any relevant sentence guidelines, case law or statutory authorities. If the prosecutor makes reference to the guidelines and specifies what they say are the aggravating and mitigating features of the offence and where in the guidelines this offence falls, then make sure that you take a note of it and be prepared to argue against it if you disagree.

If your client has pleaded guilty on a basis of plea the prosecutor will outline the basis to the court and will indicate whether this is acceptable to the Crown.

The prosecutor will then make an application for any costs or compensation sought and/or any ancillary orders. Finally the prosecutor will hand the magistrates a copy of your client's previous convictions. The legal adviser will ask you whether you have seen them. Make sure that you have remembered to check with your client that they are agreed. If they are not agreed, you should indicate those that are in dispute. In reality, this happens rarely and is something that you should already have raised and preferably resolved with the prosecutor prior to the hearing.

DEFENCE MITIGATION

For a full discussion about how to prepare your client's plea in mitigation, please refer to chapter 10.

DISPUTED BASIS OF PLEA

If your client has pleaded guilty on a basis of plea that has not been agreed by the prosecutor then before the court proceeds to sentence, the magistrates must first decide whether the defendant's basis of plea will make a material difference to sentence such that a Newton Hearing is required.

As discussed earlier Newton hearings should be avoided where possible due to the likely loss of credit for a guilty plea if the court finds against the defendant.

Your job here is to try and persuade the court that to sentence upon your client's basis of plea would not make a material difference to sentence. In order to argue this you should make reference to the magistrates' guidelines assuming of course that they help your case. If the case is one where the defendant's basis will clearly make a material difference to sentence then there is little point arguing otherwise and you should instead simply ask for the matter to be adjourned for a contested Newton hearing.

MITIGATION – IMMEDIATE SENTENCE
WITHOUT A PRE-SENTENCE REPORT

In general terms it is at this stage of the hearing that you will conduct your mitigation on behalf of your client. If you are before a District Judge then he or she will rarely retire to deliberate and will proceed immediately to sentence. Incidentally, if your client has been in a non-secure dock throughout the hearing and before announcing sentence the district judge retires, almost without exception this means that your client will receive a custodial sentence. The district judge will have retired just to allow the jailers to attend court in readiness for the pronouncement of an immediate custodial sentence. A lay bench will (usually) retire to consider sentence. When they rise, you should stand up whilst they are leaving the court. Your client will be permitted to leave the dock but should stay within the court premises. If you have not already done this, make sure that you remember to get the client to complete a means form whilst the magistrates are out.

If necessary, the magistrates will then ask the legal adviser to join them in their retiring room if they need any guidance on law or procedure. The legal adviser cannot tell them what sentence they should give but given how likely it is that the advice of the legal adviser will be followed, you may want to ask him/her what advice has been given. You will not always be told but if the justices impose a ludicrous sentence it might help to know whether they did so, on advice. The magistrates will return to the court (again, stand up whilst they do and remain standing until they sit down) and try to ensure that your client is in court when this happens. Your client should remain standing whilst the magistrates pass sentence. Advise him not to react to the sentence.

If the magistrates make an order for costs or compensation then they will ask your client whether he can pay that sum today and if your client is unable to pay the full amount within the timescale ordered by the court, instead ask the magistrates to make a collection order in respect of the total amount.

If however the court is not persuaded to deal with your client in the method that you have asked and instead requires a pre-sentence report then the magistrates will indicate the level of report that they require from probation. Depending on the timings, the matter will either be put back in the court list for a verbal report or adjourned to a new date for a fast delivery report or a standard pre-sentence report.

MITIGATION WHERE YOU ARE ASKING FOR
A PRE-SENTENCE REPORT

In the magistrates court even where a pre-sentence report is necessary you should address the magistrates in mitigation prior to their ordering the report.

The purpose of this is to make submissions about the level and type of sentence likely and the type of pre-sentence report required. At this stage you do not need to tell the court the client's mitigation in its entirety, the focus of your submissions should be based on:

1. The offence
2. Any aggravating and mitigating features of it.
3. The sentence guidelines if applicable and where your client's case falls within the sentencing range.
4. Limited personal mitigation – for example, drink/drugs or whether your client is fit and able to comply with unpaid work.

If you have spoken to the court liaison probation officer and they can deal with the matter by way of a verbal report today, inform the magistrates, similarly if they have indicated that a fuller report will be necessary.

If the matter is an either way offence *and* you think it is appropriate on the guidelines when putting the matter back for a report, invite the magistrates to rule out committal to the Crown Court for sentence. In all cases, *unless* custody is a realistic prospect when putting the matter back for a report, the magistrates should be invited to rule out custody. If the magistrates rule out committal for sentence or custody at this stage *unless* there is a change of circumstances, the sentencing bench will be bound by this decision. The advantage of doing this for the client is obvious but it also relieves the pressure placed upon you for the sentencing hearing.

I recently dealt with a young man who was before the court having pleaded guilty to offences of criminal damage and two Bail Act offences. Whilst his antecedent history was not that extensive, he had breached every single order that the court had given him and it did not take a crystal ball to work out on that basis that the probation officer would be unlikely to recommend a further community based penalty. With that in mind, I mitigated fully and asked the magistrates to deal with the offences by way of a conditional discharge. Having consulted their guidelines, the magistrates thought the case was serious enough to justify a community penalty and they were right. They therefore put the case back and asked the probation service to look at a medium level community order and it was then that I invited them to rule out custody – they agreed to do so. Two hours later my client was seen by the probation officer who then presented her verbal report to the magistrates. Unsurprisingly she concluded by saying that whilst the client had indicated that he was willing to comply with a community based penalty, given his history of non-compliance with previous orders in her view he was not suitable. The magistrates then asked the legal adviser whether they could rescind their decision to rule and custody and were quite properly advised that they could not. When making the decision to rule out custody they were in possession of my clients previous convictions where his history of non-compliance was self-evident. Three hours later he was sentenced to a conditional discharge.

Be warned however that the magistrates' guidance on the point is that *unless* they will be dealing with sentence themselves, they should not rule out custody and in doing so tie their colleagues' hands. Notwithstanding this, it is still worth you making the application.

If the client is plainly at risk of custody then do not bother, as with any aspect of advocacy, in making a futile submission.

In more complex cases the magistrates will retire to consider what type of report they require and what level of seriousness they attribute to the offence and what type/level of sentence they will be asking the probation officer to assess within their report. In all cases the magistrates must provide reasons for their decision. The magistrates should give a clear indication as to what level of sentence they are considering. It is not sufficient for them just to say 'an all options report'. If they are not clear then you should invite them to clarify what sentence or at least sentence category they are considering.

Your case will then either be put back in the days list or adjourned to another date, depending upon the level of pre-sentence report required.

On a practical note, do remember to remind the client that their conversation with the probation officer is not confidential and, good or bad what he says will be included in the report and will be read or heard by the magistrates.

MITIGATION/PROCEDURE FOR COMMITTAL TO THE CROWN COURT FOR SENTENCE

In most cases it will be very clear when a case should be committed to the Crown Court for sentence. If on the guidelines the starting point is that the case should be heard in the Crown Court then there is little point addressing the magistrates at any length and instead you need just concede that the case will inevitably be committed to the Crown Court for sentence. You should still ask the court to order a pre-sentence report in preparation for the Crown Court hearing. In some but not all courts this will be done routinely, but if in doubt then make the application.

On occasion however it will be less obvious to you that your client is at risk of being committed to the Crown Court for sentence. When you are dealing with an either way offence it is important that you always bear in mind the possibility of committal for sentence so that you are prepared to make any submissions on the point should the need arise. A common example of this is where your client pleads guilty to a relatively high value theft and has a number of previous convictions for offences of dishonesty. A District Judge in particular, will often commit those types of cases to the Crown Court for sentence. Where you think that committal for sentence is arguable, then argue it. Do not just concede and sit down. Your client will inevitably want his sentence dealt with at the Magistrates' Court because their sentencing powers are lower and will expect to see you trying to keep his case down. If there are any cases or guidelines that assist you then use them to bolster your argument. A good tactic where the case is border-line is to ask the court to retain jurisdiction for now and to instead adjourn for a pre-sentence report keeping all their sentencing options open including committal to the Crown Court for sentence. This will not tie a future sentencing benches hand and the case could still be committed for sentence at the next hearing but if on the next occasion there is a sympathetic report that recommends a sentence within the magistrates' powers you will have a stronger chance of persuading them to retain jurisdiction. Be warned however, particularly when in front a district judge who has quite obviously made up his mind whilst you should still make your point, you should make it succinctly.

BAIL POSITION

If your client is sentenced immediately, bail is no longer an issue and your client is no longer subject to any conditions of bail that he may have been previously. If your client appeared in custody and received an immediate but non-custodial sentence, he will be released from the cells and free to leave the court (assuming he is not in custody on other matters).

One of the most important things to remember after a guilty plea or conviction is that whilst the prosecutor is under an ongoing duty to assist the court with any information that may be relevant in terms of bail and can make observations, he cannot formally make a remand application, unless there is some exceptional reason for him to do so, therefore a conversation with him or her to find out what they will be saying maybe useful.

If your client is in custody and the matter is being adjourned for a pre-sentence report then when the magistrates have announced their decision about the order of the report, you will need to make an application for bail. On a tactical note in a case where I know my client is likely to plead guilty but is in custody I will ask the prosecutor for their view on bail. If the prosecutor has told you that he can agree bail conditional or otherwise, it can be a very useful tool to use this by way of observation in your subsequent bail application to the magistrates. If the prosecutor is busy and knows it is going to be a guilty plea then they will often brush off your question and tell you that it is post plea and not their concern but, still, it is worth a try.

When making your bail application, remember to keep your mind on the indication of sentence seriousness and level given by the magistrates. If they have indicated a report looking at a medium level community order you would have a good argument for saying that to remand in custody would therefore be disproportionate to the likely sentence. Whilst this is not something that appears in the Bail Act the magistrates will take it into account.

If your client is subject to bail conditions and you are instructed to make an application to vary those conditions, you should do so now. In certain circumstances your client will not formally instruct you to apply to vary the conditions, maybe because he doesn't know that he can. However you should always be alive to pointless and erroneous conditions that may no longer apply and invite the court to adjust his conditions accordingly.

Beware that the court may consider a condition of co-operating with the probation service in the preparation of a pre-sentence report and it is unlikely that there can be any sensible opposition to this.

Advocates are often lazy about bail conditions and often fail to apply to remove those which are unnecessary. Merely because your client has complied with every condition does not mean that they should continue to remain, in fact this maybe a strong argument for the removal of one or more, especially in cases where the defendant has been on bail for many months.

Once you have made your application for bail if it is a district judge, it is unlikely that he will retire and will instead give his decision and reasons immediately. If it is a lay bench and the decision to grant bail is obvious, they will not usually retire. If the issue is more complex then they will usually retire to make their decision and prepare their reasons before returning to court to announce their decision.

CHAPTER 13
THE FIRST COURT HEARING – NOT GUILTY PLEA – SUMMARY ONLY OFFENCE

ENTERING THE PLEA

At the beginning of the hearing your client will stand in the dock and the legal adviser will then introduce the case to the magistrates and your client will be asked to tell the court his name and address. The legal adviser will then ask you whether he is ready to enter a plea. Assuming your answer is yes the charge will then be put to the client and he will enter his plea saying simply the words 'not guilty' to each charge put and will then be invited to sit down (check that this is done as sometimes the magistrates forget and the client is left not knowing what to do). The court will then examine the case management form completed by you and the prosecutor before proceeding to fix a trial date.

CRIMINAL PROCEDURE RULES (CPR) AND CASE MANAGEMENT

Particularly when dealing with not guilty pleas, it is essential that you read, understand and have the Criminal Procedure Rules firmly in your mind at all times. It is the duty of the defence to make the defence and the issues it raises clear to the prosecution and to the court at an early stage. The duty is implicit in r. 3.3 of the CPR, which requires the parties to actively assist in the exercise by the courts of its case management powers, the exercise of which requires early identification of the real issues.' [per Stanley Brunton J at para 31 *Narrinder v DPP* [2007] EWCH 363 (QB)]. The court may require issues in the case to be identified in writing; that they should be determined separately and in what order they will be determined.

Having entered a not guilty plea the expectation is that all cases will be fully case managed at the first hearing and disposed of at the second – i.e. the trial. Magistrates and district judges have been rigorously trained to 'stop delaying justice'. Any attempt to do so, by any party, will not be tolerated. As part of the initiative the Lord Chief Justice said:

> 'We need referees who will go into the changing rooms before hand, tell each side how the game will be played, warn the players who may go offside that they are being watched, and as for those who foul, that they will be sent off. And having prepared the teams for the kind of refereeing they

will expect, to lead the teams out on to the pitch and put the ball down in the middle of the centre circle at the time when kick off is supposed to take place. And the proceedings played once.' [Lord Chief Justice speech 'Summary Justice in and out of Court – 7th July 2011]

Despite the sporting analogy, criminal defence is not a game [*R v Gleeson* [2003] WCA 3357] and you will be robustly examined by the court about the nature of your client's defence, the contested issues in the case and precisely why you require each specific witness to come to court and you must be prepared for this.

In short, the overriding objective of the CPR is to ensure that all cases are dealt with justly and it is your duty to:

1. Prepare and conduct the case in accordance with the overriding objective.
2. Comply with the CPR, Practice Directions and any directions given by the court.
3. Inform the court and parties of any significant failure to take any procedural step as required in (2) above.

It is the duty of the court to pursue the early identification of 'the real issues' and to actively manage cases and be warned, this is precisely what they will do. What this means in practice is that at the first hearing [*unless it would be contrary to the overriding objective*] the court is under a duty to:

1. Identify the real issues
2. Identify the needs of witnesses
3. Set a timetable for the case detailing what must be done, by whom and when.
4. Ensure that evidence whether disputed or not is presented in the shortest clearest way.
5. Discourage delay by dealing with as many aspects of the case on the same occasion and avoiding unnecessary hearings.
6. To give directions appropriate to the needs of the case as early as possible.

Rule 3.10 CP(Amendment)R 2011 requires that, in order to actively manage a trial, the court must establish, with the active assistance of the parties, what are the disputed issues.

This means that the court will examine everything that you have put on the case management form and you must be prepared to deal with any questions arising from it. The court's aim is to agree as much evidence as possible and to reduce as many issues into agreed admissions thus reducing the length of the trial and the reduction of unnecessary witnesses attending for trial, in particular, police officers. You will be expected to have a comprehensive knowledge of the evidence and to have taken your client's instructions on it. Any attempt to bypass the questions by saying that you have not yet had the time to take instructions or consider the evidence in all but exceptional cases, will be given short shrift and you will find your case put back to enable you to take those instructions.

Issues in the case

When identifying the real issues you will be expected to tell the court what the defence is and to do so in some detail. For example if your client has been charged with an assault where it is alleged that he has punched the victim twice and kicked him to the head and the issue is partially factual and partially self defence you will be required to expand on this and to make clear to the court and all parties what this means, including, where appropriate accepting and denying the important allegations.

Ambush defence

The defendant is no longer able to rely on an ambush defence and the nature of it must be clearly set out. Your duty to make the defence clear is implicit in Rule 3.3 CPR. If you [and by extension your client] fail to comply with this the court can issue the following sanctions:

1. Adjourn the trial to enable the prosecution to deal with the issue/correct any defects in their case.
2. If convicted make an increased order for costs.
3. Make a wasted costs order against you or the client. A wasted costs order will not only result in an order for you to pay the costs of the other party *but* will mean that you have no right to be paid for the work that you have undertaken for the client during the hearing that has resulted in the wasted costs.
4. The wasted costs order will also be referred to your professional body and could leave a black mark permanently.

The message is now very clear – the ambush defence has gone. If you do not comply with the CPR not only will your client gain no advantage from it, but there will be sanctions – potentially for you.

Prosecution witness requirements

You will be taken through the witness list and asked why you require each specific witness's attendance at trial and what is the disputed issue within their evidence? Where possible the court will try and get you to agree the witness's evidence. You are under no obligation to agree witnesses nor can the court force you to do so (be warned however the court can 'refuse' to justify that witness's attendance and could allow a s.114 hearsay application to adduce their evidence at the first hearing). As to how you should answer – you should identify the contentious part of the evidence and why your client disputes it, i.e. the witness says your client punched the victim three times to the head and your client says once, in self defence. You will also be asked to identify how long you think you will be with each witness. It is impossible to give a definitive time but as long as your time estimation is realistic, you will not be criticised if you are slightly out.

If a witnesses' evidence does not go directly to the issue in the case you will be asked why that witness is necessary and whether for example you could agree the evidence subject to the editing of the contentious part of it. Likewise if the disputed part of the evidence is hearsay and that hearsay is dealt with by direct evidence from another witness, the court will ask both you and the prosecutor whether the witness can be agreed subject to the deletion of the hearsay.

Do not assume that just because you and the prosecutor agree that certain witnesses are required, that the court will be content with that. The court will still go through each witness and scrutinise whether they are actually necessary.

Continuity evidence

Unless there is anything contentious contained within the evidence, you will be expected to agree this evidence either by way of a s9 statement or a s10 admission.

Directions sought

A list of the standard directions is attached at the end of this section and you should bear them in mind when conducting the hearing as they will form part of the timetabling of the case. The court can add to or vary the standard directions upon an application by any party.

Defence case statement (DCS)

There is no obligation on a defendant to file a defence case statement for a Magistrates' Court trial. At this stage it is unlikely that you will know whether, your advice will be to serve a DCS, and if the court asks you whether your client intends to serve one it is perfectly proper to say that that is a matter that will be decided in due course and served if necessary in accordance with the standard directions.

Interview summary

If your client gave an account in interview *unless* you were the solicitor present for the police interview it is extremely unlikely that you will be in a position to agree the interview summary at this stage and you should not do so. Interview summaries are prepared by the police and are routinely misleading. If the Crown is relying on your client's police interview as part of their case then it is crucial that you listen to the tape of interview and make any edits required to the summary or transcript before agreeing it. If the court asks you to agree it at this hearing (unless you have had the unlikely opportunity to listen to the tape of interview prior to going into court), you should stand your ground and tell the court that you cannot agree the summary of interview until you have listened to the tape and ask for a direction of 14 days to agree it.

Defence witnesses

If your client intends to call defence witnesses then you are required to tell the court that this is your intention and for obvious reasons of trial management, as best you can you will be required to say how many witnesses will be called. You are not required to give their names and addresses at this hearing or go into detail about the evidence they will give and if asked on the point, you should respond by saying that the defence will serve the requisite notice in due course in accordance with the CPR. It is unlikely at this stage in your case preparation that you will have spoken to the witness yet, let alone taken a statement from him and in those circumstances it would be unwise to tell the court what it is that they are likely to say.

Remember that if you are relying on an expert witness you are required to serve their statement on both the court and the prosecution. If you are relying on lay witnesses, you are not.

CPR and legal privilege

The CPR requires you to disclose what is going to happen at trial. It does not require you to disclose confidential discussions with your client. CPR rule 1.1 (2) (c) preserves legal professional privilege as a fundamental right of the client.

Professional guidance from the Law Society on the point can be found on its website.

What do I say where my client is putting the crown to proof?

If your client has admitted the offence to you but intends to plead not guilty it can make the conduct of this hearing difficult, however, the prosecution must prove that your client is guilty and he *is* entitled to put the prosecution to proof. The CPR cannot force the client to incriminate himself and it does not place any obligation on you to waive privilege. When asked what the trial issue is your answer must be restricted to words to the effect that 'that Mr X does not admit the offence (or the relevant part of it) and calls for the Crown to prove it. He raises no positive defence'. If the court presses you for further clarification of this you are under no obligation to expand upon your answer and can quite properly tell the court that you are bound by legal privilege.

In terms of witness requirements the court cannot force you to agree witnesses and when asked what the disputed issue is, again you should simply say. The defendant puts that witness to proof.

Credit for guilty plea/trial proceed in absence

As the defence advocate you will be asked by the court whether you have advised your client that:

1. If he pleads guilty he will receive credit for his guilty plea; and
2. If he fails to attend for his trial, the likelihood is that it will proceed in his absence.

Setting the trial date

The court must set the date as soon as possible. The timing will vary depending upon the backlog of the court and whether your client is remanded in custody.

If you are intending to rely on expert evidence you should ask the court to give the case a priority listing.

Do not forget to check that your client is available to attend court on the proposed date and if he is not, ask him why – for example, he has a pre-booked holiday or a hospital appointment.

If you are fixing the trial date without knowing your potential defence witnesses dates to avoid then tell the court this and that if necessary, you will bring the matter back for an application to vacate the trial date immediately the issue arises.

Immediate trial

As part of the 'Stop delaying justice' initiative the court will consider whether an immediate trial is possible. This will only happen if:

1. The prosecution has served all the evidence and initial disclosure at the first hearing
2. The prosecution evidence is all agreed under the provisions of s9 or by way of a s10 admission.
3. The prosecutor is competent to conduct the trial
4. The court can accommodate an immediate trial
5. The defendant does not wish to call any additional evidence other than himself
6. There is no disclosure issues

In deciding whether this is in accordance with the overriding objective the court will take into account:

1. The gravity of the offence
2. The complexity of what is in issue
3. The severity of the consequences for the defendant and others affected, and
4. The needs of other cases.

At the time of writing, this is not something that I have seen in practice but it is certainly within the foresight of the initiative and something therefore that you must bear in mind.

Unless the issue is a simple and discreet one, an immediate trial is something you should argue against. Your client has the right to prepare his trial and to have a properly prepared defence and unless there is genuinely nothing further that would or could be gained by adjourning the matter you should resist any such attempt by the court. Even if the trial involves no challenge to the prosecution evidence, for example a bladed article trial in which the defence of reasonable excuse is being advanced, it maybe that character witnesses or witnesses to fact are vital to the defendant's case. So, resist any application to rush through a trial on the basis that on the face of it the trial is straightforward and the Crown submit that they are trial ready.

BAIL

Contested bail application

If your client is in custody the court will then deal with the issue of bail. In terms of how to prepare your bail application please see chapter 10.

As to the procedure, the court clerk will ask the prosecutor whether they are making a remand application. Assuming the answer is 'yes' then the prosecutor will make their remand application. Make sure that you listen carefully as you need to be ready to respond to what they have said. The prosecutor will then pass a copy of the client's antecedents to the magistrates and you will be asked whether they are agreed and you will have taken instructions on any dispute within the list of convictions and you will be ready to address the court about it

The prosecutor will then sit down and now it is your turn. (If there are any co-defendants whose advocates are also making a bail application then you go in the order that your client appears on the charge sheet.)

Firstly, give the magistrates some time to read your clients previous convictions. You can usually tell when they are ready to hear from you as they will look up from the previous convictions and towards you. When you are nervous it is so tempting to speak as quickly as you can just to get it over and done with so every now and then, remind yourself to slow down. You do not want the magistrates to miss your good points.

If the magistrates or district judge interrupts you with a question, pause, think about what they are asking and then answer it. Do not blurt out the first thing that comes in to your head or say, 'I'll come back to that later'. If they have asked you a question, it is because they want the answer now. Especially in the early days, judicial interruption can be very off putting but if you listen to what they are saying, you can often get an indication of what they are thinking and where you need to go with your application. Learning to tailor your application to deal with the court's concerns is a very important skill and once learnt, will improve the efficacy of your arguments immeasurably.

Make sure that if the prosecutor has raised something in his remand application that you have not already included in your prepared bail application, that you deal with it and answer it.

Once you have finished your bail application ask the court whether you can assist any further and if the answer is, 'yes' respond to whatever questions they have and if they say 'no', sit down.

If you are before a district judge he will rarely retire to consider the question of bail and will instead give an immediate decision with reasons. If you are before a lay bench then as a general rule of thumb, they will retire to make a decision.

When the magistrates refuse bail they must announce their reasons in open court and specify which of the exceptions to bail exist. Once the magistrates have remanded your client the trial date will be formally fixed and your client will then be taken to the cells.

If your client is granted bail, again the trial date will be formally announced and your client taken back down to the cells before release.

Client in custody but prosecutor has agreed bail

Do not forget that even if the prosecutor has agreed bail with you ultimately it is a matter for the court and you must still be ready to address any questions that they have.

As to the procedure, again the legal adviser will ask the prosecutor whether he is making a remand application and the prosecutor will respond saying words to the effect that bail has been agreed subject to the following conditions (or unconditionally if applicable). The prosecutor will then hand the magistrates a copy of the client's previous convictions and sit down.

What you say here largely depends on the indication given to you by the bench. A good way to gauge it is to start by saying that your client is content to be bailed subject to whatever conditions have been agreed between you, that he understands the implications of breaching those conditions and then ask the magistrates or district judge whether there is any issue that they wish you to address them on regarding the question of bail. If they say 'no', sit down, you need say no more. If they say 'yes' almost without exception, they will tell you what it is they are concerned about and you must address your response to those issues. If it is clear that notwithstanding the prosecutor's views they are considering a remand in custody you should make a full bail application on behalf of your client. This is rare but it does happen and you need to be prepared for it.

Application to vary your clients bail conditions

Remember that this is your application and therefore you go first. You should start by outlining to the court what conditions of bail your client is subject to and which of those conditions you are asking the court to lift or vary. The court should only impose bail conditions that are necessary and therefore tailor your submissions in accordance with the Bail Act. For example, if your client has no previous convictions and has been bailed subject to a residence condition which goes to the risk of failing to surrender, there is no necessity for this as there is nothing to substantiate the fear that he is going to fail to surrender.

If the prosecutor has agreed to lift or vary the conditions then tell the court that you have spoken to your friend from the prosecution and the application is unopposed.

If the application is opposed then the court will ask to hear from the prosecutor for their views. If there is anything arising out of the prosecutors submissions, you can re-address the magistrates.

The magistrates will then announce their decision, either from the bench or less usually, they will retire.

Standard case preparation time limits

The court can vary any of these time limits. Time limits marked * are not prescribed by rules.

The total time needed to comply with all these time limits is 6 weeks (9 weeks if paragraph m applies).

Written admissions (Criminal Procedure Rules, r.37.6; Criminal Justice Act 1967, s.10)

a. The parties must serve any written admissions of agreed facts within **14 days.***

   Defence statement (Criminal Procedure Rules, r.22.4; Criminal Procedure and Investigations Act 1996, s.6)

b. Any defence statement must be served within **14 days** of the prosecutor completing or purporting to complete initial disclosure.

   Defence witnesses (Criminal Procedure and Investigations Act 1996, s.6C)

c. Defence witness names, etc. must be notified within **14 days** of the prosecutor completing or purporting to complete initial disclosure.

   Application for disclosure (Criminal Procedure Rules, rr.22.2 & 22.5; Criminal Procedure and Investigations Act 1996, s.8)

d. The defendant must serve any application for prosecution disclosure when serving any defence statement.*

e. The prosecutor must serve any representations in response within **14 days** after that.

   Witness statements (Criminal Procedure Rules, r.27.4; Criminal Justice Act 1967, s.9)

f. The defendant must serve any defence witness statement to be read at trial at least **14 days before** the trial.*

g. Any objection to a witness statement being read at trial must be made within **7 days of service of the statement.** *This does not apply to the statements listed in paragraph 10.1.*

   Measures to assist a witness or defendant to give evidence (Criminal Procedure Rules, rr.29.3, 29.13, 29.17, 29.22, 29.26)

h. Any [further] application for special or other measures must be served within 28 days.

i. Any representations in response must be served within **14 days after that.**

   Cross-examination where defendant not represented (Criminal Procedure Rules, rr.31.1, 31.4)

j. The defendant must serve notice of any representative appointed to cross-examine within 7 days.

k. The prosecutor must serve any application to prohibit cross-examination by the defendant in person as soon as reasonably practicable.

l. Any representations in response must be served within **14 days after that.**

   Expert evidence (Criminal Procedure Rules, rr.33.4, 33.6)

m. If either party relies on expert evidence, the directions below apply.

   (i)   The expert's report must be served within **28 days.***
   (ii) A party who wants that expert to attend the trial must give notice within **7 days after (i).***
   (iii) A party who relies on expert evidence in response must serve it within **14 days after (ii).***
   (iv) There must be a meeting of experts under rule 33.6 within **14 days after (iii).***
   (v)   The parties must notify the court **immediately after (iv)** if the length of the trial is affected by the outcome of the meeting.*

   Hearsay evidence (Criminal Procedure Rules, rr.34.2, 34.3)

n. The prosecutor must serve any notice to introduce hearsay evidence within 28 days.

o. The defendant must serve any notice to introduce hearsay evidence as soon as reasonably practicable.

p. Any application to determine an objection to hearsay evidence must be served within **14 days of service** of the notice or evidence.

Bad character evidence (Criminal Procedure Rules, rr.35.2, 35.3, 35.4)

q. The prosecutor must serve any notice to introduce evidence of the defendant's bad character within 28 days.

r. Any application to determine an objection to that notice must be served within 14 days after that.

s. Any application to introduce evidence of a non-defendant's bad character must be served within 14 days of prosecution disclosure.

t. Any notice of objection to that evidence must be served within **14 days after that.**

Previous sexual behaviour evidence (Criminal Procedure Rules, rr.36.2, 36.3, 36.4. 36.5)

u. The defendant must serve any application for permission to introduce evidence of a complainant's previous sexual behaviour within **28 days** of prosecution disclosure.

v. The prosecutor must serve any representations in response within **14 days after that.**

Point of law (Criminal Procedure Rules, rr.3.3, 3.9)

w. Any skeleton argument must be served at least 14 days before the trial.*

x. Any skeleton argument in reply must be served within **7 days after that.***

Trial readiness (Criminal Procedure Rules, rr.3.3, 3.9)

y. The parties must certify readiness for trial at least **14 days before the trial,** confirming which witnesses will give evidence in person and the trial time estimate.*

CHAPTER 14
FIRST HEARING – EITHER WAY OFFENCE –
NOT GUILTY PLEA

In terms of the preliminaries of the hearing they are exactly as described earlier. The two main differences between this and the hearing for a summary only offence are:

1. The magistrates must deal with plea before venue.
2. Your client has the option of indicating no plea (unless he consents to summary trial in which case he must plead guilty or not guilty).

Note: During the life of this book it is anticipated that there will two systems relating to either way offences. The existing system is that the case will be committed to the Crown Court for trial, the new system will mean that committal proceedings are abolished and instead the case will be sent to the Crown Court for trial once plea before venue has been dealt with (this new procedure is in force as of 18 June 2012 in 12 criminal justice areas). For the purposes of this book therefore we will deal with both scenarios.

Remember also to watch out for the following either way offences:

- **Certain domestic burglary offences or specified drug offences:** if your client already has two or more previous convictions for the same offence, committed after a certain date, this charge will become indictable only.
- **Criminal damage and aggravated vehicle taking** where the only damage caused is to property or the vehicle: if the value is £5,000 or below both offences can only be dealt with summarily.

The purpose of plea before venue is for the magistrates to decide whether their sentencing powers are sufficient to deal with the matter. When making this decision the magistrates will apply the Allocation Guideline, which emphasises the following considerations:

1. The nature of the offence.
2. The circumstances of the case including the aggravating and mitigating features of it.
3. In light of both of the above, whether their sentencing powers are adequate in the event of conviction?
4. Any other circumstance which might appear to the court to make it more suitable for the offence to be tried in one way rather than the other (for example; where a subsequent POCA application is likely).

Magistrates' Court Act 1980 s19(1)–(3)

Previously for the purpose of this decision the prosecution's case is taken at its highest and your client's previous convictions, defence and mitigation were irrelevant. Since 18 June 2012 that situation has changed, both previous convictions and defence representations are now considered. Unless it is likely that the court's sentencing powers will be insufficient OR the case involves a complicated issue of law or fact the guidance from the Lord Chief Justice is that cases should be tried by the magistrates. *Sentence Council Allocation guideline pg 18c.* Remember however that even if the magistrates retain jurisdiction of the case, your client still has the right to elect to have his trial dealt with by the Crown Court.

TAKING THE PLEA

The legal advisor will read out the charge/s and will explain to your client that this is a matter that can be dealt with in either the magistrates' or the Crown Court. Your client will then be invited to indicate a plea and before he does so, warned that if he pleads guilty to the offence today the magistrates could still commit the case to the Crown Court for sentence if they consider their sentencing powers are insufficient.

Your client will then be asked to indicate his plea.

If he indicates a guilty plea he will be treated as convicted and the court will either proceed to sentence, adjourn the case for a pre-sentence report and sentence either later that day or at a future date, or commit the case to the Crown Court for sentence.

If he indicates a not guilty plea or indicates 'no plea' the magistrates will then hear representations from you (and any co-defending advocates) and the prosecutor about where the case should be tried.

REPRESENTATIONS ON VENUE

The prosecutor makes his submission first and will start by outlining the facts of the case, highlighting the features of the case that make it more or less suitable for summary or Crown Court trial.

If you agree with the representations made by the prosecutor you need only say so in a few words. If you disagree with the prosecutor then you will need to make your representations as to why the magistrates can quite properly retain jurisdiction of the case. In doing so you will need to address them on:

- The offence

- The mitigating features of it highlighting those matters which make it less serious
- The relevant sentencing guidelines that demonstrate that the likely sentence is within the magistrates' sentencing powers.

In reality it is rare for there to be much disagreement between you and the prosecutor as most offences are now covered by sentence guidelines and therefore to a large extent you are restricted by those guidelines. If the sentence guideline recommends Crown Court sentence, there is no point trying to convince the magistrates otherwise. You have to pick your battles and if you become known as an advocate who takes every point good and bad, it will undermine your credibility when actually you do have a good one. So if for example, the case is one that is inevitably going to the Crown Court then just concede the point. Incidentally, make sure that you have given the client clear advice about venue and whether or not you will be making representations. If you have not but then proceed to say very little on his behalf at the hearing he will inevitably wonder why not and will likely question the quality of your representation. A large part of the job is about communicating with the client about what you are going to do and why.

THE MAGISTRATES' DECISION

The magistrates will then decide whether they accept jurisdiction of the case. Only rarely will they retire to make this decision.

Make sure that you take a clear note for your file as to whether or not the magistrates have declined jurisdiction as it will affect the Crown Court payment of the case. In cases where the magistrates have declined jurisdiction, the Crown Court fee is billed at a higher rate. On a practical note you should also mark your file note/brief with a reminder for you or the advocate on the next occasion to complete form LAC1 and to get it signed by the legal adviser. You will need this signed document for billing purposes. If your case is being sent today under the new provisions (see below) then you will need to complete LAC1 today and get it signed by the legal adviser. The legal adviser cannot sign it retrospectively so this is very important.

How the hearing will proceed from this point will depend upon whether the new committal provisions are yet in force for your local court. As from June 2012 the new provisions will be introduced incrementally depending on your geographical area. The new provisions will phase out the current committal proceedings and instead all cases where either the court has declined jurisdiction of the case or the client elects to have his trial dealt with at the Crown Court will be sent to the Crown Court for trial at the first hearing and the committal procedure abolished.

Once the new provisions are in force the following changes are anticipated:

1. If the magistrates accept jurisdiction of the case, prior to electing where he wants his trial, the defendant can ask for an indication of sentence if he were to plead guilty today and be sentenced by the magistrates'.
2. If a co-defendant elects Crown Court trial then the court must send all linked defendants to the Crown Court for trial if they appear on the same occasion and *may* do so if they appear subsequently (in practical terms they will be sent in all but the rarest of cases).

PROCEDURE IF MAGISTRATES ACCEPT JURISDICTION

If the magistrates accept jurisdiction of the case then your client will be asked to stand up and will be asked where he wishes to have his trial.

If he elects to have his trial at the Magistrates' Court then the hearing will continue in exactly the same way as for a summary only not guilty plea hearing and the magistrates will proceed to set a trial date. If the magistrates retain jurisdiction of the case and your client has consented to have his trial in the Magistrates' Court it is likely that the court will instantly proceed to begin case management of the trial and you ought therefore to have the case management form completed and ready for the court.

If he elects to have his case tried at the Crown Court then under the existing provisions the magistrates will adjourn the case for the preparation of the committal bundle. Generally speaking the adjournment will be for four weeks if your client is in custody and six if he is on bail but do check your local arrangements on these timings. If the new committal provisions are in place for your court then the case will simply be sent to the Crown Court for trial and adjourned for a plea and case management hearing or early first hearing.

PROCEDURE WHEN MAGISTRATES DECLINE JURISDICTION

If the magistrates decline jurisdiction of the case then under the existing provisions it will be adjourned for the preparation of committal papers and under the new provisions sent to the Crown Court for trial as described above.

MULTIPLE DEFENDANTS

Currently if there is more than one defendant then each defendant has an individual right of election to the Crown Court. As stated above, this will change with the new provisions and if one elects to have a Crown Court trial then all will follow.

LINKED OFFENCES

If your client is charged with linked summary only offences that are either imprisonable or endorsable and the court has *either* declined jurisdiction of the substantive either way offence *or* the client has elected then the linked summary only matters will also (in due course) be committed to the Crown Court together with the substantive offence and for the purpose of this hearing no plea will be taken in respect of the summary only matters.

If the summary only matter is not linked to the substantive offence then the court will deal with that or those unrelated summary only offences in the usual manner.

BAIL

The issue of bail will be dealt with at the end of the hearing in exactly the same manner as described in chapter 13.

CHAPTER 15
INDICTABLE ONLY FIRST HEARINGS

If your client has been charged with an indictable only matter then the Magistrates' Court hearing is very simple. The magistrates have no jurisdiction to deal with the matter other than to formally send it to the Crown Court under s51 Crime and Disorder Act 1998 for either a preliminary hearing or a plea and case management hearing. The magistrates are not concerned with whether there is sufficient evidence or a prima facie case simply whether the substantive matter is indictable only. Indictable only offences should be sent *forthwith* and adjournments of such cases are extremely rare and would usually only occur at the application of the prosecutor where, for example, it is clear to the prosecutor that the offence is in reality is a lesser one or there are serious evidential issues. A successful defence application would be rare and limited to an application to adjourn for the determination of legal aid or for a short period to enable them to make bail enquiries. Whilst both of these defence applications are possible – in reality they are unlikely to be granted by the court.

The legal advisor will put the charge to him in open court and whilst your client will be asked if he wishes to indicate a plea, no plea will be formally taken. Indications of plea at this stage are unlikely because of the gravity of the offence and the limited amount of disclosure that you will have received on it at this stage. Alternatively if your client has for example admitted the offence in interview and the evidence is overwhelming then to indicate a guilty plea at this very early stage is powerful mitigation at the Crown Court upon sentence and it will usually result in a much quicker hearing at the Crown Court.

If your client is charged with offences that are linked to the indictable only matter (and they are either-way offences or summary only offences which are either imprisonable or involve obligatory or discretionary disqualification from driving) then they will be sent to the Crown Court together with the indictable only matter.

If you are representing a defendant who is charged with an either-way offence and his co-defendant is charged with a linked indictable only offence, the court must also send your client's case to the Crown Court for trial.

The primary issue for the magistrates to determine is the question of bail. If your client is in custody and the prosecution is applying for a remand in custody then please refer to chapter 10 for how to prepare your bail application and conduct the hearing. Note the specific provisions relating to the exceptions to the right of bail for indictable only offences. Remember, if your client has been charged with murder then the magistrates have no jurisdiction to deal with bail and you cannot make a bail application.

Once the issue of bail has been decided then the case will be formally sent to the Crown Court and listed either for a preliminary hearing or more usually, adjourned for a plea and case management hearing at the Crown Court. Preliminary hearings are generally reserved for the most serious offences, for example, murder.

If your client is remanded in custody for an indictable offence the relevant custody time limit is 182 days starting from the day after his remand in custody, continuing through to the first date of the Crown Court trial. Where a case has been sent to the Crown Court for trial there is no right to a second bail application in the Magistrates' Court. If your client wishes to make a further bail application, this must be done on application to the Crown Court Judge in chambers.

CHAPTER 16
APPLICATION TO ADJOURN

When I discussed this section with a colleague her response was, 'what are you going to say? Do not bother?' She was half joking but actually it is representative of the complete sea change in attitude towards adjournments. When I first started, adjournments were given out routinely and nothing substantive really happened until the second or third hearing. Those days have gone and getting an adjournment is very much the exception and not the norm. Most cases *will* be concluded in one or two hearings and if you need to deviate from that you will have to have the CPR firmly in your mind when making your application.

The starting point for any application to adjourn is the overriding objective that all cases are dealt with justly whilst:–

- *being fair to the prosecution and the defence,*
- *recognising the rights of the defendant,*
- *respecting the interests of victims and witnesses ,*
- *dealing with the case in ways which reflect the gravity of the offence,*
- *the complexity of the case,*
- *the severity of the consequences to the defendant and others,*
- *bearing in mind the needs of other cases and*
- *dealing with cases efficiently and expeditiously.*

Persaud v DPP [2010] EWHC 1682 (Admin)

It is the duty of the court to actively manage cases and to discourage delay and the use of unnecessary hearings [Part 3.2(g) CPR]. If you have an application to adjourn the court will scrutinise whether it is necessary. The decision about whether to adjourn a case is at the magistrates' discretion and your job when making that application is to persuade them that it is in the interests of justice to exercise that discretion.

APPLICATIONS TO ADJOURN THE FIRST HEARING

The five applications to adjourn that you are likely to face or be considering at the first hearing are:

1. For legal aid to be determined.
2. For further time to take instructions

3. To make representations to the Crown that they cannot prove their case or that it is not in the public interest to proceed.
4. To make representations to the Crown that your client should be dealt with by way of a caution or community resolution.
5. That the crown have served insufficient evidence to advise on plea.

APPLICATION TO ADJOURN FOR LEGAL AID

See chapter 4.

APPLICATION FOR FURTHER TIME
TO TAKE INSTRUCTIONS

Unless the case is very complex or involves multiple witness statements it is unlikely that the court will grant such an adjournment and far more likely that your case will instead be put back in the court's list to allow you time to take those instructions. The application will always be considered as to whether it is in the interests of justice.

There will be cases where through no fault of yours, or your clients, you are simply unable to take instructions at court and therefore an application to adjourn will be necessary for example, if your client has a learning difficulty such that renders him incapable of concentrating for any length of time, or he requires an interpreter and the court appointed interpreter is dealing with other cases that day and unable to spend sufficient time with you to enable you to take those instructions, or your client is unwell or unfit to give those instructions. If your client is unfit because he is drunk or on drugs and you make the application on that basis, be warned, there is a risk that the court will consider remanding him overnight to sober up sufficiently to give you those instructions at an adjourned hearing the following day.

Each application depends on its own facts so if there is a genuine need for the application, do not be afraid to make it but do expect to have to argue it. As an example; I had a case recently where the client had been charged with theft to the value of £1.50. The evidence against him from 5 police officers was overwhelming. The client was a French national who had recently suffered a severe stroke which affected his speech to the extent that the court interpreter was simply unable to understand him and therefore I was unable to take any instructions. In those circumstances I had no choice but to ask the court to adjourn the matter to enable his usual interpreter to attend who, despite the speech impediment, could understand him. My application was on that basis, and despite the minor nature of the offence, the overwhelming evidence against him and the perhaps inevitability of the plea, it was in the interests of justice that I was able to take his instructions and communicate with him.

If the magistrates refuse your application then ask them instead to put the matter back in the list to give you some more time to go through the case with your client and take his instructions on it.

If, for some very genuine reason you are unable to take instructions or to advise properly on plea *and* the court insists upon a plea being entered then you will have no choice but to advise your client to plead not guilty until such time as you are in a position to do so. If you are advising the client to plead not guilty on this basis then do not forget that you will have to complete a trial management form as best you can and that the court will go through the form with you as described in chapter 13. If this happens in your case then you should ask for it to be noted on the court file that you are not in a position to advise your client and the reason for that. The purpose of doing this is in the event of a guilty plea being entered at the next hearing is to salvage as much credit for his guilty plea as you can.

APPLICATION TO ADJOURN TO MAKE REPRESENTATIONS TO THE CROWN THAT THEY CANNOT PROVE THEIR CASE OR THAT IT IS NOT IN THE PUBLIC INTEREST TO PROCEED

This is often the type of application that you will have agreed with the prosecutor in advance of the hearing. However, do not be misled this does not mean that the court will agree to it. More likely the court will ask you why you cannot enter your plea and make written representations to the crown following the hearing. If your application to adjourn is to enable you to make representations to the prosecution that they cannot prove the case against your client then in reality, there is not much that you can say in response to this. If you do not feel that there is sufficient evidence to prove the case against your client (and nor will there be) then you should speak to the prosecutor at court and ask firstly whether the matter can be reviewed at court. If so, you should ask the court to put the matter back in the list to enable the prosecutor to conduct that review. More likely, the prosecutor will not have time to do this at court and you should therefore advise your client to plead not guilty and proceed to set a trial date. Following the hearing either you or your instructing solicitor should write to the prosecution with those representations.

If on the other hand your application to adjourn is on the basis that it is not in the public interest to proceed with your case, your application is on much stronger ground. If on your client's instructions he is not guilty then it is difficult to see a valid argument for not proceeding to plea as described above and making written representations following the hearing. Your client is caused no prejudice. However, if your client has admitted his guilt to you but for reasons to do with his personal circumstances, the likely sentence or some other compelling reasons you think that it is not in the public interest to proceed with this matter then your application has far more weight. Assuming that the prosecutor is not in a position to make that decision today (and that would be unlikely since they will not only have to review the file but also seek the views of the police and the victim) then you should make an application to adjourn the plea. In making your application you should set out the following (which is by no means exhaustive and depends entirely on the circumstances of your case):

1. The reason for your request to adjourn.
2. The nature of your proposed representations to the prosecution i.e. why it may not be in the public interest to prosecute.
3. The proposed time estimate for your representations, including consideration by the prosecution (emphasising that this will be done as expeditiously as possible).
4. Make it clear that you are mindful of the CPR but that in your submission, this application is entirely consistent with the overriding objective i.e. to deal with cases justly including the rights of, and consequences for, the defendant; and
5. Conclude your application by outlining the prejudice to the defendant should a plea be forced today i.e. either he will be forced to plead guilty which in this case would or could be contrary to the interests of justice for the reasons outlined above *or* that he will be forced to plead not guilty to await the outcome of your representations which if unsuccessful, could result in a loss of credit for his guilty plea.

The full Code for Crown Prosecutors' can be accessed via the CPS website.

APPLICATION TO ADJOURN TO MAKE REPRESENTATIONS TO THE CROWN THAT YOUR CLIENT SHOULD BE DEALT WITH BY WAY OF A CAUTION/COMMUNITY RESOLUTION

In my view this is a perfectly proper application to make and if you encounter any resistance from the bench when making it you should stand your ground and be prepared to argue the application. As part of the 'Stop delaying justice' training magistrates are being asked to consider:

1. *Is there any advantage to this?*
2. *Whilst a caution rather than a conviction will be recorded, if it is a comparatively minor first offence, then the court is likely to deal with the case by way of a discharge anyway*
3. *If the case is too serious for a discharge, why is it in the public interests to adjourn for a caution?*
4. *If the case is delayed on more than one occasion for the caution to be administered then the defendant has prolonged exposure to the criminal justice process when the case could have been concluded at the first hearing; and*
5. *In those cases the defendant will often have been on bail, with the risks that brings if the defendant fails to attend a subsequent hearing.*

In addition to the CPR generally you will have to bear this in mind and be prepared to address it.

An absolute discharge will become spent 6 months after the date it was imposed and a conditional discharge will become spent either 12 months after the date it was imposed or at the end of the discharge period whichever is longer. A caution becomes spent immediately and a conditional caution, within 3 months of its imposition (assuming the conditions have been satisfied). Convictions and cautions will both stay on his criminal record for ever and may impact on future decisions about whether to caution, or the likely sentence imposed or potential bad character applications.

If the client is employed (and under a duty to inform his employer of the fact that he has received a conviction) or is applying for a job until that conviction becomes spent then he will have to declare it. Unless the existing or proposed job is one where either it specifies cautions or an enhanced CRB (Criminal Records Bureau) check is required, he will not have to declare the fact of a caution.

If your client is applying for a new job, visa or whatever it may be, the reality is the fact of a criminal conviction will always be more detrimental than a caution.

If your client is eligible for a caution and through no fault of his, the police did not deal with him as such it will always be in the interests of justice that the caution should be administered and that is your argument. Why otherwise is the caution system in place? It is not as simple as saying 'he will just get a discharge anyway so lets proceed to do it that way'. There is prejudice to your client.

The CPS guide to adult cautions can be viewed on its website.

As to the fact that the client is at risk if the matter is adjourned and subject to the requirements of bail, this seems a non-argument where in the alternative to adjourning for a caution the court is considering a conditional discharge or a financial penalty. There are risks and consequences for the defendant inherent in both of these either re-sentence for the offence upon breach of the conditional discharge or (ultimately), a custodial sentence for non-payment of fines. Absolute discharges are rarely imposed.

Whist it is true that some clients will want the matter dealt with there and then and are willing to forgo the opportunity of a caution for the convenience of getting the matter concluded, most will be content with the delay if the outcome is the lesser penalty of a caution.

APPLICATION TO ADJOURN ON THE BASIS THAT THE CROWN HAVE SERVED INSUFFICIENT EVIDENCE TO ADVISE ON

In accordance with Part 21 of the CPR, in summary cases the CPS must disclose initial details of the prosecution case and include—

(a) a summary of the evidence on which that case will be based; or

(b) any statement, document or extract setting out facts or other matters on which that case will be based; or

(c) any combination of such a summary, statement, document or extract; and

(d) the defendant's previous convictions.

There is no requirement for the prosecution to serve any more than this at the first hearing and therefore any application to adjourn on the basis that the prosecution has served *only* this will be met with short shrift by the Crown and the Court. Good practice suggests particularly when a not guilty plea is anticipated that the prosecution should serve at the very least, the key witness statements and ordinarily they do. If the prosecution has complied with their duty it is extremely unlikely that the court will adjourn the case for any further information and will expect a plea to be taken.

If the prosecution has not complied with their obligations then the court will first make enquiries as to whether the prosecutor has that information within their file or they can obtain it within the course of the court's sitting. If so, the case will be put back in the list for the prosecutor to obtain the evidence for you and thereafter for you take instructions on it.

If, but only if, the prosecution is unable to provide sufficient information will the hearing will be adjourned.

There is ongoing debate as to whether CCTV is a 'document' and should therefore form part of advanced information (initial details) however the courts are increasingly reluctant to adjourn for the service of CCTV. If your application is based on the fact that you need to view the CCTV before advising your client as to plea (save in exceptional circumstances) it is unlikely to be granted. An example of an exceptional circumstance may be where your client is charged with an affray and the primary evidence is the CCTV however, even in this circumstance, the magistrates will still be inclined to refuse your application and therefore your argument needs to compelling.

APPLICATION TO ADJOURN THE COMMITTAL HEARING

Prosecutor's application to adjourn

This is a very common prosecution application. Far too often the committal papers have not been prepared in time for the hearing and far too regularly, the application is granted. Whether the defendant is in custody or on bail, magistrates will sometimes take the view that another couple of weeks will not matter. In the light of 'stop delaying justice' this should change and is an example of where the initiative can work to the advantage of the defendant if a more robust approach is taken by the courts to routine applications to adjourn this type of hearing.

An application to adjourn because the committal papers are not ready should be treated with the same scrutiny that is applied to any other adjournment application and the court should have regard for the need for expedition. If you find yourself faced with this application then make sure that you speak to the prosecutor in advance of the hearing and find out:

1. Why they are not ready?
2. What is it that is unavailable?
3. When were the enquiries started?
4. When will the material be available?

Do not be deterred by a prosecutor who tries to justify the need for the adjournment on the basis that it is a serious charge. Whilst the severity of the charge is something that the magistrates will have to consider when deciding upon the application, it is not in itself, a justification for it. If the application is through the fault of the prosecution or one of its limbs, namely the police or the Benefits Agency, that is a factor against granting the application.

You should always oppose a prosecution application to adjourn the committal hearing unless you are persuaded that the reason for the delay and the adjournment are compelling. As to how strongly you do so will of course depend on the merits of the application. Arguments of being short of staff, the relevant CPS lawyer being on annual leave or the officer in the case is on long term sick leave are regrettably common and you should object as strongly as possible if this is the basis of the Crown's application.

If the prosecutor is not in a position to apply to commit the case and the magistrates refuse the application then the court will discharge the case and it is for this reason that the courts have been inherently reluctant to refuse the application. Whilst of course the consequence of this for any victim or loser is not to be disregarded, the court *must* weigh this against the interests of your client who maybe in custody or at the least been on bail with the matter hanging over him for some weeks by this stage. If your client is charged with a serious offence, the public interest will almost always lean in favour of the victim and not your client. The focus of the CPR is to convict the guilty and limits those acquitted by virtue of a technicality.

When you argue the application have in your mind:

1. The overriding objective
2. The gravity of the offence
3. The complexity of the issues
4. The duties of the parties to comply with court directions and the reason for the non-compliance

5. The duty of the court to ensure compliance with directions and to discourage delay and avoid unnecessary hearings; and
6. To balance the consequences to the victim and the defendant fairly

If the Crown are seeking a two week adjournment for the preparation of the papers, invite the court, in circumstances where they are likely to grant to rule against you, to instead consider granting it for a shorter period sought. This is will have the obvious impact of lessening the delay for your client but importantly, if the crown is still not ready on the next occasion, the magistrates are less likely to grant a further adjournment.

If the Crown is seeking an adjournment of the committal hearing, do make sure you take the client's instructions about how they want you to deal with it. You must advise him that if the case is discharged the prosecution may still summons him to court for the offence once they have the relevant outstanding evidence. Some clients would rather agree to the adjournment than have their case discharged and potentially have to go through the whole thing all over again if they are re-summonsed. If your client can bear the delay he is probably better served pushing for the discharge and instructing you to oppose any application to adjourn, you never know what may occur in the intervening period that prevents the Crown getting its act together, there may never be a re-summons.

If you are representing a client whose case was originally discharged by the magistrates because the prosecution were not ready to apply to commit and who now appears in answer to a summons for the same offence, do not agree to an adjournment at the first hearing for the preparation of committal papers. The prosecution has already had more than enough time to get the case ready. You should instead ask the magistrates to refuse the adjournment and if the prosecution is not in a position to commit the case to the Crown Court that day, to again discharge the client. If this happens there is nothing to prevent a re-summons in due course and you will again need to warn the client of this.

Defence application to adjourn

This can be dealt with briefly, if you are applying to adjourn for time to read the committal papers, it is unlikely to be successful and instead, you will find your case put back in the list for more time to read. You are not expected to take the client's full instructions on each and every piece of evidence, simply to advise him whether there is a case for him to answer and in reality, you do not need a week to do this. If it is a paper heavy case, ask the prosecutor to refer you to the salient pieces of evidence which will help you. Paper heavy cases can be a bit overwhelming in the early days but remember, for the purposes of this hearing, you are not conducting the trial just deciding whether or not there is a prima facie case.

APPLICATION TO VACATE THE TRIAL

It is a central tenet of this initiative that it is normally more unjust to adjourn a trial, particularly on the day of trial, than to proceed. An innocent defendant is entitled to an early acquittal. Anxious witnesses and victims are entitled to be heard without delay. The best route to a fair verdict is to hear the evidence when fresh. (Stop delaying justice training pack p. 34).

It is not impossible to adjourn a trial but the applicant, whether you, a co-defendant or the prosecutor will have to have very good reason for it.

The following guidance can be found in the case of *CPS v Picton* [2006] EWHC 1108:

1. The decision to adjourn is one within the discretion of the court and with which the Administrative Court will be slow to interfere unless clear grounds for doing so are shown.
2. The court must have regard for the need for expedition. Delays bring the system into disrepute and proceedings in the Magistrates Court are supposed to be simple and speedy.
3. Applications for adjournments should be rigorously scrutinised.
4. Where an adjournment is sought by the prosecution, magistrates must consider both the interest of the defendant in getting the matter dealt with, and the interest of the public that criminal charges should be adjudicated upon, and the guilty convicted as well as the innocent acquitted.
5. With a more serious charge the public interest that there be a trial will carry greater weight.
6. Where an adjournment is sought by the accused, the court must consider whether he will be able fully to present his defence and, if he will not be able to do so, the degree to which his ability to do so is compromised.
7. The court must look at the consequences of an adjournment and its impact on the ability of those involved to remember salient facts.
8. The reason that the adjournment is required should be examined and, if it arises through the fault of the party asking for the adjournment that is a factor against granting the adjournment. If that party was not at fault that may favour an adjournment. Likewise if the party opposing the adjournment has been at fault, that will favour an adjournment.
9. The court must look at the history of the case.
10. The court's duty is to do justice between the parties.

APPLICATION WHERE THE DEFENDANT HAS NOT ATTENDED/IS UNABLE TO ATTEND FOR TRIAL

The general rule is that if your client voluntarily absents himself from trial then it will proceed in his absence.

If your client has a genuine reason for being unable to attend the trial then as long as he can evidence it, for example, by a doctor's certificate stating he is unfit for *court*, in most cases it will be in the interests of justice to vacate the trial. If, on the other hand your client has not attended because he cannot afford the bus fare or does not want to take the time off work, the trial will proceed regardless (see the section on trials in absence for information on the role of the advocate in these circumstances).

APPLICATION TO ADJOURN WHERE A PROSECUTION WITNESS HAS NOT ATTENDED

If a prosecution witness has not attended for trial then there are a number of factors that the court will take into account when deciding to adjourn.

1. Why the witness has not attended. Is there a genuine reason that he is unable to? If so, what is it?
2. Was the witness warned to attend for trial in a timely manner or is the prosecution at fault?
3. Can investigations be made today to locate the witness and secure his attendance at court?
4. Is the witness crucial to the Crown's case?

All of this will of course be considered in the context of the CPR and the guidance set out above. If the witness has not attended through the fault of the prosecution, this will be a factor against granting the application.

Often it depends whether the witness is crucial and how much they add to the case. If the prosecution can proceed without that witness the court will normally direct that they should. If that particular witness helps an aspect of your clients' defence then you should support the prosecutor's application and resist any attempt by the court to abandon the evidence of that witness or put pressure on the prosecution to read the sections of the witnesses' statement that supports your client.

If the witness is crucial to the Crowns' case and they are unable to prove it without him then the court's starting point will be to give the prosecutor some time to make enquiries about what has happened to the witness and whether their attendance can be secured. If the witness is running late then the court is likely to put the matter back or consider taking evidence out of turn whilst they are waiting for this witness. If the witness is one whose non-attendance should have been foreseen at a much earlier stage by the prosecution and despite that knowledge, they did not apply for a witness summons or other special arrangements, then this will be a factor against granting an adjournment but not a bar.

As to what you do if a crucial prosecution witness fails to attend, if the Crown is unable to prove their case without that witness you should oppose the application to adjourn and this is where the new initiative is helpful to you. Have the 'stop delaying justice' training pack with you, quote the relevant sections, which particularly where the Crown is at fault, will help you and urge the magistrates to make a brave decision and refuse the application.

If the Crown decides that they can proceed without a certain witness and will understandably not agree the parts that you need from the statement, you may have to ask for the adjournment. As frustrated as the justices will be, if it is a witness that you were expecting to be in attendance and your case is seriously prejudiced by the absence of that witness, they may well be forced to grant your application.

APPLICATION TO ADJOURN TRIAL WHERE A DEFENCE WITNESS HAS NOT OR IS NOT ABLE TO ATTEND

If one of your witnesses has not attended then what you do about it will depend on who the witness is and what evidence they give. If for example, the witness is merely a character witness whose evidence is not contentious then speak to the prosecutor and show him a copy of the witness statement and see whether the evidence can be agreed. Usually you will be able to agree all or part of the statement with the prosecution.

If the witness is in any way contentious then the prosecutor will not agree him and you must decide whether you can proceed without him. Take instructions from your client on the point and be prepared to advise him what you think he should do, whether it is to proceed without him or apply to adjourn in order to secure his attendance. If your advice is to apply to adjourn the trial but against that advice, your client wants to proceed then make sure you get a signed endorsement on the point in the event of conviction and a potential complaint.

If you are ready to proceed to trial but for that witness, another option to consider is to proceed today but to make an application to go part heard [if the need arises] to deal with the absent witnesses evidence at a future date when he is available to attend. This is a good tactic if you think the defendant may succeed with a submission of no case to answer at the end of the prosecution case, concluding the case that day in his favour rather than a lengthy adjournment for a second trial listing.

As to whether your application will be granted, each case turns on its own facts. The magistrates will consider the following factors (Stop delaying justice training pack p. 35):

- *How important is the witness to the defence case? The more central the evidence to the disputed issue, the greater the importance of hearing the witness.*
- *Why has the witness not attended? If the defendant has done everything possible to secure the witness's attendance, including taking a statement from him, providing proper details of the time and place of the hearing, and in appropriate cases seeking a witness summons to compel attendance, then he cannot be faulted for the failure of the witness to attend. This is an important factor. Arrangements need to be made to hear the evidence (see below). If on the other hand there is no statement, no warning to the witness to attend, and no action taken to secure his witness' attendance, then fault can be attributed to the defendant. This is an important factor. After all, if a defendant through his own negligence fails to attend trial, then almost certainly the case will proceed in his absence. The same principle can apply where the defendant fails to take proper steps to secure the attendance of a witness.*
- *Can the case proceed part heard? It is submitted that this possibility should be considered more frequently than in the past. It may be that there will be no case to answer, or that the bench would acquit even in the absence of the witness. In these circumstances an adjournment would have been a mistake. Even if the bench needs to hear from a witness, that need occupy very little court time at a future hearing. It may be inconvenient to the bench, or the prosecutor, or the defence lawyer, or the defendant himself, but nevertheless a part heard trial can often be accommodated at fairly short notice, before other business begins (possibly of a list to be heard before a differently constituted bench). This may be less than ideal. The defence advocate may want to know what the witness says before cross-examining other witnesses. The bench may need to come to court when not otherwise sitting. The prosecution may prefer not to leave a gap between cross-examining the defendant and hearing from his witness. However in almost all cases it will be better than the alternative of sending witnesses away unheard to come back on a later occasion. A witness summons should be considered.*
- *Can the witness's statement be admitted as hearsay? Again this is not normally ideal but may be better than the alternatives. It might be particularly appropriate where the witness gives peripheral evidence. Of course the bench will be alert to the weight to attach to a hearsay statement from a witness who has not been cross-examined.*

CHAPTER 17
THE COMMITTAL HEARING

Committal hearings relate to either way offences where *either* the magistrates have declined jurisdiction of the case *or* the client has elected Crown Court trial. The purpose of the committal hearing is for the case to be formally committed to the Crown Court. At the time of writing there are two types of committal hearing:

- S6(1) Magistrates'' Courts Act 1980 (MCA) – a contested hearing to determine whether there is a prima facie case against the defendant.
- S6(2) MCA – a non-contested hearing where the defendant consents to his case being committed to the Crown Court on the papers.

However, as from June 2012 the existing committal proceedings will be phased out and instead the above cases will be sent to the Crown Court at the first hearing in exactly the same way as described in Chapter 15. The new provisions will be introduced on an incremental basis and it will depend on your geographical area as to when they are in force. It is therefore essential that you check which provisions are relevant for your court. It will vary.

Below is an outline of the existing provisions. For an outline of the sending provisions please see chapter 15.

THE COMMITTAL HEARING

You will need to obtain a copy of the committal papers from the prosecutor. If the committal papers are not ready and the Crown is seeking an adjournment of the hearing, please see chapter 16.

If you are supplied with the papers in readiness for an effective committal consider them carefully to decide whether there is a prima facie case against your client (a case to answer). Remember at this stage your client's defence is irrelevant, no matter how strong you may think that it is, the court is just concerned with whether the papers disclose a case against him.

In reality, contested committal hearings are rare and more usually cases are committed to the Crown Court by consent.

If the court has declined jurisdiction of the case make sure that you get form LAC1 signed by the legal advisor. This is very important; you will need it for submission with the Crown Court bill to get paid at the higher rate. In cases where the magistrates have accepted jurisdiction of the case but your client has elected Crown Court trial, the Crown Court fee is paid at a lower rate.

For the purpose of this hearing you are not required to take your client's instructions on the evidence, simply to advise him what it is, summarise any new evidence not previously served within advanced information and tell him whether there is a case for him to answer and whether he should consent to his case being committed to the Crown Court. Your client will want to know the ongoing procedure and you should be prepared to give him a summary of what will happen from here on in. Despite the fact that you or a colleague will no doubt have advised on the procedure at the first hearing and followed it up in a letter, it is surprising how few clients really understand the procedure, particularly first time offenders.

A summary of what happens following the hearing is as follows:

- The case will be adjourned to a plea and case management hearing at the Crown Court and the client will be remanded to that date, either on bail or in custody.
- The defendant will meet with his Crown Court advocate and he should be advised when, within reason, this is likely to happen.
- In the meantime he will need to meet with his solicitors to take his full instructions on the committal bundle and (if applicable) prepare his defence case statement/defence witness notification and it is therefore essential that he remains in contact.
- At the plea and case management hearing he will formally enter his plea at the Crown Court. If he pleads guilty he will either be sentenced there and then or more likely his case adjourned for the preparation of a pre sentence report and he will be given a future specified date for the sentence hearing. If he pleads not guilty, the judge will make directions as to how the case should proceed and the case will be adjourned for trial, either placed in a warned list or given a fixed date.

S6(1) MCA CONTESTED COMMITTAL HEARING

If having read the papers it is your view that there is no case to answer then you should advise your client not to consent to having his case committed to the Crown Court on the papers and instead request a contested committal.

At the beginning of the hearing the legal adviser will introduce the case to the magistrates and read out the history of the case and outline the charge. Your client will then be asked to give the court his name and address and will then be invited to sit down. The legal adviser will ask the prosecutor whether the matter is ready for committal to the Crown Court. Assuming for this section that the answer is yes (for how to respond if they are seeking an adjournment see chapter

16) you will be asked whether your client consents for his case to be committed to the Crown Court. Your response is 'no', he does not accept that there is a prima facie case against him and requires a read out committal.

Depending on the court, the issues and the complexity of the case, the contested committal will either be dealt with there and then or adjourned to another date. Check with the legal adviser prior to the hearing which is likely in your case so that you can prepare for an immediate hearing if necessary, do not assume that the hearing will be adjourned and then face the embarrassment of not being prepared to make your submissions when called upon to do so.

The procedure for the contested hearing follows a similar patter no matter where you are, the prosecutor will read out the statements and exhibits either in their entirety or an agreed summary of them. There is no provision for you to ask for prosecution witnesses to attend court to give live evidence or for to you cross-examine them. The hearing is based on paper evidence alone. If you are before a district judge in reality he will often have had and read the papers in advance avoiding the need for the papers to be read out in court. Strictly speaking, procedurally the papers should be read in open court but in practice, this is often dispensed with depending on your tribunal.

At the end of the evidence both you and the prosecutor will have the opportunity to make representations to the magistrates, the prosecutor first and then you. If there are co-defendants involved in the application, the advocates go in the order that their respective clients appear on the indictment. Your representations must be based on the prosecution evidence alone. Submissions relating to either the defence or the defendant are irrelevant for the purpose of this hearing. The only issue before the court is whether or not there is a case for the defendant to answer, in a case alleging that the defendant caused grievous bodily harm, no evidence that any such harm was caused.

If the magistrates find that there is a case to answer the case will be committed to the Crown Court for trial and adjourned for a plea and case management hearing to place at the Crown Court at a future specified date. If the magistrates find that there is no case to answer, your client will be discharged.

S6(2) MCA – COMMITTAL BY CONSENT

If, on the papers, you are satisfied that there is a case to answer then this hearing is very simple. It is an administrative hearing where you will be asked on behalf of your client whether he consents for his case to be committed to the Crown Court. Your answer is yes. The case is then formally committed to the Crown Court for trial and adjourned to a specified date at the Crown Court for a plea and case management hearing. The hearing will usually take about two minutes.

By the committal stage your client will almost certainly have exhausted both his bail applications and therefore *unless* there is a change of circumstances, if you client was produced for this hearing in custody then he will be committed to the Crown Court in custody.

CHAPTER 18
THE SENTENCING HEARING

Prior to the hearing beginning it is crucial that you have a conversation with the prosecutor about some of the important details of the hearing. Start by getting clear in your mind how you understand the crown to be opening the case against the defendant including any basis of plea that may have been submitted and accepted on earlier occasions. It is surprising how common it is to have not been told by a colleague about a basis of plea or it being agreed but not reduced to writing and nobody has a note and so on. The way in which the case is going to be opened is crucial to how you prepare your mitigation submission so make sure you know precisely how they put their case. See Appendix 3 for a standard preparation template.

Once the basis for the opening is established, if appropriate, ask what sentencing bracket the prosecution will submit that the case falls into. So many offences now have sentencing guidelines and finding the appropriate bracket is not always a straightforward exercise. The new assault guidelines are an example of a category of offending where there is considerable room for manoeuvre and it is important to know what the prosecutor is going to submit to the court and, very importantly, why they will say it. Although it is a matter for the sentencing tribunal, if both parties are in agreement about the bracket then, subject to it not being ludicrous, then the court is likely to be persuaded by the joint position. Therefore, do not leave this discussion to submissions in court when battle lines have been drawn, speak to the prosecutor and ask them to justify to you why they are placing the case in a higher or more serious category than you will submit. Polite but firm negotiations with the prosecutor on this topic often bear fruit and you might just be able to persuade him to soften his stance. Do not try to do this unless you really feel you are right having considered the guidelines properly, we have all seen the irritating advocates who try it on with the prosecution at every opportunity and it doesn't work. It is very easy to get a reputation as a bit of a chancer or a troublemaker and when it then comes to trying to negotiate, the crown advocate will not even be listening to you as they will have heard it all before. However, if you are someone who is starting to build a reputation as being trustworthy, reliable and sensible, when you speak to the prosecutor and explain your reasoning they will be far more likely to be receptive to your attempts to change their mind. If you cannot change the prosecutor's mind, it does not matter you can still make your submissions to the court but in cases where you have a properly held view, it is always worth a try.

Thirdly, check what the up-to-date list of previous convictions reveals. You may have an outdated copy in your brief and in between plea and the date of the sentencing hearing he may have acquired himself a relevant conviction that wipes out half of your intended mitigation remarks. It is all too common for the court, the prosecution and the defence to be working from three different versions. It is embarrassing when it happens especially when if it sounds as though you are deliberately misleading. I recently conducted a bail application and had been given a list of previous convictions supplied within my brief. I checked with the prosecutor that he just had the three convictions one in 2006, one in 2007 and one in 2008 and we agreed verbally what those convictions were. The copy I had was not complete, not that it left off the list other convictions, it did not include the rather important detail that each of his three previous convictions had been offences committed whilst on bail. So, when I was boring the judge with my lengthy submissions about how the defendant has always respected his previous bail conditions and had certainly never committed the cardinal sin of offending whilst on court bail, I could see the prosecutor itching to get to her feet, which she did and to devastating effect. It was embarrassing and maybe a little pessimistically I felt that the judge thought I was being a touch sharp. So check the document the prosecutor will be using and ask for a copy.

Fourthly, check what ancilliary orders the prosecution will be seeking. Football banning orders, restraining orders, sexual offences prevention orders and exclusion orders are all common sentencing add-ons and you must be alive to them and advise your client about their affect and the implications of not complying with them, which often can result in far heavier punishment than the original sentence.

You should also provide to the prosecution a copy of any document you intend to supply to the court and that includes character references. Most prosecutors will not be particularly interested in their contents but you should at the very least give them an opportunity to consider what they say.

In court, the procedure will tend to follow a pretty set pattern. The prosecutor will open the facts of the case, provide a copy of the defendant's previous convictions to the court and apply for any orders that they feel are appropriate. You will then make your submissions in mitigation, the court will hear any input from the court liaison probation officer (if applicable) and will then pass sentence.

During the course of the hearing, and in particular when the prosecutor is opening the facts and the clerk to the court is advising the justices, make sure that you are listening. There are mistakes made and you must be in a position to correct any errors as they are advanced and not after the hearing when your client advises you of the mistake. It may then be too late.

Although you must correct any mistakes that are made during the hearing, there is a time to do this. Do not interrupt your opponent's submissions or the clerk's advice, this is rude and unnecessary and will only irritate the tribunal. At the end of the submission or the advice from the clerk, then stand and make your submission. There will be times when you are furious at the behaviour of the prosecutor or the clerk but you must never show this to the court, no matter how cross you are, always make proper submissions to the court, free from emotion or personal issues and at an appropriate stage. Persistently interrupting your opponents or the clerks and unseemly bickering is unprofessional and will do your client absolutely no favours.

Following the hearing, you must explain to your client the effect of the sentence that has been passed. This can sometimes feel like an onerous and thankless task – especially when the result has not gone quite to plan but it is a task that you mustn't shy away from. Defendants who have received prison sentences, particularly for the first time, will be terrified and you have a duty to try to console them and reassure them that HMP High Down is in fact the ideal place to spend Christmas.

Other defendants will be eager to leave court and may not want to listen to what you have to say but if the sentence involves a number of different aspects, then you must take the time to explain what it entails especially if there are fines and/or compensation to be paid and certain ancilliary orders have been made. If the defendant is required to see the court liaison probation officer before he leaves court then take him to the office, do not just leave him to fend for himself as he'll probably just go home or to the pub to celebrate.

If you are counsel or instructed as an agent you must then make contact with your instructing solicitor who will expect to know the outcome. Do not delay doing this so the solicitor is forced to call you. Remember, your solicitor maybe receiving calls from the defendant's family about the result so the sooner he knows the better. Make this call as soon as the hearing is finished and then follow it up on the train or at chambers with an attendance note, solicitors expect this to be done as a routine part of representation.

NOTE TO ASSIST IN SENTENCING CASES

The sentencer must start by considering the seriousness of the offence

1. Must be commensurate with the seriousness of the offence

2. Seriousness defined by culpability of defendant and harm caused or risked being caused by the offence.

ABSOLUTE/CONDITIONAL DISCHARGE

'Inexpedient to impose any further penalty'.

Maximum length of con dis + 3 years.

COMMUNITY ORDER THRESHOLD

S148 CJA = serious enough

Or S151 age 16 + 3 or more previous fines and in interests of justice

COMMUNITY ORDER REQUIREMENTS (max length 3 years)

- Unpaid work requirement (minimum 40 hours/maximum 300)
- Activity requirement (max 60 days)
- Programme requirement (length must be same length as overall order and must be combined with supervision)
- Prohibited activity requirement (maximum 3 years)
- Curfew requirement (maximum 6 months)
- Exclusion requirement (maximum 2 years)
- Residence requirement (maximum 3 years)
- Mental health treatment (maximum 3 years)
- Drug rehabilitation treatment (minimum 6 months/maximum 3 years)
- Alcohol treatment (minimum 6 months/maximum 3 years)
- Attendance centre (minimum 12 hours/maximum 36 hours)
- Supervision requirement (will be length of overall order)

COURT MUST HAVE REGARD TO PURPOSES OF SENTENCING

1. Punishment of offender
2. Reduction of crime (including its reduction by deterrence)
3. Reform and rehabilitation of offender
4. Protection of public
5. Reparation by offender to persons affected by their offence

CUSTODY THRESHOLD

Is the offence so serious no fine or community order can be justified for the offence. Is it unavoidable a custodial sentence be imposed, if so can it be suspended.

SUSPENDED SENTENCE

NB equals a prison sentence and therefore appropriate only for offences passing custody threshold and for which imprisonment is the only option.

1. Has the custody threshold been passed?

2. If so, is it unavoidable that a custodial sentence be imposed?
3. If so, can that sentence be suspended?

NB Sentencers should be clear that they would have imposed a custodial sentence if the power to suspend had not been available.

Length: A prison sentence that is suspended should be for the same time it would have applied if the offender had been sentenced to immediate custody.

Magistrates must impose one or more requirement but NB because of the very clear deterrent threat, the requirement should generally be less onerous than those imposed as part of community sentence.

DANGEROUS OFFENDERS

Is it a Section 224 CJA 2003 specified offence? See Schedule 15 part 1, Schedule 15 part 2, for specified violent offences and specified sexual offences.

Note: Convicted of a specified offence <u>and</u> the Court considers there is a significant risk to members of the public of of serious harm occasioned by the commission by him of further such offences (taking into account all such information about the nature and circumstances of the offence and the offender). If so, magistrates have no jurisdiction to deal with the case and it will be committed to the Crown Court for sentence.

BREACH PROCEEDINGS

Community orders

Remind Magistrates, having decided community sentence is commensurate with the seriousness of the offence, the primary objective when sentencing for breach of the requirements is to ensure those requirements are completed.

The Court must either increase the severity of the existing sentence or revoke the sentence and re-sentence for the original primary objective.

The Act allows a custodial sentence to be imposed in response to a breach but custody should be the last resort reserved for those cases of deliberate and repeated breach where all reasonable efforts to ensure that the offender complies have failed.

Before making the requirements more onerous, sentencers should take account of the offender's ability to comply and should avoid precipitating further breach by overloading the offender with too many, or conflicting, requirements.

What were the circumstances of the breach? What has been the compliance to date?

Breach suspended sentence order

Expectation is that the court will activate in full or in part UNLESS unjust to do so.

If court likely to activate custodial element, ensure you ask for appropriate reduction in length taking into account defendant's compliance if any with order to date.

CHAPTER 19
THE SECOND BAIL APPLICATION

For a full discussion on how to prepare your bail application, see chapter 10.

In the Magistrates' Court there does not need to be a change of circumstances for you to make a second bail application, it is the defendant's right. In order to make a third or subsequent bail application however, a change of circumstances is required. If your first bail application failed, do not look at this as a pointless exercise as with a different bench and more persuasive information in support of your application, you can achieve a different outcome.

Whilst this is a complete re-hearing insofar as bail is concerned and the justices are not bound by their colleagues' earlier decision, they will inevitably have in their minds the fact that bail was refused on the last occasion and providing them with a new suggested condition or reason may realistically be the only way that you will persuade this new bench to depart from the previous decision of their colleagues. If there is nothing different about your application, the prosecution will quite understandably remind the justices of the fact so a dull repeat of the first application is likely to do no more than raise the hopes of your client, without any justification. Notwithstanding this advice, be prepared, when the client wants you to, to make a forceful, punchy bail application that captures the interest of the court for its style and delivery, even if the content sounds remarkably similar to the time before.

In most courts, this hearing will take place via a live video link-up with whichever prison your client is detained at. The court will sit as normal and your client will be deemed present at the hearing via the video link. The main difference so far as you are concerned is that you (and any other party) will be seated throughout the hearing (all the other rules of etiquette remain the same). The reason for this is purely logistical to ensure that your client can see everyone present in the court-room on the television screen. Remember to talk into the microphone so that your client can hear you.

If the hearing is not conducted by way of a video link then your client will be brought to court from the prison and (save for any reference to the video link) the hearing conducted as described below.

If the hearing is via the video link, it will start once the live link has been connected with the prison. Your client will sit in a room at the prison accompanied by a prison officer and will also remain seated throughout. The legal advisor will introduce the case to the magistrates. He will then explain to the client that whilst he is not physically present in the courtroom the proceedings will be conducted exactly as if he was. If he wishes to speak to you at any point during the course of the hearing, he need simply raise his hand and the proceedings will be paused to enable you to have a private consultation with him (also via a live video link).

The legal advisor will then introduce everyone in the court room by turning the video camera to each individual present in the court room and identifying them. In the course of the hearing the camera will be turned towards whoever is speaking.

Whether your client appears by video link or in person the hearing will proceed in the same way from here on in. The legal advisor will tell the magistrates the history of the case and will then ask you whether you will intend to make a second bail application.

Whether you are making a bail application or not the prosecutor must still make his remand in custody application to the magistrates. If you are opposing the application, make sure that you take a note of any points made by the prosecutor that you need to address by response.

Once the prosecutor has made his application, he will hand a copy of your client's previous convictions to the magistrates and you will be asked whether they have been seen.

In terms of your advocacy, you should make your bail application in exactly the same way as described in chapter 8.

If on the last occasion, your client was remanded in custody for the first time, it is often worth making the point that having had his first experience of custody he has learnt a salutary lesson as to the likely outcome were he to find himself back before the court either in breach of his bail conditions or having committed further offences.

At the end of your bail application remember to ask the magistrates or District Judge whether you can be of any further assistance. If the magistrates have questions for you, remember to think carefully before you answer them. When you are first on your feet you can feel enormous pressure to answer everything immediately but in fact you will find that not only is it acceptable to take your time, it can often make your submissions more effective.

If the prosecutor wishes to address the magistrates on anything arising out of your application he will do so at the conclusion of your application. If in turn you need to respond, then do.

If you need to take instructions from your client at any point throughout the hearing, do not be afraid to ask and the proceedings will be paused to enable you to have a private consultation with him via the video link (or through the dock if he is present at court).

Once the bail application is completed, the bench will either retire to make their decision or proceed straight to their announcement with reasons.

If your client is remanded into custody, make sure you ask the legal advisor for a certificate of full argument as you will need this document if you intend to make a judge in chambers bail application at the Crown Court.

CHAPTER 20
THE TRIAL

INTRODUCTION

The most exciting and interesting aspect of being an advocate is representing a defendant at his trial and anyone who has experienced the thrill of the 'not guilty' verdict will testify to this. In what is usually no more than one day in the Magistrates' Court each and every one of your skills as an advocate and lawyer is called upon. Negotiating, advising, making submissions and speeches, witness handling and tactics will all be required in almost every trial.

When you start your preparation get it into your head that the case will be an effective trial as this is the only way that you will do things properly. It is so easy to read the prosecution witness statements and think that the case is so overwhelmingly strong that your client will inevitably plead guilty, especially having listened to your gold-plated advice.

This is a serious mistake as it has two profound effects on you and the case. Firstly, it means that your preparation is far less thorough than it should be, you will not scrutinise the crown's case properly, you will ignore the unused material, you will fail to spot the potentially winning point and if the matter does proceed to trial your examination of witnesses and speeches will be all the poorer for it.

Secondly, if at court your client tells you that he has no intention of pleading guilty your judgment can become skewed. Your advice regarding the strength of the evidence will become more forceful verging on pressure being applied, you will try to strike deals with the prosecutor to lesser charges without instructions in the hope that your client succumbs to the offer, you will even start to drum up spurious ways of having the trial adjourned, just because you think he should be pleading guilty and your preparation was poor as a result. The advocates that behave in this way are usually repeat offenders and think nobody knows that they are doing it but it is so obvious as to sometimes be embarrassing. In any advocates room it is usually the same people whose trial once again could not be effective because of some appalling lack of disclosure, witness unavailability or a client suddenly deciding that the case against him was too strong for him to fight. This sort of awful reputation sticks like glue and it is one that you should avoid, other lawyers joke about a person's reputation for 'cracking cases' but deep down nobody admires it at all. It shows a lack of preparation, but worse, a lack of fight, not ideal traits for any advocate.

There is another problem with getting a reputation like this; other lawyers have you down as a bit of a soft touch. We all know prosecutors who do not really like conducting trials and it is to those people that you make ridiculous offers of pleas or bind-overs and often come out with what you want. You may love to be prosecuted by those lawyers but you have absolutely no respect for them. It is the same when you defend, prosecutors know who they can and cannot take a chance with and if your reputation is someone with a lack of fight or courage then wily old Magistrates' Court prosecutors are more likely to try it on with leading questions, inappropriate applications, adducing inadmissible evidence and so on.

So, when you open that brief to begin the trial preparation, always have it firmly in mind that the hearing will be effective and that you will be required utilise all the skills of a trial advocate. If in the end the trial does not go ahead then it matters not, you will have gained valuable experience in trial preparation, you never know your clerks may call you the following week needing you to cover a Crown Court trial and you will be all the better equipped for that if you have at least approached the preparation of a Magistrates' Court trial in the proper way.

As with almost every aspect of the job, preparation is the key. There will be occasions when you receive the papers for a trial a couple of hours before the case is listed, maybe because of an administrative error in chambers or a case has not made its way to your firm's diary and in those cases preparation will be hurried and less detailed than it should be, but manageable. However, in most case you will have at least the night before to read and prepare the case and for almost all cases before the justices, a night's preparation should be ample.

The key to preparing for a trial is to not waste time on irrelevant issues and to focus on what really counts, this will cut the time required in half. Identify at the outset what the salient issues are and direct your preparation at those. In a case where the defendant is charged with common assault and his interview (or proof if you are lucky) says he acted at all times in self-defence, do not spend time worrying about issues relating to defences that he is not advancing, for example no forensic evidence linking him to the scene or the fact that no identification procedures were carried out. It never fails to surprise me how much time is wasted by advocates discussing things that do not matter and issues that have no bearing on whether the defendant is guilty or not guilty, and believe it or not, that is what the whole process is about.

There is no set way to prepare a trial and over time you will develop a unique way of approaching a brief. There are some basic rules that are worth applying to every case.

Firstly, read everything once before you begin to prepare submissions and examination of witnesses. A thorough read of the papers so as to ensure that you have an overall understanding of the case, cuts down the time it takes in the long-run to complete your more detailed preparation. Of course you can highlight anything that stands out as something that needs further consideration but, if time permits, read everything thoroughly as a starting point.

Secondly, understand your instructions. It maybe that these come from his rambling interview or if you are lucky, from a proof of evidence. It is likely that one, other or both are lacking some of the detail that is required to finalise your preparation but they will almost certainly be a good starting point. When I say understand your instructions I mean try to make clear in your own mind what it is the defendant accepts and what he disputes. This will save an awful lot of wasted preparation time. For example if the defendant accepts that he caused the victim's broken nose but he did so in self defence, do not spend hours preparing cross examination of the complainant about his injuries, worse still questions for the doctor who for some reason is a fully-bound witness. I should mention at this stage that when inheriting a case from another, one of the most common occurrences is to find that a certain witness has been warned to attend to give live evidence at the trial. Do not worry if this happens and you are utterly unable to see why the witness's evidence has not been agreed. The first thing to do is to make contact with the advocate who made the decision to warn the witness as it maybe once you have spoken to him or her, the reason becomes clear. However, as is often the case that person will now be on a beach somewhere and you will not be able to fathom their decision. Be brave, if you have no questions for a witness; tell the prosecutor that the witness can be sent away, even at that late stage. That is far more acceptable than to ignore the problem, leave the consultant pediatrician hanging around at court until 330pm, only to ask him no questions. Most witnesses are glad to be released early without having given evidence and although you may have to put up with a snotty prosecutor complaining about how this all could have been done sooner, you have done what you can as soon as you could.

Thirdly, consider the prosecution witness statements in detail, and prepare your cross-examination for each witness. Preparing the examination of witnesses is a personal thing and what works for you is unlikely to work for anyone else. However, it is pretty safe advice to say that you should try not to write out each and every question that you propose to ask, especially not in a fixed order. This all too common approach is wrong for two very important reasons. Firstly, to write out your questions in a sequential list is to presume the answer to the previous question, this, if you have ever conducted any trial, is a serious mistake to make. Most witnesses at some stage during their evidence give an unexpected answer and some witnesses never give the answer that is expected. In these situations your endless preparation of writing out questions will be thrown into chaos – and this is the second reason for not doing it this way. If your fifth question has been determined by your anticipated answer to the fourth question and that one does not come, it will unsettle you and your handling of the witness will suffer. We have all seen advocates struggle to control a witness or fail to deal with a strange answer and this often is due to a rigidity in the preparation which hampers the ability to improvise and to think on one's feet.

You should of course have a structure to the cross-examination and you must be absolutely clear what areas you want to cover by the time you sit down. However, you must be able to improvise and to change the order in which you deal with issues as the witness will almost certainly throw you from time to time by raising an issue you want to deal with but not at the time that you wanted to deal with it. Take the consumption of alcohol as a good example. It is often a fruitful area for cross-examination to remind the witness that they told the police in the statement that they made the day after the incident that they had consumed 12 pints of Stella Artois and it maybe you have decided that it is the final matter with which you will deal. However, within two minutes of questioning by you, completely unprompted the witness says that he had three halves of lager at the pub that night. The time to deal with that apparent fib is there and then. Do not say 'we'll return to the issue of your alcohol later'; meet him head on with it. It shows a command of the papers and a fluidity to your cross-examination. The impact of this point will be lost if you deal with it an hour later after the witness has come to terms with you and managed to bat back your other points. If you have an inflexible method for your witness handling it not only can unsettle you when things do not go as planned but worse than that, it can lessen the impact of the good points that you do have.

As a general guide I draw up a list of areas that I need to cover, very often with sub-headings within those areas and I do have them in an order but the order is changeable and rarely stuck to. If you know the papers inside out, you will have absolutely no difficulty in altering the order you will deal with things. It also looks very impressive to the justices if your knowledge of the witnesses' statement and testimony is such that you are able to instantly spot where an inconsistency has arisen and you are then able to cross-examine on the point immediately.

Remember when preparing your cross-examination to ensure that you have covered every area that is specifically challenged by the defendant, it can be very embarrassing when a witness has finished giving evidence and you realise that part of the defendant's case has not been put. Some, kind prosecutors, if the point is not overwhelmingly important, will not make a fuss or worse still require that the witness be brought back to court for you to put the questions, however, some will not be so generous. Make sure your preparation includes all the specific challenges that must be put and that you do put each of the matters to the witness. If you have not put a matter to a witness you cannot comment on that matter in your closing address to the justices, this is because the witness has not been given an opportunity to deal with your challenge to their evidence.

It can appear sneaky or lacking in courage if you are not prepared to put your case, however fanciful it maybe.

If you do, as a genuine oversight miss something during the trial that should have been put, as embarrassing as it is to raise the matter, you must do so and do so as soon as possible. Your error must never become something which adversely affects your client's case, in this example by not putting your error right, then not being able to deal with a potentially important issue in closing. Everyone makes mistakes and they can be forgiven but it is how you deal with the error that is the important thing.

Fourthly, consider the defendant's police interview and do so very carefully. The defendant's interview is often an area where the prosecution can make a great deal of head way as often they will include inconsistencies and lies. You must consider how, if at all, you can limit the impact of the negative parts of your client's interview by properly arguing the admissibility of some or all of it. In particular, be alive to comment from the police officers, answers given to questions that have no evidential basis, repetitive questioning, answers that may have elicited your client's previous convictions (either by creating a false impression or attacking the character of another), reference by the police to your client's previous convictions or other investigations, the defendant's mental and physical health and in particular whether an appropriate adult should have been sought, the advice given to the defendant prior to interview, pre-interview disclosure (particularly in the context of an inference being sought for failing to mention certain facts) and the custody record. This is by no means an exhaustive list but it does feature some of the more common areas to look out for.

Fifthly, consider in detail the schedule of unused material. With a trial in the Magistrates' Court, the schedule of material is unlikely to be particularly voluminous but it still may contain a tiny piece of information or evidence that completely changes the case. Just by reading crime reports, police serials and minute sheets, first accounts from witnesses contained within officer's pocket note books or the more obvious areas such as antecedents of a prosecution witness, you may uncover something that will really help your cross-examination of witnesses and the overall presentation of the case. So many cases are won by proper consideration of the unused material and often prosecutors, who have had to prepare three trials that morning, have not had sufficient time to consider the unused material and you can gain a huge advantage if you have. Do not take the lazy option and ignore the unused material thinking that its unlikely to help, you have absolutely nothing to lose in checking it and you may be pleasantly surprised by what you find.

MISCELLANEOUS TRIAL ISSUES

Special measures

Most people take completely the wrong approach to special measures, namely just oppose for the sake of opposing. That 'object to everything' approach might sound good to your client and his family but is it actually in his best interests? I speak as someone who over the course of the last five years has done countless serious sex cases all of which have in some form involved the use of special measures. By far the most powerful and persuasive witnesses have, without exception, been those that have been prepared to give evidence live in court, with or without a screen. It seems to be the Crown's default position is to ask for a remote TV link for young witness or those perceived to be vulnerable. Of course, in 90% of cases such measures are completely unnecessary but just because they are excessive and over-the-top, it does not mean that they are necessarily harmful to the defendant. I rarely oppose such an application as I am mindful of the alternative, namely, the witness in court, often upset and distressed in full view of the tribunal and from the defendant's point of view this can only be a bad thing. Even if a witness is not telling the truth to see him or her sobbing pulls at the heart strings of even the sternest of magistrates.

There can be no objection, moral or legal, to a defence advocate, whilst acknowledging that special measures are a necessary tool in ensuring that witnesses give their evidence in the best possible environment, doing his or her best to limit the negative impact of the measures put in place and if that means suggesting or agreeing to a remote TV link rather than screens then that must be the stance taken.

Hearsay

How do we know its hearsay? Because someone told us. Although the rules regarding hearsay are far more relaxed since 2003, there is still a process to be followed and you should not just give up the fight because the feeling now is that hearsay 'goes in'. It does not and proper objection can still be taken even in those cases where the notice has been served and on time, especially with fair-minded prosecutors. Where a notice has not been served but hearsay and multiple hearsay appears throughout the papers, edit the statements accordingly and when you are having your pre-trial discussion with the prosecution, remind him that there is to be no hearsay adduced and if certain paragraphs particularly offend you, then draw them to his attention. It is no good expecting the prosecutor to play fair and to not adduce any hearsay evidence, some will do this but plenty will not and before you know it, the complainant's girlfriend's, sister's neighbour has told the court that she heard through a friend's cousin, that had read it on Facebook, that the person who committed the burglary was the defendant.

As with any application, only take objection where it is sensible to do so. Becoming known as the advocate who takes the bad point and does so regularly is not a reputation to be proud of. Take objections when appropriate and do so with as much force as you can muster but pick your fights and you will find that you may well have considerable success.

Bad character

So many cases now involve the prosecution serving notice of their intention to adduce the defendant's bad character and the ramifications of such an application can be devastating to your client's case. Therefore, from a very early stage in your career as an advocate, you must get used to responding to these applications properly.

Bad character covers so many different forms of behaviour and do not be fooled into thinking that your client of good character may not be the subject of an application to adduce evidence of his reprehensible conduct. Telling lies and taking drugs are good examples of established types of 'bad character' so be warned that applications may flow as a result of this type of conduct as well as his previous convictions.

The most common form of application relates to the defendant's propensity to commit offences of the type with which he is now charged, (which falls under Criminal Justice Act 2003, s101 (1)(d), namely an important matter in issue between the defendant and the prosecution.) This is always arguable, in one of two ways. Firstly, in certain circumstances you will want to argue that his skinny list of previous convictions does not establish the requisite propensity but be sure to be sensible about this point. If your client does have eight convictions for theft and he is charged with his ninth, it is a foregone conclusion that the justices will find that the propensity test is easily passed. So, it may be in these circumstances you will prefer to consider the second way in which you can argue the propensity point; by objecting to the admissibility of the bad character on the basis that once evidence of his eight convictions is admitted, there will be no proper scrutiny of the evidence in the current trial as he will be deemed to be guilty by virtue of his unpleasant past.

The other common form relates to an attack made by your client on another person's character (which falls under section 101 (1)(g)). This can arise pre-trial, namely in the defendant's interview or more commonly, mid-trial by virtue of your cross-examination or the defendant's evidence, so be very careful to advise the defendant about this pitfall. Very often defendants are unaware of the implications of attacking another person's character and will complain to you when, as a result of the way the case has been conducted, the justices learn of an extensive criminal past. The best way to deal with it is by speaking to the prosecutor and asking him what his attitude will be to the defendant's bad character if his case is conducted in a certain way. It maybe that your client could not care less and will still want the witnesses attacked and the police accused of planting evidence, nevertheless, you must advise him of the possible implications of the line he wants to take.

Another more common gateway for admittance of bad character is to correct a false impression given by the defendant (which falls under s101 (1) (f)). It is important to remember that this can be done by the defendant's actions (for example wearing an armed forces uniform despite having convictions for dishonesty and no longer being a serving soldier, or by is words, suggesting in evidence that he is of good character. Be careful with some of the more subtle ways in which this gateway can be engaged and two examples that I have seen first hand, spring to mind.

Firstly, I was involved in a case where a defendant was asked by his barrister at the beginning of his evidence in chief, if he was nervous, when the defendant answered yes, he was asked why. The defendant said 'because I have never given evidence before'. Now, factually that was absolutely accurate but the impression it created was misleading and false as it left the jury with the impression that he had never been before the courts, which could not have been further from the truth. He was on trial for non-dwelling burglary, namely a computer games shop and he had fifteen similar convictions, they all went in and he was convicted.

Secondly, on another occasion as I stood up to cross-examine a defendant who was charged with a sexual offence he removed from underneath his shirt a huge crucifix. He had numerous convictions for offences of dishonesty all of which were admitted to correct the false impression he had tried to create by suggesting he had led a god-fearing and blameless life.

On both occasions the hammer-blow of the admittance of the defendant's good character was utterly avoidable. Were it not for on one occasion the appalling questions asked by his barrister and on the other his own silly attempt to bolster his own credibility, the jury would have known nothing of the damning list of previous convictions.

The bad character provisions also relate to non-defendants and co-defendants and as such there will be times when you are making an application to adduce the evidence of another person's bad character. These applications should usually have been made well before the trial date as there is a strict regime for the admittance of bad character evidence and often in cases involving more than one defendant the court will be slow to admit evidence of a co-defendant's bad character if that co-defendant has been ambushed by the late application.

Admissions and agreed facts

The popular approach to agreed facts and admissions is one of my pet-hates. Agreed facts are precisely what they say they are – facts. Unless and until you are in a position to agree them as such, you should never do so. Agreeing a set of admissions because you think they are probably accurate or because you have got nothing to controvert what is suggested is completely wrong.

Never agree any fact until you know it as a fact. Remember the wording of the s.10 of the Criminal Justice Act 1967 could not be clearer, if you make an admission then the court will treat the fact as 'conclusive evidence of the fact admitted'. The date and time of arrest, client's date of birth, timings of police interviews and date of charge are all the sorts of things that can quite easily be agreed and there is unlikely to be any controversy about such detail.

However, there is an approach creeping into the trial process that sees prosecutors asking for, and defence advocates agreeing to, admissions that simply should not and cannot be made. It seems that there is some confusion between agreeing a statement under the provisions of section 9 of the Criminal Justice Act 1967 and agreeing facts or making admissions.

For example in a case involving toxicology, when an expert says that he found 200 mililitres of alcohol in the defendant's sample of blood, that can be admitted as a fact. However when he goes on to say that that quantity of alcohol usually means that someone will be unable to walk straight, that is opinion, albeit based on his expertise and that is more properly agreed, should you be inclined to, under the provisions of s9 CJA 1967.

I have been asked recently in a case in which identification was the primary issue if I would be prepared to agree as a fact a police officer's commentary of what he purports to see on CCTV including his opinion that it was the defendant seen on the footage. The reasoning was this; the officer is going to give the evidence from the witness box about what he says he saw and it is his opinion, you cannot argue with what he says is his opinion so why do not you just make an admission about what he says he saw?!

I could not admit what he says is his opinion (even if I wanted to) as it is his opinion and his opinion is not a fact, but my attempts to get the prosecutor to understand the difference failed. There is of course a difference between this sort of admission and those commonly and quite properly drafted that merely sets out that witness A attended the identification parade and when asked to identify his attacker he said that it was number 4 and the person positioned at number 4 was the defendant. This is an admission about the facts of what happened at the identification procedure and nothing more.

The case of *R v Lewis* [1971] Crim LR 414 CA. makes clear the requirement that the tribunal of fact must be able to understand the distinction between that which is fact, law and opinion. Remember this when drafting or agreeing admissions.

IN THE BRIGHTON COURT

B E T W E E N:

REGINA

-V-

JOE BLOGGS

SECTION 10 ADMISSION

Pursuant to Section 10 of the Criminal Justice Act 1967 the Crown admits that:

1] The defendant's date of birth is 10th May 1975

2] The defendant was arrested on the 12th March 2012 by PC Smith and made no reply to the caution.

3] The defendant was interviewed at Brighton Police Station at 11.30am on the 13th March 2012 and the defendant answered no comment to all questions asked.

Signed ....   Signed ....

Crown Prosecution Service

Dated ....   Dated ....

THE FIRST MEETING WITH THE DEFENDANT

This may well be the first time that you have met your client, particularly if you are counsel and have been instructed fairly late in the proceedings. The first thing to do, client's attendance permitting, is to have a conference with the defendant during which you will discuss with him the strengths of the Crown's case, the merits of his defence, whether he is likely to give evidence, any defence witnesses he may want to call, likely sentence upon conviction and whether he wants, even at this late stage, to plead to the charge(s), some of them or less serious alternatives.

At this discussion you must have the courage to advise him in accordance with how you see the case against him and his prospects of success at the trial.

Notwithstanding any earlier advice given to him about how no court in the land could convict him of these trumped up charges, if you feel differently you must tell him. You may have to deal at a later stage with an irate instructing solicitor or colleague when word gets back to him that you have told the defendant to ignore the advice that that lawyer has given him and to instead take your word for how dire his chances are. Do not concern yourself with that problem at this stage, concentrate on ensuring that the defendant understands the case against him and the trial process.

You will be amazed how many defendants say to you on the morning of the trial that they had no idea that at a trial they may have to give evidence as part of their defence. It is a fact that by the time the trial is listed; defendants still might not have been advised fully and properly about all manner of issues and you must not be frightened to reveal to them something that they should have been told about at the first appearance. It is tempting but do not shirk from being straight with your advice and robust where necessary. The Court of Appeal have said many times and in particular in the case of *R v Hall* 52 Cr App R.528, CA, that it is the duty of defence counsel to impress upon a defendant the implications of certain courses of action, if needs be, in forceful language.

You may be faced with a client who for whatever reason is reluctant to plead to the current charge but may well consider a lesser alternative. Explore how far he is prepared to accept guilt and upon what basis and then you have a foundation upon which to begin negotiations with the prosecutor.

There will be times when your client is late or later to court than your opponent and there is nothing wrong in that situation with exploring with the crown what their 'bottom line' is, regarding acceptable pleas. Even if they want a plea to the current charge on the full facts, at least you know precisely where you stand when you do have that first meeting with the defendant.

Remember, no matter how bad your client's predicament appears to be, he has already pleaded not guilty and will, in most circumstances have been readying himself for a trial, so be firm in your advice but be understanding and sympathetic to what will be a worrying situation and try not to ride roughshod over his concerns and fears, no matter how inconsequential they sound to you.

NEGOTIATING WITH THE PROSECUTION

You will develop and hone your own way of negotiating and there is no textbook that can show the definitive way to negotiate successfully. However, there are techniques that are unlikely to work and, especially in the early days, are best avoided.

Take the example of a defendant charged with ABH, who is seen by three independent witnesses and the local CCTV camera to approach the victim from behind and hit him on the head with a bottle, which does not break but causes a small bump. The injury is so slight that the correct charge is probably Common Assault, but the decision has been made and he faces the ABH trial. Certain advocates, and I include in this certain experienced advocates, would take the view that the right approach is to confront the prosecutor, probably in a robing room full of people, about how utterly hopeless his case is and that only a moron would continue with the charge as it stands. Avoid this approach, even if you think it. If a defending advocate mocks the prosecutor, the case against his client, the charging decision, the prosecution witnesses or the reviewing lawyer, it is likely that they will become offended, maybe embarrassed but more importantly, very reluctant to negotiate with you.

In the example given, it should be your target to persuade the prosecutor that a Common Assault is a fair disposal and on these rather obvious facts. It is more likely that he would be willing to agree that course, if approached politely and reasonably. If not, and he feels that you have been rude, notwithstanding the weakness in his case, he is likely to proceed with the ABH with the obvious risk to your client that in the witness box, that the complainant gives some additional evidence that satisfies the justices that he was in fact occasioned actual bodily harm.

It can often help if you begin your negotiations with a concession, for example in this case, maybe tell crown counsel that you acknowledge that self-defence is a non-starter in light of the CCTV. If the prosecutor thinks from the outset that you are being reasonable and not blindly one-sided, he is far more likely to soften his position. After the concession, point out the obvious flaw or weakness in his case and then suggest the obvious lesser alternative being firm but at all times courteous. There will be occasions when you can be light-hearted and more jovial about the negotiating and this is another good way of relaxing your opponent, thereby improving his view of you. These little things can sometimes help.

We have all been involved in cases when your opponent is rude, aggressive and obtuse from the outset and when this happens you become reluctant, stubborn and awkward yourself to combat it. When you are defending people you do not want a hostile opponent who, in the Magistrates' Court, can make your life difficult but, much more importantly, make life for your client immeasurably trickier, whether that is pre-trial, in refusing to accept sensible pleas or within a trial by conducting the case differently than he had once intended.

Many cases may involve negotiations far less obvious than this example and in each case you will have to think very carefully about how to approach your opponent. However, the fundamentals of being courteous, prepared to make concessions, firm, realistic and not overly confrontational will always stand you in very good stead.

THE SECOND CONFERENCE WITH YOUR CLIENT

Having heard the Crown's view regarding your offer(s), unless it has been agreed at that stage that the case will not be an effective trial, you will have to communicate to your client what has been said. It maybe that he is prepared to agree to their suggestion or it may be that you have to return to speak to your opponent with another, slightly lesser offer. It is not advisable to do this too many times as it begins to appear as though you are trying to shoe horn the defendant's instructions into the basis or the charge that the crown want.

If there is a particular sticking point, finalise your client's instructions on the point, check with the prosecutor whether the defendant's version/plea is acceptable and then leave it. Do not unsettle the defendant by obviously trying so hard to persuade him to abandon his objection or plead to a certain charge. Always remember he must have complete faith in you, particularly if the matter may result in a trial, and if you have told him twenty times that his instructions on a point are more stupid than anything you have ever heard, he is unlikely to feel entirely confident that you will be doing your utmost to secure his acquittal at trial.

If your negotiations with the Crown have borne fruit and agreement has been reached then you must ask your client to sign an endorsement on your brief or file. This is something that you must explain to your client, as he will often be suspicious of the need to sign something that admits his guilt in rather irrefutable terms. Explain that he is signing a declaration for your benefit and you (and possibly your solicitor) will be the only person to see it, the court and the prosecution will not see the document. Remember it is a protection for you and nothing more, it is not something you can force the defendant to sign, nor is it something that if he refuses to sign, should change the course of events.

THE OPENING SPEECH

If there is a subject that you want left out of the opening speech make sure you raise this with the prosecutor before he begins his opening address to the justices. Do not presume that just because something is so obviously inadmissible or it is going to be the subject of argument, that the prosecutor will automatically remove it from his opening. Raise it with him, make clear your objection and most will then leave it out of their opening submissions.

If you do not raise the matter and it is then mentioned in opening, you will be on rather shaky ground when it comes to applying to discharge the justices on the basis that they have had inadmissible and prejudicial material that they should not have heard. Magistrates' Courts are not inclined to waste a day of court time just because an advocate failed to do his job properly so be sure to deal with any objections that you may have from the outset. Then, if the prosecutor mentions the contentious issue, having agreed not to, you will be in a stronger position to argue any application to discharge.

When the prosecutor is opening the case to the justices, pay attention. Mistakes are made and at that very early stage of the proceedings when the attention of the court is at its best, it is important that any mistakes are rectified immediately. When I say immediately, the time to rectify a mistake is at the end of the address. Do not interrupt your opponent during his opening speech, this is rude and it will not impress the justices or the court clerk. However, there are exceptions to this and if a significant error is being made repeatedly then it may be appropriate to wait for the right moment, get your opponent's attention, inform him of the mistake and he can then rectify it for the court.

Choosing when to object to things is one of the areas that most troubles newly qualified advocates, as whilst you do not want to appear rude by interrupting, you will be concerned not to let something go unchallenged that could be damaging to your client.

How to object is the other worry. Do not stand up and shout 'objection' and definitely do not approach the front of the court like a scene from the film, A Few Good Men. Choose your moment to stand up, tell the justices the nature of your objection, allow the prosecutor to make his submission and then respond to what has been said. No matter how cross you are about the conduct of the prosecutor, do not let this show and never personalise your submissions. Object when it is appropriate and do so firmly, but do so politely.

PROSECUTION WITNESSES GIVING EVIDENCE IN-CHIEF

There will be areas of evidence that are uncontroversial and I am never one for insisting that prosecutors ask non-leading questions about every single topic. However, there is a tendency in the Magistrates' Court for people not to be troubled by non-leading questions on very important issues and this is wrong. It is still the job of the prosecutor to get *from* his witness the evidence and not to give the evidence himself by suggesting answers in leading questions. Make it clear to him before the witness is called which areas you are content to allow leading but then do not allow him to lead on any other area.

If you have agreed with the prosecutor that certain material is not admissible and it relates to the evidence of a specific witness, there is no harm in asking your opponent to ask the witness not to refer to the offending material. If the witness ignores the warning and appears to do so deliberately, you may want to cross-examine him about that. Further, if it relates to a very important matter that seriously prejudices your client, then it may be persuasive on the matter of whether the justices should be discharged.

CROSS-EXAMINATION OF PROSECUTION WITNESSES

This is the part of the trial that you should relish because the reality is, it is where cases are won and lost. If you work on the basis that most witnesses are able to satisfy the court that their memory of an incident six months ago was better when they made their statement than it is on the day they give evidence, will come up to proof then it is your cross-examination that will have to be the undoing of the witness.

Your cross-examination should leave nobody in any doubt about what your case is and you should challenge every aspect of a witnesses' testimony that your client refutes. If, when you first begin, you remember these two principles you will at least have the correct foundation for your own style and approach to develop.

The way in which you cross-examine a witness will depend on many factors. Your client, the attitude of the witness, the evidence in chief, what needs to be put and your tribunal all may affect the style and approach to your examination and as time goes by you will get a feeling for the way in which you handle a witness.

Regardless of style, you must always remain in control of the witness and yourself. There are some witnesses that are impossible to control and no advocate in the land would be able to do anything about it but most are manageable and providing you are prepared to be firm, very firm at times, most witnesses can be kept on the leash.

The best way to control any witness is to have a structure to your examination; if you are lurching from one point to the next without any direction and you are faced with a witness who is being particularly difficult you will never be in control of the witness and if he senses that you are struggling (this can be the case with experienced police officers, store detectives etc) he will begin to control you and this should never happen. Just because you have a completely hopeless case to put and one which the witness is never going to agree with, that does not mean you should not be in control – quite the opposite. When putting a hopeless case appearing in control may be the only thing that gives your examination some credence.

As has already been mentioned in the trial preparation section, the structure must be flexible and allow for the witness or your tribunal knocking you off your course but a structure there should always be. The structure need be no more than a list of headings of the areas that you know you must cover in an order that is logical and easily followed and this should be done for every cross-examination. As part of this structure you should know where you want to get to with each witness, it may not always be achievable but you should have that aim as it gives your examination some purpose.

There are times when your structure has to be disregarded altogether and this can happen for a variety of reasons. This can sometimes occur when you sense that a witness is wobbling during examination-in-chief and you get the feeling he may give you the answers you need far quicker than you had imagined. You may decide therefore to get straight to the point at the beginning of your cross-examination and sometimes, just sometimes you get the answer you want. If this happens, do not, whatever else you do, carry on with all the other points that you had listed that were designed to chip away at the credibility of the witness. Once you have achieved your target, sit down and say no more.

Although this sounds like boringly obvious advice, you would be surprised how often it is advice that is not followed and usually that is for one of two reasons; either because there was no established target with a certain witness so the advocate does not realise when the situation is as good as it needs to be or alternatively where the structure for the cross-examination is so rigidly relied upon that the advocate feels too frightened to abandon it. So, have a structure that is focused but one that allows you to add and omit as the evidence develops.

The other occasion when the structure might have to be shelved is when you realise that the end target you had with a certain witness is never going to be reached. This can be because you get utterly unexpected answers or some vital information that your client has given you is palpably not true. The classic example is when a defendant tells you that a certain witness is a lying, drunken, drug addict who will be utterly incomprehensible due to alcohol and heroin. The man walks into court and is in fact more presentable and eloquent than your opponent. Your entire cross-examination was based on the witnesses' supposed unreliability and lack of credibility and so you have a problem that you must address immediately. Do you carry on with your client's obviously incorrect assessment of the witness and put all manner of ridiculous suggestions to him? No, of course you do not do that. Test the witness in the early part of your cross-examination to see if what your client told you has any foundation whatsoever but if it does not, abandon it, put your case to him and sit down.

Another very important aspect of cross-examination is listening. Too often advocates do not listen to answers given and as a consequence the basis upon which they ask their follow-up questions or prepare their speech is wrong. It can be embarrassing to be corrected time and time again by your opponent, the clerk, or worse the justices, because you have not listened properly to the evidence. One of the problems with not listening properly to the evidence is that you begin to put a more positive slant on the evidence than actually was the case. The witness that says he 'thinks it was the man in black who threw the first punch' becomes the witness who said 'it was the man in black who threw the first punch'. These may appear to be minor differences but nonetheless they are important ones and these mistakes will not be made if you listen to the evidence.

Controlling yourself is also a much understated requirement. You must never show your emotions no matter how a witness is behaving or what answers he is giving you as to do so adds a personal element to the examination that has no place in the courtroom. It is important that you stay focused on asking proper questions that are relevant and have a purpose, getting upset and annoyed will invariably mean a loss of focus and a lack of clarity. Even if you feel your blood boiling, keep your cool and let nobody see your emotions.

HALF TIME SUBMISSION

At the close of the prosecution case you must consider whether there is an argument that your client has no case to answer. The threshold for this is very high and you should not make anything other than proper submissions at this stage, based on the witnesses and their evidence.

It used to be the case that prosecutors were not able to make closing speeches and would welcome a hopeless half-time submission as an opportunity to make what was effectively a closing speech. Now that prosecutors can make closing speeches you have a little more leeway to make your submission at the close of the crown's case but do not make one for the sake of it if you know it to be hopeless.

Each case will be fact specific and making submissions at this stage is a judgment call. You may feel that the judge or the justices has given you an indication that they would be receptive to such a submission and if this is so, even if you had not prepared one, get on your feet and make one. Equally, you may always have planned to make one but the tribunal may have been awkward and unpleasant to you throughout the trial. Do not let this put you off if you feel that your submission is valid, but gauge the mood of the court and if you feel it would be pointless, do not make the submission.

If you decide to make a submission of no case to answer in front of the justices you should start by reminding them of what the test at this stage is and where it comes from, namely R v Galbraith 73 Cr App R 124, CA. This is the proper approach:

'1) If there is no evidence that the crime alleged has been committed by the defendant, there is no difficulty – the judge will stop the case.

2) The difficulty arises where there is some evidence but it is of a tenuous character, for example, because of inherent weakness or vagueness or because it is inconsistent with other evidence. a) Where the Judge concludes that the prosecution evidence taken at its highest, is such that a jury properly directed could not properly convict on it, it is his duty, on a submission being made, to stop the case. b) Where however the prosecution evidence is such that It is strength or weakness depends

on the view to be taken of a witnesses reliability, or other matters which are generally speaking within the province of the jury and where on one possible view of the facts there is evidence on which the jury can properly come to the conclusion that the defendant is guilty, then the Judge should allow the matter to be tried by the jury' (per Lord Lane CJ at p127).

The most common mistake is to think that there is a valid submission of no case to answer merely because there are inconsistencies between what was said by a witness in his statement and in evidence or as between two witnesses. There will be occasions when the inconsistency is so marked and/or important that a submission based on this is perfectly proper but usually these sorts of issues are matters for the justices at the end of the case and not at half-time.

CALLING YOUR CLIENT TO GIVE EVIDENCE

The decision about whether to call your client will depend on the circumstances of the case and there is not a scientific method regarding when to and when not to call your client. In certain circumstances the decision will be simple because the defendant wants to give evidence and needs to give evidence because his case requires it.

Equally, there are cases in which the defendant never has the slightest inclination to give evidence and even after you have advised him of the adverse inference direction he still does not want to go into the witness box. In this scenario you should endorse your brief with the advice you have given the defendant and his decision to not to give evidence.

However, some cases will not be so straightforward and the decision for the defendant is complicated by his understandable concerns about his ability to give evidence, whether he or his account will stand up to the rigours of cross-examination or whether he really needs to give evidence if the case is tenuous or weak, acknowledging that very often the defence case can be at its strongest at the close of the prosecution case.

Do not fret about this issue as providing the defendant has been properly advised about the potential consequences for each course, you can do no more. You will have as many cases where the defendant makes a good witness as cases when he is an unmitigated disaster and sometimes there is no telling which it is likely to be. Most defendants do give evidence and most come through it alive.

If your client has decided that he is going to give evidence then you must prepare him for the experience. This does not mean telling him what to say but it certainly does mean you should discuss with him what he can expect to be asked. There is nothing wrong with discussing in detail what areas the crown are most likely to focus on and importantly, why they will do so. If there is a very difficult area issue about which your client will certainly get asked, deal with it with him, do not shy away from it as he will not thank you when he has to cope with it for the first time in the witness box. It may be that no answer he gives will deal with the problem but it is important that you know what answer he is going to give – regardless how implausible it seems.

It is also important to advise your client about how to deal with the pressure of giving evidence, in particular; impressing upon him how he must be polite at all times to the prosecutor, the magistrates and the court staff, never to lose his temper or become aggressive, not to try to be funny or to show off, never to ask questions of the prosecutor when answering his questions and at all times to try to be likeable.

Your examination of your client, and indeed any witnesses, should be controlled and delivered at a measured pace, a pace that you set. Keep the witness under control and try to ensure that he answers the questions, speaks slowly and clearly and does not ramble about irrelevant matters. There is nothing wrong with being firm with a client who seems not to be listening or who seems to be unable to answer the question- the magistrates will thank you for it. You are not, however, permitted to rescue a defendant who appears to be hanging himself by interrupting his evidence when you do not like the sound of an answer. There is a fine line between controlling a witness and saving his skin, be sure to know where the line is.

When the defendant is being cross-examined listen, take notes and if the examination becomes overly hostile, rude or on an incorrect factual basis, wait for an opportune moment, get on your feet and make your objection known. However, persistent interruption of your opponent can appear rude and will do your client no favours, if however, you feel that your objections are valid, ask the justices to retire and discuss your concerns with the prosecutor and the clerk, this may have the effect of diffusing the situation without irritating the justices.

RE-EXAMINATION

As a general rule, do not do it. It rarely makes the situation any better and it can appear as a desperate attempt to salvage a lost cause. Sometimes you just have to accept that your client has conceded something in cross-examination that destroys his case and there is no coming back from it. Trying to manoeuvre your client back to his original instructions will almost always make the situation worse whilst highlighting the bombshell that he dropped under cross-examination.

There will be times when you do need to clarify or correct something that he has said and in those situations you must of course do so. The best example of this is when a prosecutor questions your client about answers he gave to the police in interview but does so by only highlighting some of the questions and answers he has given on that subject. This can be very misleading and you should be ready to balance matters by adducing in re-examination the more favourable answers on the topic.

THE COURT CLERK'S ADVICE

This is very important as the justices, quite properly, will almost always take the advice of their clerk on matters of law and procedure. Prior to the advice being given, take the time to discuss with the clerk what his/her advice will be, that way you can discuss anything with the clerk that you disagree with and make submissions to the justices if necessary. Ask the clerk of the court to give the advice in open court as it is equally important that your client hears what is being said. There is a tendency for clerks to retire with the justices to give a bit of additional advice and guidance, this will unsettle you and your client and is to be discouraged wherever possible.

The advice given will almost always be correct but that should not stop you wanting to listen to it and correcting it if needs be. Having been on the end of the advice of a clerk who once told the justices that because the defendant had raised the issue of self-defence it was for him to prove on the balance of probabilities that he was, you will understand how important it is to hear the guidance being given.

The justices will often ask to see the clerk of the court during the course of their retirement, usually for further explanation on matters of also or procedure. The court will not reconvene for the advice to be given in open court and when the clerk returns having given the advice backstage you will be told by the clerk what the question and the advice was. If the clerk does not volunteer any information be sure to ask.

CLOSING SPEECH

You should be considering your closing speech from an early stage and as the trial proceeds you should make notes of points to consider making in your closing address. There is no advocate in the world who has not sat down and realised almost straight away that there is a point that should have been made and there is very little in this job that is more annoying than that feeling.

Most Magistrates' Court trials are finished within a day, so your planning for your speech should be done as part of your trial preparation the night or day before the trial begins. This should be a framework within which you can knit additional points that arise during the trial and in the same way that your notes for cross-examination should be fluid allowing for amendments and additions so should your structure for a closing speech.

In particular you should listen to your opponent's closing speech and where necessary deal with the points that are made, including any mistakes about the law or the facts. Your framework should allow for this as a prosecutor's closing speech is now a common part of a Magistrates' Court trial and you must anticipate the points he is likely to make and deal with them. Remember, the fluidity of your speech framework should of course allow for leaving matters out if an anticipated point is not made by the prosecutor or does not develop in the way in which you had thought it would.

Always remember that in the course of a closing speech you must only refer to matters that have featured in evidence. You are not entitled to speculate or invite speculation by the justices nor should you represent something to the justices that on the evidence is correct but you know from the unused material is factually inaccurate. Both of these are sadly all too common.

There will be occasions when you will want to deal with matters of law, a common example being the good character of your client. Just because the clerk of the court will advise the justices how they should use the defendant's hitherto crime-free life, should not stop you from making the submissions yourself. This can be your best and most powerful point and you should make the most of it, do not rely on the clerk to do it as persuasively as you can.

Another area of law that you will want to address the justices on is a defendant's decision to answer no comment to the questions asked of him in his police interview. Do not leave this issue to the clerk of the court who is required to give the justices the full, very negative, direction regarding the defendant's failure to answer questions. There will almost always be a more positive slant on this issue and you must address what is, if left unanswered, a very powerful part of the crown's case.

Draw up headings that will cover all the necessary points that need to be made and even sub-headings within each section but be prepared to alter the order if whilst you are on your feet you think of an improved order for the points to be made.

The delivery of your speech should be measured and delivered at a pace that everyone can follow. Rushing your submissions is the best way to ensure that good points are lost and as it is likely that you will only have two or three genuinely good submissions you cannot afford to lose any of them to bad advocacy.

Many advocates start, maybe having dealt with some basic introductory matters, by telling the court, whether it be a jury or the justices, how many points they propose to make in their closing and this can be a very effective way of keeping the attention of the audience, particularly when you intend to make just a few points. A recent Crown Court trial I conducted involved a barrister who began his closing speech by telling the jury that he had 16 points maybe stretching the effectiveness of that technique beyond its limits.

Try not to be long-winded, by the time the closing speech arrives the justices will be very familiar with the issues arising in the case and they do not need a recital of the facts from you. In the same way that mitigation should not drag on and on, nor should closing addresses, long speeches are boring and unnecessary and do your client no favours. You should be thorough at all times and detailed where necessary but you should not try to turn obviously bad points into good ones and you should never repeat yourself, these are the two things that increase the length of most advocate's speeches.

WAITING FOR THE JUSTICES TO REACH A DECISION

This is an awkward time for the defendant so you should spend a little time with him after the justices have retired to relax him and to ensure that he understands what might happen. You do not need to spend the entire retirement time with him but just enough to explain fully what the options for the court are on conviction and acquittal. This advice should extend to the defendant's family if needs be and remember to advise the defendant and his family that no matter what the outcome they should avoid reacting noisily or inappropriately.

If you have not already done so, be sure to use this time to take instructions from your client in mitigation and make sure that you ask him to complete a means form. Explain to the client when doing this that just because you are preparing for the worst it does not automatically mean that you think he will be convicted, just that is in his best interests that you are fully prepared should the worst happen. Whilst of course some cases will be put back to later in the day or adjourned to a different day pending the preparation of a pre-sentence report, many cases will proceed to sentence as soon as the magistrates have convicted and if you have not already prepared for sentence, you must do so now.

APPEALS FROM THE MAGISTRATES' COURT

Unlike an appeal from the Crown Court to the Court of Appeal, there is no need for grounds of appeal to be drafted and submitted for an appeal from the Magistrates' Court to the Crown Court. However, your advice should be no less robust when considering the defendant's prospects of an appeal following a conviction by the justices and if he has no realistic prospect then do not advise him to just 'give it a go'.

Not only are you duty-bound to give him proper advice about his prospects, if you advise him to pursue an appeal that you know to be frivolous, there may be serious consequences for him. Firstly, remember that the hearing is *de novo* and if the defendant is convicted at his appeal, the issue of sentence remains open and may well be increased and not all judges will warn you of their intention to increase the sentence if the defendant is convicted. Secondly, the issue of costs should be considered. Crown Court hearings are expensive and the costs of a failed appeal are likely to be borne by the defendant, at least in part.

This application form (available from the Criminal Procedure Rules section of www.justice.gov.uk) needs to be completed on behalf of the defendant and it can be submitted on the day of sentence and no later than 21 days of his sentence for the offence. This should be served on the court and all relevant parties.

BAIL PENDING APPEAL

If your client has received a custodial sentence for the offence/s and he is appealing against either the conviction or sentence, provided he has served his notice of appeal on the court and all relevant parties you can apply for bail pending an appeal on his behalf and particularly if your client has been on bail throughout the proceedings you should consider doing so. The Bail Act 1976 does not apply to bail applications pending appeal and your client no longer has the right to bail. If bail is refused by the justices, your client can apply for bail at the Crown Court.

TRIAL IN ABSENCE

This is not an easy issue and each time you are faced with a defendant who fails to turn up to his trial it will be slightly different from the last and slightly different considerations will apply.

Courts are now under severe pressure to ensure that trials are effective on the day they are listed and consequently the defendant who deliberately absents himself is unlikely to de-rail the trial process as a result, he can expect his trial to take place in his absence. The question for you is whether you can and should stay to represent him and some situations are far simpler than others. In other words do you still have instructions?

Take the example of an advocate turning up to a trial for which the defendant fails to attend and does so with no good reason. The advocate is blessed with a signed proof of evidence and in addition a full written commentary on the prosecution witness statements. Unless there is something quite out of the ordinary this would be an example of when you as his advocate should stay and represent the defendant's interests – notwithstanding any opposition you would have made about how the trial should not proceed in his absence due to the inherent unfairness of it all. You have the material to cross-examine, object to any applications that the Crown may make about his character and you can make a speech. His absence maybe a blessing!

The other extreme is when you have not met the defendant, there is no proof of evidence, in his interview he answered 'no comment' and the solicitor's file is silent on what his case maybe. In these circumstances you are without instructions and it is difficult to envisage a situation where you could stay and represent the defendant. I should say at this stage that this section is solely about the issue of whether you continue to act for a defendant, professional conduct and/or ethical issues that may arise from a solicitor's failure to notify the court of a loss of contact with their client until the morning of the trial is a separate issue and not one to be considered here.

However, the difficulty arises (and these situations are far more common than the clear-cut examples) when the defendant has provided a full-comment interview and some unsigned instructions in accordance with that interview, however neither the proof or the interview goes quite far enough and there are no comments on prosecution witness statements.

These situations become a matter for your professional judgment on the facts of each individual case, however, you should beware that your professional body and the courts are encouraging people to err on the side of remaining and representing defendants even in less than ideal circumstances and you should be prepared to do this.

You should try to find a way, giving proper consideration to your professional obligations, to stay to represent the client that has given some instructions. If you are a solicitor and you took the proof of evidence from the defendant that remains in the file unsigned, you should continue to act for him unless there be some reason why you now think his instructions have changed or been withdrawn. The mere fact of no signature on the proof of evidence should be no bar to you continuing to act for him in circumstances where you have no reason to think his instructions have changed.

If you are counsel in this situation, make contact with your instructing solicitor to see what handwritten notes they have from the occasion when the proof was signed, better still, speak to the relevant lawyer to find out if the proof reflects what he was told by the defendant and whether anything has come to their attention that suggests a change or withdrawal of instructions.

If you do decide to stay to continue to act for the defendant, you should continue to conduct the case as if the defendant had attended his trial but had decided not to give evidence and on the basis of any instructions he has received from the defendant.

If you had intended to call witnesses as part of the defence case and they have attended court in circumstances where the defendant has not, you can still call those witnesses as part of his case, do not forget this as it maybe an important part of salvaging the defence case in difficult circumstances.

One last thing, if you are counsel and your instructing solicitor withdraws from the case on the basis of a withdrawal of instructions, you have no choice but to withdraw too.

CHAPTER 21
THE YOUTH COURT

INTRODUCTION

Appearing in the youth court for the first time can be daunting. Proceedings in the youth court are closed and in most cases only parties connected to the hearing are allowed in to the courtroom during the hearing. This means that the first time you represent a client in the youth court will almost certainly be the first time that you will experience a hearing in it. Unlike the adult court, you cannot sit in the back of the court and watch and learn. However, as you begin your career in the youth court you will quickly realise that in fact the hearing is much more relaxed than in the adult court and as long as you have done all the necessary preparation and applied the relevant provisions and principles, you will probably find the hearing itself less pressurised.

The youth court is designed to deal with children as young as ten years old. With the exception of your client when giving his name to the court, entering his plea and receiving his sentence, everyone in the courtroom remains seated throughout. If you are someone who likes to write your submissions out in detail this makes your advocacy much easier as you will have your notes on the table in front of you. Your client is referred to by his first name and the language used by everyone is simpler so that the defendant can understand it. If you are dealing with a bail application or sentence, the Youth Offending Team (YOT) has far more input in the hearing than the probation service do in the adult court and quite often you will find that the representative from the YOT will do most of the talking for you and assuming of course that you agree with their proposals, this makes your job much easier.

Your role, how you approach your case preparation and analysis, case management and advocacy, is exactly the same as for the adult court. For the purpose of this section of the book, we do not intend to rehearse all the principles that relate to both courts and it is essential that you read this part of the book in the context of those earlier chapters.

SUMMARY OF THE MAIN DIFFERENCES FOR YOU BETWEEN THE ADULT AND THE YOUTH COURT

Fundamentally your job is the same as for the adult court. The main differences are:

173

1. Your client's name will not appear on the court list. The courtroom number of the youth court will be on the public list. You should then go to the courtroom, speak to the usher, ensure that your client is in that court and if so, sign in.

2. The probation service does not deal with youths, their function is instead dealt with by the Youth Offending Team (YOT)/Youth Offending Service (YOS) [see below]

3. The court is closed which means that only parties to the proceedings are allowed to be present during the hearing. With the exception of the parents or guardian, friends and wider family members are not allowed to watch the proceedings (except with leave of the court).

4. The courtroom layout is less formal than the adult court and in most courts the magistrates sit at the same level as everyone else in the court.

5. Your client will sit next to his parent or guardian and usually, behind or next to you.

6. All advocates in court remain seated throughout the hearing.

7. If your client is under the age of 16 his parent or guardian must attend the hearing, if he is 16 or over, they may attend.

8. In court you refer to your client by his first name.

9. Everyone in court is expected to use simple language so that the defendant can understand the proceedings.

10. Particularly during the sentencing exercise, the magistrates/district judge will talk directly to your client and ask him questions.

11. An additional exception to the right of bail applies.

12. Different sentencing principles apply.

13. All cases (including most indictable only offences) will be dealt with summarily *unless* the offence is deemed a grave crime, the dangerousness provisions apply or in some cases, where your client is jointly charged with an adult whose case has either been committed to or sent to the Crown Court for trial.

14. Your client does not have the right to elect Crown Court trial.

15. Reporting restrictions apply in almost every case.

16. A lay magistrate can only sit in the youth court if he or she is authorised to do so and if you are before a lay bench it should be comprised of at least one man and one woman. District Judges (Magistrates' Court) have full jurisdiction in both courts.

JURISDICTION OF THE YOUTH COURT

The youth court deals with defendants aged between 10 and 17.

All youth cases will start in the youth court unless:

1. The youth is jointly charged with an adult.

2. The youth is charged with aiding and abetting an adult to commit an offence, or the adult charged with adding or abetting the youth.
3. The youth is charged with an offence which relates to the charge of an adult.
4. No youth court is sitting on that day and your client has been remanded by the police.

The statutory presumption is that all youths will be tried summarily (i.e. in the youth court) *unless*:

1. He is charged with homicide (murder, attempted murder, manslaughter, causing or allowing the death of a child or vulnerable adult or infanticide)
2. He is aged 16 or over and is charged with an offence/s to which a mandatory minimum sentence term applies under s51A Firearms Act 1968.
3. He is aged 16 or over and is charged with an offence/s to which s29(3) Violent Crime Reduction Act applies.
4. He is charged with a grave crime and the youth court has determined that if he is convicted he would or could receive a sentence beyond their powers.
5. He has been assessed as dangerous within dangerous offender provisions.

AIMS AND OBJECTIVES OF YOUTH JUSTICE

The welfare of your client is very much at the forefront of everyone's minds and the court *shall* have regard to it (*Children and Young Persons Act 1933, s44(1)*).

In terms of welfare, every court in dealing with a child or young person who is brought before it, either as an offender or otherwise, shall have proper regard to the welfare of the child or young person, and shall in a proper case take steps for removing him from undesirable surroundings, and for securing that proper provision is made for his education and training (*Children and Young Persons Act 1933, s44*).

In applying this principle the court should ensure that it is alert to:

- The high incidence of mental health problems amongst young people in the criminal justice system.
- The high incidence of those with learning disabilities amongst young people in the criminal justice system.
- The effect that speech and language difficulties might have on the ability of the young person (or any adult with them) to communicate with the court, to understand the sanction imposed or to fulfil the obligations resulting from that sanction.
- The extent to which young people anticipate that they will be discriminated against by those in authority and the effect that it has on the way that they conduct themselves during court proceedings.
- The vulnerability of young people to self-harm, particularly within a custodial environment.

- The extent to which changes taking place during adolescence can lead to experimentation.
- The effect of young people of experience of loss or abuse.

You will find many of your clients are affected by these issues and you should refer the justices to these overarching principles when making your submissions.

The aim of the youth court is to prevent offending (*Crime and Disorder Act 1998, s37(1)*) and in applying this aim it is recognised by the courts that whilst the offender must be punished in a manner that it is proportionate to the crime and demonstrates that their conduct is unacceptable; as important is the need to address the underlying issues that led to the offending behaviour in this case and, makes it more likely in the future. A custodial sentence must be imposed only as a measure of last resort (*Sentencing Guidelines Council Overarching Principles – Sentencing Youths 11.5 p 22*).

The Youth Justice Board has identified six key objectives of the youth justice system:

a) Swift administration of justice
b) Confronting young offenders with their offending behaviour
c) Intervention that tackles particular factors that leads youths to offence
d) Punishment proportionate to the offending
e) Encouraging reparation
f) Reinforcing the responsibilities of parents/guardians

This approach is reflected by and incorporated into the Sentencing Guidelines Council Overarching Principles.

THE AGE OF YOUR CLIENT

Defendants who are between the ages of 10 and 13 are referred to as 'children'. Those between the ages of 14 and 17 are referred to as 'young people'. A child under the age of 10 cannot be prosecuted.

The age of your client is crucial in the youth court as it can affect where his case is dealt with and how he is sentenced. It is therefore essential that you remember to check his age. The relevant age is his age at the first court hearing or, for grave crimes, his age at the point the court makes its decision about mode of trial (ordinarily this will be the first hearing in any event).

In short:

- A young person becomes an adult for the purpose of court jurisdiction when he attains the age of 18.
- If your client was aged 17 at the time of the offence but aged 18 on or before his first court hearing for it, his case will be dealt with by the adult court.

- If he is aged 17 at the first hearing but turns 18 during the course of the proceedings (unless he has been charged with murder or certain firearms offences *or* his case is a grave crime *or* in certain cases, he is jointly charged with an adult) his case will be dealt with at the youth court.
- If he is aged 17 at the time of the first hearing but aged 18 by the time of the sentencing hearing, in dealing with sentence the court may make any order that it could have made, had he still been.
- If it subsequently materialises that your client's true age is different to that known to the court at the time of dealing with him, it does not invalidate any order or judgement made by it. *Children and Young Persons Act 1933 s99(1).*
- If the true age of your client is discovered during the proceedings both courts have the discretion to continue dealing with the case.

DETERMINING AGE

In most cases the court will accept the age of your client as given by him to the police or the court but on rare occasions it will be disputed by the police or prosecution. If this happens you should endeavour to obtain evidence of his age, usually by calling a parent or guardian to give evidence on it and/or produce his birth certificate. If your client or his parent or guardian is unable to provide proof of his true age, ask the prosecution to assist by enquiring into your client's antecedent history or any previous custody records available for him. In all but exceptional cases, the court will accept the evidence of the parent or guardian on the point but can order further enquiries. Where age is in issue, 'it shall be deemed to be or to have been that which appears to the court after considering any available evidence to be or to have been his age at that time' (Magistrates' Courts Act 1980, s 150).

THE ROLE OF THE CROWN PROSECUTION IN YOUTH CASES

The Crown Prosecution Service works closely with other agencies in the youth justice system and (amongst other things) is committed to:

1. Deal with cases expeditiously.
2. Consider whether an out of court disposal would be appropriate.
3. Consider the interests of the child or young person as part of the public interest consideration when deciding whether a prosecution is necessary.

In doing this they must balance the statutory duty to prevent further offending.

Particularly if your client has been charged with a minor matter and is in the early stages of his criminal career you must always consider whether there is any merit in making representations to the prosecutor that it is not in the public interest to proceed and/or the case could more properly be dealt with in another way, for example, an acceptable behaviour contract, a reprimand, final warning or if the offence relates to your client's school, by an internal school disciplinary.

If your client is eligible for a reprimand or final warning and has fully admitted the offence in his police interview, then in most cases, the starting point for the prosecutor is that the case should be dealt with as such and he should consider an adjournment for enquiries to be made in conjunction with the police and YOT as to whether this would be an appropriate disposal. Be aware that (subject to the gravity of the offence and the requisite admission of guilt) your client is only entitled to one reprimand and one warning. A second and final warning *may* be imposed but only if two years have passed since the imposition of the first warning. Remember, simple cautions are not available for youths but in some cases, conditional cautions are.

The full Crown Prosecution legal Guidance for Youth Offenders can be found on its website (www.cps.gov.uk).

Prosecutors should follow this guidance and apply it to each case. It is therefore important that you have read it too so that you can make representations to the prosecutor in accordance with their guidance where appropriate.

THE ROLE OF THE YOUTH OFFENDING TEAM

Each local authority must establish a Youth Offending Team (YOT) or as they are called in some areas, Youth Offending Service (YOS). For the purpose of this book we will refer to them as YOT. The YOT must consist of the following:

1. A probation officer,
2. A person with experience of social work in relation to children, nominated by the director of children's services appointed by the local authority,
3. A social worker,
4. A police officer,
5. A person nominated by a Primary Care Trust or Local Health Board any part whose area lies within the local authority's area; and
6. A person with experience in education nominated by the director of children's services.

In addition it may include the following:

7. A housing officer,
8. A psychiatrist/psychologist; or
9. A substance misuse worker.

However, at the court hearing it is likely that only member of the YOT will be present, usually the probation officer.

In terms of their overall function the YOT is responsible for:

1. Identifying the needs of the child or young person.
2. Identifying the underlying problems of the offender.
3. Measuring the risk that the offender poses to others.
4. Preventative intervention: Working with children and young people and other agencies in the community towards preventing offending.
5. Restorative justice: Working with children and young people and their families in order to help them understand the consequences of their offending and assisting them where appropriate in making amends to the victim for it.
6. Attending the police station as an appropriate adult.
7. Liaising with the police pre-court with a view to diversions such as a reprimand or a final warning.
8. Attending court hearings and playing an active role in the proceedings with regards to bail and sentencing.
9. The preparation of pre-sentence reports, including written and verbal reports for the magistrates.
10. Supervising community based sentences.
11. Supervising children and young people who have been admitted to bail.
12. Supervising children and young people upon release from custody.

They may also provide advice and support on:

1. Housing
2. Education
3. Employment
4. Substance misuse
5. Mental health
6. Parenting programs
7. Mentoring programs
8. Offender behaviour programs

The above list is by no means exhaustive.

In terms of your interaction with the YOT it is essential that you liaise with them in any case where:

1. Bail is an issue.
2. Your client is already subject to an order.
3. Your client is intending to plead guilty.
4. Your client has been convicted.

The YOT can be invaluable to you particularly in the early stages of your career where you can find yourself baffled by the relevant bail provisions, various bail support packages or which the most appropriate sentence is for your client. To some extent since the introduction of the Youth Rehabilitation Order sentencing has been simplified but you should make no apology for taking the time to speak to the YOT, remember that they are experts and do a very good job in difficult circumstances. No matter how stuck you are for ways to argue that your client should yet again be admitted to bail or for the fifteenth mitigation submission in a row why he should not receive a detention and training order, the YOT always manage to assist with realistic, non-custodial proposals or bail packages. The magistrates do pay attention to their proposals and very often follow them. If you have submissions for bail or sentence and they are endorsed by the YOT, you are far more likely to succeed with them.

That being said, if you disagree with them, do not be shy about saying so or arguing against their proposals in court but do it only with good reason and as always, in a polite and courteous manner.

Your local Youth Offending Team will have its own website and it is a good idea for you to look at it for full information about the services offered by your local area.

RECOMMENDED READING

The following are recommended resources for you to read in addition to the primary texts prior to representing in the youth court:

1. The Youth Court Bench Book
2. The Sentencing Guidelines Council Overarching Principles – Sentencing Youths

THE ROLE OF THE PARENT OR GUARDIAN IN YOUTH CASES

If your client is under the age of 16 he must have a parent or guardian with him in court unless the court thinks it is unreasonable, for example, the parent is in hospital or inappropriate, for example, the parent is the alleged victim. At least one parent must attend.

If your client is 16 or over he may be accompanied by a parent or guardian.

If your client attends without a parent or guardian, speak to him and find out why not and whether one is able to attend. If your client has a contact number for his parent or guardian then telephone him/her and ask them to attend. Explain to them implications of not doing so, namely that the court may summons them to attend court on the next occasion and if your client is convicted of the offence, the fact of their non-attendance at court *may* make a parenting order or a bind over more likely. If they have a genuine reason for being unable to attend, ask them when they can attend, be prepared to make an application to the magistrates (if you think it is appropriate) for the case to be adjourned to that future date. Sometimes you will be faced with a parent who flatly refuses to attend and if this happens there is little you can do. If your client has a social worker, contact him or her to see if he can attend instead. If there really is no-one who can or will attend on his behalf then speak to the YOT as they may be able to assist.

If you are satisfied that your client is capable of giving you instructions and of understanding the proceedings without an adult present then it is in his best interests for you to try and persuade the magistrates to proceed in the absence of the parent or guardian. This will avoid unnecessary delays and court appearances for your client. If you are not satisfied that he is able to understand sufficiently you should not proceed and instead you should apply for the case to be adjourned to a date when his parent or guardian can attend. Generally speaking however, the magistrates will not deal with the plea, trial or sentencing hearing in the absence of a parent or guardian.

Note the following extract from the Sentencing Guidelines Council – Overarching Principles – Sentencing Youths pg 12:

> 7.2: The statutory framework clearly envisages the attendance of an adult with a degree of responsibility for the young offender; this obligation reflects the principle aim of reducing offending, recognising that it is unlikely to be achieved by the young person alone. A court must be aware of a risk that a young person will seek to avoid this requirement either by urging the court to proceed in the absence of an adult or in arranging for a person to come to court who purport to have (but in reality does not) the necessary degree of responsibility.

> 7.3: Insistence on attendance may produce a delay in the case before the court; however, it is important that this obligation is maintained and that it is widely recognised that a court will require such attendance, especially when imposing sentence. If a court proceeds in the absence of a responsible adult, it should ensure that the outcome of the hearing is properly communicated.

If your client is not previously known to you then it is a good idea to speak to the parent or guardian alone before seeing your client, to ascertain whether he has any problems that you should be aware of prior to your meeting with him. It may be that the answer they give you affects the manner in which you advise your client and indeed the advice that you give him.

If your client has told you that he would rather see you alone then tell his parent this but be careful when doing so. For most parents, the experience of attending court for their son or daughter is extremely upsetting and for those who have no previous experience of the justice system, terrifying. If the parent or guardian is present during your meeting with your client be sure to take control of it.

Parents are often inclined to talk on behalf of their children, especially when the child or young person has clammed up. You cannot take instructions from the parent or guardian. If the parent or guardian persists, close the conversation down and explain to him or her that it is your client, their son or daughter, who has to give the instructions and that the evidence cannot come from him or her. In other words, politely but firmly, ask them to be quiet. If they persist in talking over you or on behalf of their child then consider asking them to leave the room so that you can speak to your client alone. You will often find that in the absence of the parent your client will speak far more freely and articulately.

Assuming the parent or guardian is co-operative with you and then use them to obtain background information about your client, in particular about his education including any educational problems or any learning difficulties. If your client is seeing a child psychologist it is far more likely that his parent will know the details similarly any medication he is on.

At sentencing hearings, part of the sentencing process involves the magistrates asking parents direct questions about their child and their attitude towards his behaviour. Warn the parent or guardian that the court *may* consider a parenting order or a bind over (see below) and it is therefore in their best interests to co-operate as fully as possible with any questions the magistrates may have.

If your mitigation is partly based upon the defendant's difficult family circumstances, the prominent role played by the parents at court hearings in the youth court can make things a little awkward. Take the example of the defendant's mother being an alcoholic who is never at home and when she is she is too drunk to care for him, however his mother is at court and seemingly interested in her son's case. If the defendant tells you this and it is clear to you that it is a relevant consideration for the justices, then the safest course is to raise the issue, as sensitively as you can, with the defendant's mother, not for permission from her but out of courtesy. The public pronouncement of such an embarrassing piece of information may cause your client even more problems at home so tread carefully but if it really is relevant and persuasive mitigation, do not be dissuaded by the angry and shamed parent.

The situation is slightly trickier when the information does not come from your young client instead from the author of the PSR. In these circumstances, the first person you must raise the issue with is the defendant. Check the accuracy of the suggestion and explain to the defendant how it maybe used to support his mitigation. If he has not volunteered this to you, it is likely that he will not want you to use it and his understandable stance should be the end of the matter providing it has been explained to him the value (if there really is value) in you being permitted to use it.

FINES/COSTS AND COMPENSATION TO BE PAID BY PARENT OR GUARDIAN

Under s137 of the Powers of Criminal Courts (Sentencing) Act 2000 s137 the court can order that the parent or guardian pays any costs, compensation or fines imposed in respect of the youth's offence (including costs imposed in respect of a breach of court order) *unless* having regard to the circumstances of the case it would be unreasonable to do so or the parent or guardian cannot be found.

If your client is under 16 and the court imposes an order for costs or fines it *will* make the order in respect of the parent or guardian. If he is 16 or above, it *may* make the order against the parent or guardian OR against your client. Therefore if your client is over 16, do not forget to complete a means form with him.

It is therefore essential that you take details from the parent or guardian about their means so that you are ready to address the court on them. In addition if you have not already done so take full instructions from the parent or guardian about any efforts they have made to prevent their child's offending behaviour.

If your client is 16 or under, the parent or guardian must complete a means form.

In terms of the unreasonableness of the order, you will have to persuade the magistrates that it would be unreasonable either:

1. On the basis of the family's already limited means. If there are problems within the family that may in part have contributed to your client's offending behaviour a good argument against this is that the increased burden on the family's income will or could exacerbate the problems within it that led to the offending in the first place. Remember that the court's aim is to reduce offending.
2. On the basis that the parent or guardian has done everything they possibly could in order to support their child and help to reduce or prevent his offending behaviour and he should not therefore be penalised because of it.

BIND OVER

If your client is aged 15 or younger and has been convicted of an offence the court *must* make a bind over in respect of the parent or guardian *if* in the circumstances of the case it would assist in reducing the risk of the child or young person from re-offending. If your client is 16 or over, the court may make a bind over in respect of the parent. This is a rarely used measure.

A bind over must be in clear terms and specify what the parent is required to do. In general terms the bind over is for the parent or guardian to take proper care of, and exercise proper control over, the child or young person and that is your argument against its imposition.

If the parent or guardian is already doing everything reasonable possible in an attempt to reduce the child's offending then it is difficult to see how the imposition of a bind over would be necessary in those circumstances.

PARENTING ORDER

If your client has pleaded guilty or been convicted of an offence, the court has the power to impose a parenting order on the parent or guardian (Section 8 of the *Crime and Disorder Act 1998*). A parenting order is an agreed program of activities between the parent, guardian and the YOT, including counselling and guidance sessions, and it is designed to help the parent develop the necessary skills to in order to prevent the child or young person from offending. It also requires the parent or guardian to control the child or young person's behaviour. The maximum period for the order is twelve months.

You should prepare the parent or guardian for this and advise them that the court will consider its imposition as part of the sentencing exercise. Take information from the parent or guardian about the family circumstances, what efforts they have made to prevent their child from offending and what support they give him. For example, have they already engaged in meetings with the school, local authority or YOT?

CHAPTER 22
ADVISING YOUTH CLIENTS

As with adult clients, perhaps even more so, your advice to youths must be tailored to his abilities to understand and comprehend the necessary information. Youth clients may have all manner of distractions at court that are hurdles to giving this important advice. Whether they are genuine issues such as his inability to concentrate or low intelligence or more irritating external factors such as his friends, mobile phone or IPod, you will encounter and need to deal with these problems so you can be satisfied that your advice has had the intended effect.

It is easy to forget that you are sometimes dealing with very young people who have no comprehension of the system despite their brash, street-wise image and exterior. Advising young people who appear disinterested in you and the proceedings can be infuriating, particularly when you are tight for time. As irritating as this as, and there is of course a limit, bear with the defendant whose problems maybe a little more complicated than just not paying you enough attention. A life in care or behavioural/mental health difficulties can cause huge difficulties for a young person so resist the temptation to abandon him because he appears not to be listening or bothered by your advice about who sits where in court.

If your client has concentration issues such as ADHD and if time allows, take breaks to ensure they are able to take in what you are saying and give coherent instructions. You will sometimes find that your client is far more interested in speaking to his friends in the waiting area than he is in talking to you so keep it as short as you can but do not omit vital information or advice.

If possible try to take your client somewhere private, preferably a consultation room. This will give you a better chance of holding his attention and may encourage him to talk more freely. Particularly in a case where there are multiple defendants remember that there may be members of the co-defendant's family or friends around the waiting area or friends of his and anything that hinders his willingness to engage with you should be avoided.

Whilst a parent or guardian must be present in the courtroom there is no obligation on you to have him or her present when you are advising your client and taking his instructions. Young people will respond more openly in the absence of their parent, particularly if they are guilty and wavering on admitting it for fear of getting into trouble with their mother or father. Make sure that you ask your client whether he wants his mother, father or guardian with him in the meeting and explain to him that he can speak to you alone. If he does want his parent or guardian present in your meeting then unless the parent is being particularly obstructive, you should respect his wish and allow the parent to be present. The age and maturity of the defendant will usually be the determining factors in whether you want the parents present.

In terms of what information you must take from your client and what advice you should give it is in essence the same as outlined previously for adults and it is essential that you read that chapters.

In addition you must advise where applicable about:

1. Grave crimes and dangerousness
2. Bail
3. Sentence

As a general point to note when dealing with youths, it is a good idea to advise them about their demeanour in court. For example, no hats, chewing gum, hands in pockets or laughing.

CHAPTER 23
YOUTH COURT BAIL

In general terms the provisions for youth bail are exactly the same as those that apply for adults.

The three main statutory differences are:

1. The place of detention when bail is refused (which can include a home address).
2. An additional exception to the right to bail, namely, for his own welfare or in his own interests.
3. A parent or guardian can be asked to act as a surety not only to secure attendance at court but also to ensure compliance with bail conditions.

The main practical difference as far as you are concerned is:

4. The YOT has far more input on the issue of bail. Whereas in the adult court the probation service has little or no input on the issue of bail [save for updating the court if necessary about how well your client is responding to an existing order], the YOT plays an integral role in the bail process and it is essential that you liaise with them in all cases where bail is an issue.

All youths can be remanded on:

• Unconditional bail
• Conditional bail

Certain youths can be remanded on:

• Conditional bail with Intensive Supervision and Surveillance (ISS)
• Conditional bail with a tag.
• To local authority accommodation (with or without conditions)
• To local authority accommodation (LAA) with conditions including a tag
• To a local authority accommodation with a security requirement
• To police custody, prison or remand centre.

For the criterion that applies to the above see the very useful extract from the Judicial Studies Board Youth Court Bench Book below.

The magistrates will make their decision regarding bail, based on:

• The age of your client
• The sex of your client

- The vulnerability of your client
- The offence
- Whether he is a persistent offender
- Whether an exception to the right of bail applies
- The necessity of the bail conditions/remand in custody

When dealing with a youth remand application remember the overarching principle that custody must only be imposed as a measure of last resort. For the purpose of bail your client's welfare is a 'relevant' but not 'paramount' consideration. The CPS guidance on youth bail is that all other non-custodial options of bail should be considered before an application for a remand with a security requirement or to a remand centre or prison is made.

How you approach your preparation, advice to your client and the bail application itself is exactly as set out in preceding chapters. Those chapters should be read in conjunction with this one. It is also essential that you have read, understood and applied the relevant provisions of the Bail Act 1976 together with s23(5)A of the Children and Young Persons Act 1969 and s25 of the Children Act 1989.

If your client has been remanded into custody by the police, a representative from the YOT will visit your client in the court cells prior to the court hearing in order to conduct an assessment of him and ascertain which, if any, bail support packages are available to him. They will also assess whether your client is vulnerable, i.e. at risk of self-harm if remanded in custody. Always advise your client to co-operate with this process as it is in his best interests.

Once they have completed their assessment of your client it is vital that you liaise with the YOT in order to:

1. Find out how your client is responding to any existing order or has previously responded (if applicable).
2. Discuss the suitability of your client for any non-custodial bail support packages, for example, an ISS.
3. Establish whether your client would be suitable for electronic tagging.
4. If they are recommending a remand to local authority accommodation, to find out, whether that is with a security requirement and where they are proposing to place your client.
5. Obtain a copy of their vulnerability assessment.

When you are considering your application and which conditions you will propose, be mindful of the risk of setting your client up to fail. It is always tempting to propose a raft of onerous conditions in an attempt to persuade the court to admit your client but to suggest such conditions that your client has no realistic of prospect of complying with will not help your client in the long run.

BAIL ACT EXCEPTIONS

Judicial Studies Board (JSB) Youth Court Bench Book p 23 March 2010.

	Non-imprisonable offences	Summary imprisonable offences	Either-way or indictable offences
Would not co-operate in preparation of a pre-sentence report	N/A	N/A	✓
Would not come back to court	N/A	N/A	✓
Commit offences	N/A	N/A	✓
Interfere witnesses/obstruct justice	N/A	✓	✓
Insufficient information	N/A	✓	✓
Commit offence likely to cause physical/mental injury to another	N/A	✓	N/A
Commit offences and this allegation was committed whilst on bail	N/A	✓	N/A
Would not come back to court as they have a record of not attending	✓	✓	N/A
Own welfare	✓	✓	✓
Already serving a custodial sentence	✓	✓	✓
Commit offences/would not come back to court/interfere witnesses or obstruct justice and have previously been released on conditional bail and not kept those conditions	✓	✓	N/A

GUIDE TO REMAND PROVISIONS FOR DEFENDANTS
AGED 10–17 YEARS OLD

(JSB Bench book pp 24–26)

Unconditional bail	The same criteria applies as for adults
Conditional bail	The same criteria applies as for adults
Remand on conditional bail with Intensive Supervision and Surveillance (ISS)	Conditional bail with ISS is not created by statute. It is an intensive community-based programme for young offenders that can be accessed via existing disposals, i.e. as part of a community order, conditions on bail or part of supervision following a DTO. The local YOT will indicate whether the offender is suitable for ISS but it is a matter for the court whether bail is granted and whether the ISS conditions are attached. Conditions may include tagging and voice verification. Breach of the conditional bail with ISS is dealt with like any other breach. i.e. arrest and production to the court.
Remand on Conditional bail With tagging	The offender must be at least 12 years old. The offender must be charged with or convicted of: • A violent or sexual offence, **or** • An offence punishable in the case of an adult with 14 years imprisonment or more, **or** • Have a recent history of repeatedly committing imprisonable offences while remanded on bail or to local authority accommodation. • YOT have to certify to the court that such a condition would be suitable. • In the case of a defendant who has attained the age of 17 years, the court can only impose a tagging condition if it is satisfied that it would not grant bail otherwise. Tagging is imposed to ensure compliance with other conditions.
Remand to local authority accommodation (with or without conditions)	The court must be satisfied that there are reasons to refuse bail. This is a refusal of bail even where the youth can reside at home with their parent/guardian. Where conditions are imposed, the youth can be arrested and brought back before the court for breaching those conditions. The relevant time limits for remands in custody apply i.e. eight clear days before conviction, four weeks on second appearance, 21 days after conviction etc.

Remand to local authority accommodation (LAA) with conditions including tagging	The court must be satisfied that there are reasons to refuse bail. The offender must be at least 12 years old. The offender must be charged with or convicted of: • A violent or sexual offence, **or** • An offence punishable in the case of an adult with 14 years' imprisonment or more, **or** • Is charged with or convicted of one or more imprisonable offences, which together with any other imprisonable offences of which they have been convicted in any proceedings amount to or would amount to a recent history of repeatedly committing imprisonable offences while remanded on bail or to LAA. YOT have to certify to the court that such a condition would be suitable. This is a refusal of bail even where the youth is going to reside at home with their parent or guardian. Where such conditions are imposed, the youth can be arrested and brought back before the court for breaching those conditions.
Remand to local authority accommodation with a security requirement	The court must be satisfied that there are reasons to refuse bail. The offender must be at least 12 years old. The offender must be charged with or convicted of: • A violent or sexual offence, **or** • An offence imprisonable in the case of an adult with 14 years' imprisonment or more, **or** • Have a history of repeatedly committing imprisonable offences while remanded on bail or to local authority accommodation, **and** the court must be satisfied that the security requirement is necessary for the protection of the public or to prevent the commission of imprisonable offences. YOT have to certify to the court that such a condition would be suitable. Where the youth is male and • Aged 15–16, **and** • The court would remand to a prison/remand centre but the court is of the opinion that by reason of the offender's physical or emotional immaturity or a propensity to harm himself it would be undesirable for him to be remanded to a remand centre or prison (e.g. vulnerable) **and**

Remand to local authority accommodation with a security requirement	• Secure accommodation is available the court may remand to secure accommodation instead. If the court is of the opinion that the youth is vulnerable but no secure accommodation is available, the youth will be remanded to a prison/remand centre.
Remand to police custody, prison or remand centre	The court must be satisfied that there reasons to refuse bail. Youths aged 10–16 may be remanded to police cells for a maximum of 24 hours. Where the youth is aged 17, the maximum is three days. For a 17 year old to be remanded to prison/remand centre, the same criteria applies as for adults.

CHAPTER 24
YOUTH CASES – VENUE

The presumption is that youths will be dealt with in the youth court unless one of the three exceptions exists:

1. Youth charged with an adult
2. Grave crimes
3. Dangerousness

YOUTH CHARGED WITH AN ADULT

Adult elects/court declines or indictable only offence

If your client is jointly charged with an adult and:

(a) The adult's case will be tried in the Crown Court; and
(b) The magistrates decide that it is in the interests of justice that both are tried together

His case will be sent or committed to the Crown Court together with the adults' (*S24(1) Magistrates' Court Act 1980*).

Usually the cases will be kept together but in determining whether it is the interests of justice to send or commit the youth the court will consider the following:

(a) The age of your client and his maturity
(b) The nature of the offence
(c) His role in the offence
(d) His previous convictions
(e) Whether the two cases can be quite properly severed without inconvenience to the witnesses or an injustice to the case as a whole.
(f) The likely sentence upon conviction

In practical terms if the court decides that the two cases should be kept together the procedure with dealing with the youth's case is then identical to the procedure for dealing with an adult. Remember however that if your client is 16 or under, a parent or guardian must attend the hearing. When addressing the court, you should still refer to your client by his first name but given that you are in the adult court, you do stand up to address the court. Your client is not automatically entitled to a press restriction in the adult court so if the legal advisor does not raise it, ask the magistrates to make a press restriction in respect of your client under s39 Children and Young Person Act 1933.

If the magistrates decide that it is not in the interests of justice for the youth to be sent or committed to the Crown Court then the charge will be put to him in the Magistrates' Court. If he pleads guilty the magistrates will decide whether their limited sentencing powers (absolute or conditional discharge, a fine or a bind over with regard to the parent or guardian) are sufficient. If their sentencing powers are not sufficient then your client's case will be remitted to the youth court for sentence. If he pleads not guilty then his case will be remitted to the youth court for trial.

ADULT CHARGED WITH SUMMARY ONLY MATTER OR MAGISTRATES ACCEPT JURISDICTION

If your client is jointly charged with an adult whose case will be dealt with by the magistrates and:

(a) The adult and the youth both plead not guilty; then
(b) The youth's case must be dealt with together with the adults, in the Magistrates' Court.

If:

(a) The adult and the youth both plead guilty; then
(b) The magistrates may sentence the youth if their limited powers are sufficient; or
(c) More usually, they will remit the youth to the youth court

If:

(a) The adult pleads guilty and the youth pleads not guilty; then
(b) Technically the Magistrates' Court could deal with your client's trial; but
(c) Almost without exception, your client will be remitted to the youth court for trial.

Procedurally, the charge will be put to the adult and thereafter to the youth.

CHAPTER 25
GRAVE CRIMES

A grave crime is defined by s91 Powers of Criminal Courts (Sentencing) Act 2000 as:

1. An offence that carries at least 14 years in the case of an adult offender
2. An offence of Sexual Assault contrary to s3 Sexual Offences Act 2003
3. An offence of child sex offences committed by a child or young person contrary to s13 SOA 2003
4. An offence of sexual activity with a child family member contrary to s25 SOA 2003
5. Inciting a child family member to engage in sexual activity contrary to s26 SOA 2003

S91 PCC(S)A 2000 enables the Crown Court to:

- Impose a custodial sentence on a child or young person who the youth court would not have the power to impose a custodial sentence upon. (A child between the ages of 10 and 11 or a child or young person between the ages of 12 and 14 if they are not a persistent offender),

and in all cases

- Extend the length of the custodial sentence (up to the maximum range available for the specific offence) beyond that which a youth court can impose, namely a 24 month detention and training order (DTO).

The fact that your client has been charged with a grave crime does not mean that it will automatically be sent or committed to the Crown Court for trial but it does mean that the court must consider the question of venue before they take a plea from your client.

Make sure that you check whether the offence/s that you are dealing with falls within the definition of a grave crime. Offences such as possession with intent to supply cannabis, handling stolen goods and burglary dwelling all fall within the definition. Whilst in reality it is unlikely in those cases that the court would decline jurisdiction, you will still have to deal with the issue prior to your client entering his plea.

195

DETERMINATION OF VENUE FOR A GRAVE CRIME

If your client is any age and charged with the following offences his case must be sent for trial at the Crown Court and the Youth Court has no jurisdiction to deal with it:

1. Murder
2. Attempted murder
3. Infanticide
4. Causing or allowing the death of a child or vulnerable adult

If he is aged 16 or over and he is charged with the following offences his case must be sent to the Crown Court and the Youth Court has no jurisdiction to deal with it:

5. Offences within s51 Firearms Act 1968 (for example, possession of a firearm with intent to injure)
6. An offence under s29(3) of the Violent Crime Reduction Act 2006. (minimum sentences in certain cases of using someone to mind a weapon)

For all other grave crimes, venue is determined by the 'realistic' sentence that could be imposed, whether it is a 'realistic' possibility and whether it exceeds the maximum sentence that is available in the youth court. The fact that a sentence of more than two years is hypothetically possible is not sufficient. The decision is made prior to your client entering his plea and is effectively a prediction of sentence exercise. If the magistrates retain jurisdiction of the case, *unless* your client is later found to be a dangerous offender, they cannot subsequently commit the case to the Crown Court for sentence.

The relevant test to be applied by the magistrates is dependent on your client's age and if he is under 15, whether he is a persistent offender.

Persistent offender

There is no statutory definition of 'persistent offender' but the Sentencing Guidelines Council – Overarching Principles – Sentencing Youths gives the following guidance at p 11 paragraphs 6.4 and 6.5:

6.4 A dictionary definition of "persistent offender" is "persisting or having a tendency to persist"; "persist" is defined as "to continue firmly or obstinately in a course of action in spite of difficulty or opposition".

6.5 In determining whether an offender is a persistent offender for these purposes, a court should consider the simple test of whether the young person is one who persists in offending:

  i) in most circumstances, the normal expectation is that the offender will have had some contact with authority in which the offending conduct was challenged before being classed as "persistent"; a finding of persistence in offending may be derived from information about previous convictions but may also arise from orders which require an admission of guilt – these include reprimands, warnings, restorative justice disposals and conditional cautions; since they do not require such an admission, penalty notices for disorder are unlikely to be sufficiently reliable;

ii) a young offender is certainly likely to be found to be persistent (and in relation to a custodial sentence, the test of being a measure of last resort is most likely to be satisfied) where the offender has been convicted of, or made subject to a pre-court disposal that involves an admission or finding of guilt in relation to, imprisonable offences on at least 3 occasions in the past 12 months.

The test to be applied for those aged between 10 and 11 and between 12 and 14 who are not persistent offenders:

'Is the offence of such gravity that, despite the normal prohibition on a custodial sentence for a person of this age, a sentence exceeding two years is a **realistic possibility**?' (Youth Court Bench Book p 29 para 10).

The fact that the youth court has no power to impose a custodial sentence upon these defendants is not a reason to commit (send under the new provisions) the case to the Crown Court.

The test to be applied those aged between 12 and 14 who are persistent offenders and in all cases, those aged between 15 and 17:

'Is the offence of such gravity that a sentence **substantially** beyond the two year maximum for a DTO is a realistic possibility?' (Youth Court Bench Book p 29 para 1)1.

There is no definition for the word substantially, instead the Youth Court Bench Book defines it as 'something of considerable importance' (para 12, p 29).

See also the Sentencing Guidelines Council – Overarching Principles – Sentencing Youths, P 27, paras 12.11 (i) (ii).

Application of both tests:

In making their decision about venue the court will:

- Hear a fair and accurate summary (but not evidence) of the facts of the case. (make sure that you agree the prosecution case summary)
- Hear representations from the prosecutor and you (and any co-defending advocates)
- Consider your client's previous convictions (including his good character)
- Consider your client's non-contentious mitigation

- Consider an indication if given of a guilty plea and therefore take into account the appropriate credit for that plea
- Consider any unusual aspects of the case that make it more serious (The term unusual does not include the fact that in the absence of committal to the Crown Court the youth court has no power to impose a custodial sentence)
- Consider firstly whether the custody threshold has been passed and if so – the sentencing guidelines available for the specific offence/s including any aggravating or mitigating features of it. Unless there are youth specific guidelines for the offence *and* your client is 17, the magistrates will rely on the adult sentencing guidelines but in doing so they must apply the Sentencing Guidelines Council – Overarching Principles – Sentencing Youths. In applying the guidelines for youths the 'court must consider whether a lower starting point is justified in recognition of the offenders age and maturity' (*Sentencing Guidelines Council – Overarching Principles – Sentencing Youth p 23 para 11.13*)

As an example of how this is worked out in practice:

GBH s18. Offence involves an injury which is less serious in the context of the offence and lack of premeditation. Category 3 offence.
Defendant is 16, but very immature and mixes with friends of 13 and 14.

Starting point:	4 years custody
Reduction of 50% due to immaturity	(–2 years)
Appropriate length of sentence	2 years
(Therefore not a grave crime)	

NB: reduction in sentence for guilty plea is calculated once the appropriate starting point has been established. Therefore using the above example, even if there were aggravating features present which would indicate a starting point of 5 years–

Appropriate starting point	5 years
Reduction of 50% due to immaturity	2.5 years (30 months)
Credit for early guilty plea	(–10 months)
Sentence	20 months
Appropriate DTO	18 months

Therefore not a grave crime
NB even if the indication is a not guilty plea and therefore no reduction for a guilty plea, a starting point of 2.5 years for a persistent offender is arguably not substantially beyond the two year maximum.

The court should and will start from the principle that the case should be tried in the youth court *unless* an exception to that presumption applies.

THE COURT PROCEDURE FOR DEALING WITH GRAVE CRIMES

1. At the beginning of the hearing the legal adviser will tell the magistrates the name of your client and what he has been charged with.
2. Your client will be asked to give the court his name, address and date of birth (he should stay standing for this and sit down once he has been invited to do so by the magistrates).
3. The legal adviser will then advise the magistrates that the relevant offence is a grave crime and that a decision must be made as to venue of the case before a plea can be taken.
4. The prosecutor will then summarise the facts of the case and make representations about where the case should be dealt with. He will refer the magistrates to any aggravating or mitigating features of the offence, your client's previous convictions and any relevant sentencing guidelines. In most cases whilst the offence is prima facie a grave crime the prosecutor will not ask the court to commit the case to the Crown Court and will more usually concede that the offence is one that should be dealt with by the youth court.
5. You will then make representations about venue. With the exception of those very serious cases it is rare for the magistrates to decline jurisdiction of youth cases. If the prosecutor has indicated that a summary trial would be appropriate you need say very little other than to endorse those representations. If the guideline sentence for the offence is one where it is very clear that the youth court's sentencing powers are insufficient then do not trouble the court with pointless representations and concede that the offence is one that should be dealt with by the Crown Court. In all other cases where venue is arguable your job is to try and keep the case in the youth court thus minimising the length of the custodial sentence available.

Within your representations you should include the following:

- An indication of a guilty plea if relevant and a reminder to the magistrates of your client's entitlement to credit for that plea.
- Reference to his lack of previous convictions or lack of relevant offences.
- An outline of the mitigating features of the offence making reference to the relevant sentencing guideline (if available).
- Submissions that the magistrates should consider lowering the starting point of any sentencing guideline to take account of your client's age and lack of maturity. The younger your client, the stronger your submission.
- Reference to the Overarching Principles – Sentencing Youths.
- An outline of your client's undisputed mitigation, for example; mental health issues or the fact your client is pregnant or the carer of young children. Refer yourself to the specific points made within the

Overarching Principles, which mitigate against a lengthy custodial sentence and make your submissions on those grounds.

6. The legal advisor will then advise the magistrates of any relevant law or guidelines that have not already been addressed by you or the prosecutor and will correct any errors made by either of you in your submissions.
7. The magistrates will then consider their decision. Lay magistrates will usually retire for this a District Judge will usually announce his decision immediately. The magistrates must give reasons for their decision and announce whether their decision was effected by an indication of a guilty plea.
8. The plea will then be taken.
9. If the court has accepted jurisdiction the hearing will proceed exactly as described for the adult court (first hearing (summary only) guilty or not guilty plea whichever is applicable).
10. If the court has declined jurisdiction then the hearing will proceed exactly as described for either way offences where jurisdiction has been declined or where your client has elected Crown Court trial.

DANGEROUSNESS

Your client will be considered dangerous if:

- He has been charged with a 'specified' sexual or violent offence (see sch 15 of the Criminal Justice Act 2003 for a list of specified offences), *and*
- The court is of the view that there is significant risk to members of the public of serious harm by the commission of your client of further 'specified' offences; *and*
- The Crown Court would deal with the offence by a determinate sentence of at least four years, whether by way of an extended sentence, an indefinite sentence for public protection or a life sentence.

The test for serious harm and the risk of further offences for youths must be assessed in the context of:

1. The age and maturity of the offender,
2. The possibility of change in a much shorter time than would apply for an adult, *and*
3. The wider circumstances of the young person.

Sentencing Guidelines Council – Overarching Principles – Sentencing Youths p 28 para 12.12.

Dangerousness can become an issue in the youth court either before your client has entered his plea to a relevant specified offence or following his conviction of it. Unlike grave crimes, if the youth court retains jurisdiction of the trial, it can still commit your client to the Crown Court for sentence if the dangerous provisions apply (*Powers of Criminal Courts (Sentencing) Act 2000 s3C*).

DANGEROUSNESS ASSESSMENT PRE PLEA

If the court is satisfied that if convicted of the relevant offence your client would be deemed dangerous *and* the offence merits a determinate sentence of at least four years then it must send it (and any related charges so long as for a summary only matter it is either imprisonable or involves discretionary or obligatory disqualification from driving) to the Crown Court forthwith for trial (*s51A(3) (d) Crime and Disorder Act 1998*). The procedure is exactly the same as for sending a case to the Crown Court in the Magistrates' Court. The case will not be adjourned for committal proceedings.

Such cases are exceptional and it is most unlikely at this stage that the court would have all the relevant information before it to make the dangerousness assessment which would usually include a full assessment by the YOT. If your client has recently been assessed by the YOT for and found to be a significant risk of serious harm to the public then in an exceptional case, this would be sufficient information upon which to make the assessment pre-plea. Unless the grave crimes provisions apply then the guidance from the Sentencing Council is that the case should be tried summarily and the dangerousness decision made after conviction (*Sentencing Guidelines Council – Overarching Principles – Sentencing Youths. p 28 para 12.14*) This approach is endorsed by the CPS guidance on the point and the starting point in all but exceptional cases is that prosecutor will recommend that the case is tried by the youth court.

In summary the case will only be sent to the Crown Court if:

1. There is sufficient information before the court to make the necessary dangerousness assessment; *and*
2. It is in the interests of justice that the case be tried on indictment.

DANGEROUSNESS ASSESSMENT POST GUILTY PLEA OR CONVICTION

If your client has been convicted of an offence and has been assessed as posing a significant risk of serious harm by the commission of further specified offences then as long as the above criteria is met, the court will commit sentence of the matter to the Crown Court.

201

Dangerous offender flowchart

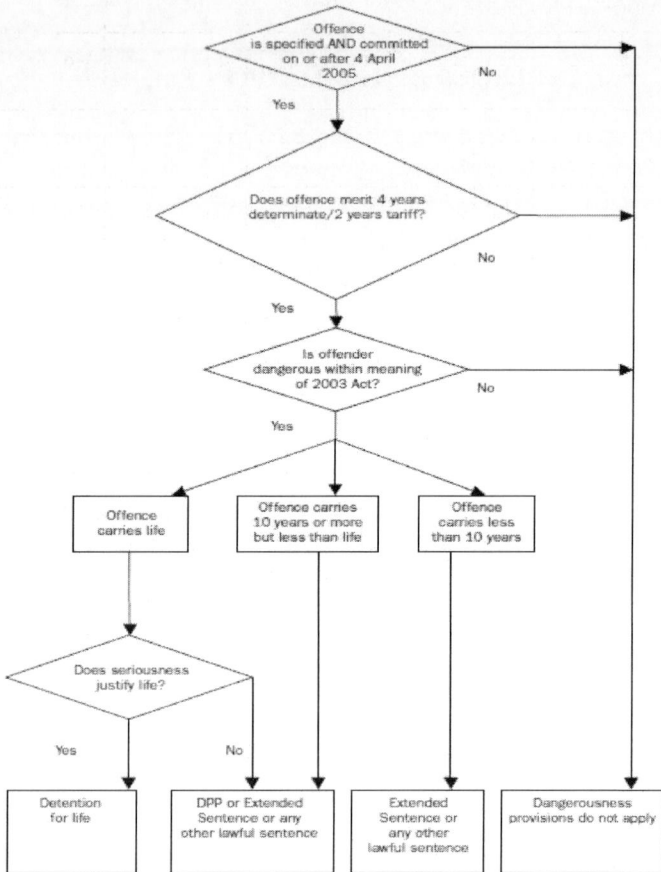

Youth Court maximum penalties summary

Assault/Violent offences	Maximum penalty in law	Maximum penalty in the youth court	Grave crime?	Dangerousness?
Assault Occasioning Actual Bodily Harm (Racially or religiously aggravated)	7 years custody	2 years DTO	No	Yes

Assault Occasioning Actual Bodily Harm	5 years custody	2 years DTO	No	Yes
Assault on a Police Constable	6 months custody	6 months DTO	No	No
Assault with intent to resist arrest	2 years custody	2 years DTO	No	No
Common Assault (Racially or religiously aggravated)	2 years custody	2 years DTO	No	No
Grievous Bodily Harm with Intent	Life	2 years DTO	Yes	Yes
Unlawful wounding/ grievous bodily harm	5 years custody	2 years DTO	No	Yes
Threats to kill	10 years custody	2 years DTO	No	Yes
Rape/Attempted rape	Life	2 years DTO	Yes	Yes
Manslaughter	Life	Not applicable	Not applicable	Not applicable
Murder	Life	Not applicable	Not applicable	Not applicable

Criminal Damage Offences	Maximum penalty in law	Maximum penalty in the youth court	Grave crime?	Dangerousness?
Criminal Damage (over £5000)	10 years custody	2 years DTO	No	No
Racially aggravated Criminal Damage	14 years custody	2 years DTO	Yes	Yes
Criminal Damage (under £5000)	3 months custody	YRO	No	No
Threats to commit Criminal Damage	10 years custody	2 years DTO	No	No

Road Traffic/vehicle offences	Maximum penalty in law	Maximum penalty in the youth court	Grave crime?	Dangerousness?
Allowing self to be carried in a vehicle taken without consent	6 months custody	6 months DTO	No	No
Causing Death by Careless or Inconsiderate Driving	5 years custody	2 years DTO	No	No
Causing Death by Dangerous Driving	14 years custody	2 years DTO	Yes	Yes
Causing Death by Driving when under the influence of drink or drugs	14 years custody	2 years DTO	Yes	Yes
Causing death by Driving unlicensed, disqualified or uninsured drivers	2 years custody	2 years DTO	No	No
Dangerous Driving	2 years custody	2 years DTO	No	No
Driving while disqualified	6 months custody	6 months DTO	No	No
Excess Alcohol/ attempting to drive	6 months custody	6 months DTO	No	No
Excess Alcohol – in charge	3 months custody	YRO	No	No
Fail to Provide Specimen for analysis (drive/attempting to drive)	6 months custody	6 months DTO	No	No
Taking vehicle without consent (TWOC)	6 months custody	6 months DTO	No	No
Vehicle interference	3 months custody	YRO	No	No

Dishonesty offences	Maximum penalty in law	Maximum penalty in the youth court	Grave crime?	Dangerousness?
Burglary (dwelling)	14 years custody	2 years DTO	Yes	No
Burglary (non dwelling)	10 years custody	2 years DTO	No	No
Handling stolen goods	14 years custody	2 years DTO	Yes	No
Making off without payment	2 years custody	2 years DTO	No	No
Theft	7 years custody	2 years DTO	No	No
Going equipped to steal	3 years custody	2 years DTO	No	No
Obtaining services dishonestly	5 years custody	2 years DTO	No	No

Drug offences	Maximum penalty in law	Maximum penalty in the youth court	Grave crime?	Dangerousness?
Possession of a Class A drug	7 years custody	2 years DTO	No	No
Possession of a Class B drug	5 years custody	2 years DTO	No	No
Possession of a Class C drug	2 years custody	2 years DTO	No	No
Possession of Class A drug with intent to supply	Life	2 years DTO	Yes	No
Possession of Class B drugs with intent to supply	14 years custody	2 years DTO	Yes	No
Possession of Class C drugs with intent to supply	14 years custody	2 years DTO	Yes	No

Drug offences	Maximum penalty in law	Maximum penalty in the youth court	Grave crime?	Dangerousness?
Cultivation of cannabis	5 years custody	2 years DTO	Yes	No

Public Order Act offences	Maximum penalty in law	Maximum penalty in the youth court	Grave crime?	Dangerousness?
Section 5 Disorderly behaviour	Level 3 fine	Fine or YRO	No	No
Racially aggravated Sec 5	Level 4 fine	Fine or RYO	No	No
Section 4	6 months custody	6 months DTO	No	No
Racially aggravated Sec 4	2 years custody	2 years DTO	No	No
Section 4A Disorderly behaviour with intent to cause harassment, alarm or distress	6 months custody	6 months DTO	No	No
Racially aggravated Section 4A	2 years custody	2 years DTO	No	No
Section 3 Affray	3 years custody	2 years DTO	No	No
Section 2 Violent Disorder	5 years custody	2 years DTO	No	Yes

Sex offences	Maximum penalty in law	Maximum penalty in the youth court	Grave crime?	Dangerousness?
Exposure	2 years custody	2 years DTO	No	No
Fail to comply with sex offenders register	5 years custody	2 years DTO	No	No

Possession Indecent Photographs of Children	5 years custody	2 years DTO	No	Yes
Sexual Assaults	Between 7 – 14 years custody	2 years DTO	Yes	Yes
Voyeurism	2 years custody	2 years DTO	No	No

Miscellaneous offences	Maximum penalty in law	Maximum penalty in the youth court	Grave crime?	Dangerousness?
Possession of an Offensive Weapon	5 years custody	2 years DTO	No	No
Possession of a Bladed Article	4 years custody	2 years DTO	No	No
Harassment – putting people in fear of violence	5 years custody	2 years DTO	No	Yes
Harassment (without violence)	6 months custody	6 months DTO	No	No
Breach of Anti Social Behaviour Order	5 years custody	2 years DTO	No	No
Breach of restraining order	5 years custody	2 years DTO	No	No
Witness intimidation	5 years custody	2 years DTO	No	No
Blackmail	14 years custody	2 years DTO	Yes	No
Bomb hoax	7 years custody	2 years DTO	No	No
Perverting the Course of Justice (common law)	Life	2 years DTO	Yes	No
Fail to Surrender to Bail	3 months custody when tried summarily	YRO	No	No

Miscellaneous offences	Maximum penalty in law	Maximum penalty in the youth court	Grave crime?	Dangerousness?
False Imprisonment	Life	2 years DTO	Yes	Yes
Firearm, carrying in a public place	7 years custody (12 months for imitation firearms)	2 year DTO (12 months for imitation firearm)	No	No
Firearm, carrying in a public place – Air Weapon	6 months custody	6 months DTO	No	No

CHAPTER 26
YOUTH COURT SENTENCE

A youth can receive the following sentences:

1. An absolute discharge
2. A conditional discharge
3. A referral order
4. A fine
5. Costs and compensation
6. A reparation order
7. A Youth Rehabilitation Order (YRO)
8. A Detention and Training Order (DTO) (subject to the defendants' age and previous offending history).

A youth cannot receive a suspended sentence order.

A youth cannot be subject to more than one YRO and therefore if your client is already subject to a YRO the court can only impose a YRO for this offence/s if it revokes the existing order and incorporates it into the new order.

Sentence, including the requirements within it, is determined by your client's age and offending history. The table below is an extract from the Youth Court Bench Book (p 53) which is a very helpful overview of youth court sentencing options:

Age next birthday	10–12	14	16	16–17
Absolute discharge	✓	✓	✓	✓
Conditional discharge Note: cannot be imposed if the youth has received a final warning in previous 24 months unless exceptional circumstances are found.	✓	✓	✓	✓

Age next birthday	10–12	14	16	16–17
Referral order Note: **Must** be imposed if first imprisonable offence and the youth pleads guilty and court is not considering a discharge or custody. **May** be imposed if the offence is non-imprisonable or the youth has one previous conviction for which no referral order was imposed or where mixed pleas have been entered. **May** be imposed if the offender has been made the subject of a referral order and it is recommended by the YOT and the court find exceptional circumstances for imposing a second order.	✓	✓	✓	✓
Fines Note: For youths aged 10 – 15 the order must be made against the parent or guardian unless unreasonable in the circumstances.	✓ Maximum £250	✓ Maximum £250	✓ Maximum £250	✓ Maximum £250
Compensation and costs Note: Compensation takes priority over any costs or fines. Costs cannot exceed any fine imposed.	✓	✓	✓	✓
Reparation order Where the court has the power to impose a reparation order but does not do so, reasons must be given.	✓	✓	✓	✓
YRO ** see table below for requirements	✓	✓	✓	✓
DTO	✗ Aged 10–11 ✓ Aged 12–13	✓ If deemed a persistent offender	✓	✓

**YRO requirements table

	10–13 years old	14 years old	15 years old	16–17 years old
1. Activity requirement	✓ Max. 90 days	✓ Max. 90 days	✓ Max. 90 days	✓ Max. 90 days
2. Attendance centre requirement	✓ Aged 10–13 at date of conviction Max 12 hours	✓ Aged 14 at date of conviction Max 12–24 hours	✓ Aged 15 at date of conviction Max 12–24 hours	✓ Aged 16+ at date of conviction Max 12–36 hours
3. Curfew requirement	✓ Max 6 months	✓ Max 6 months	✓ Max 6 months	✓ Max 6 months
4. Drug testing requirement	✓ Offender must consent	✓ Offender must consent	✓ Offender must consent	✓ Offender must consent
5. Drug treatment requirement	✓ Must be recommended and the offender must consent	✓ Must be recommended and the offender must consent	✓ Must be recommended and the offender must consent	✓ Must be recommended and the offender must consent
6. Education requirement	✓	✓	✓ Not any period after offender has ceased to be compulsory school age	✓ Not any period after offender has ceased to be compulsory school age
7. Exclusion requirement	✓ Max 3 months	✓ Max 3 months	✓ Max 3 months	✓ Max 3 months
8. Intoxicating substance treatment requirement	✓ Must be recommended and the offender must consent	✓ Must be recommended and the offender must consent	✓ Must be recommended and the offender must consent	✓ Must be recommended and the offender must consent

9. Local authority residence requirement	✓ Max 6 months	✓ Max 6 months	✓ Max 6 months	✓ Max 6 months. Not any period after offender reached 18.
10. Mental health treatment requirement	✓ Court must have medical evidence and the offender must consent	✓ Court must have medical evidence and the offender must consent	✓ Court must have medical evidence and the offender must consent	✓ Court must have medical evidence and the offender must consent
11. Programme requirement	✓ Must be recommended	✓ Must be recommended	✓ Must be recommended	✓ Must be recommended
12. Prohibited activity requirement	✓	✓	✓	✓
13. Residence requirement	✗	✗	✗	✓ Aged 16+ at date of conviction
14. Supervision requirement	✓	✓	✓	✓
15. Unpaid work requirement	✗	✗	✗	✓ 40–240 hours

PREPARATION FOR THE SENTENCING HEARING

In order to prepare for a sentence hearing, in addition to the mainstream texts, it is essential that you read The Sentencing Guidelines Council – Overarching Principles – Sentencing Youths. It is also recommended that you read pages 45 –88 of the Youth Court Bench Book which deals with sentence in great detail.

Youth sentencing is very much based on the individual and not prescribed by the adult guideline for the offence. This means that the way in which you approach your sentence preparation will differ from how you would approach your mitigation for an adult.

In the preparation of your mitigation you should consider the following:

THE AGE AND MATURITY OF YOUR CLIENT

When preparing a youth sentence, your starting point should be your client's age and emotional maturity, for example, whether he has learning difficulties or mental health problems. In most cases you will be able to ascertain this information from your client, his parent or guardian and the YOT. In some cases you will require further evidence, for example, if he has received a statement of special educational needs.

THE SERIOUSNESS OF THE OFFENCE

Then consider the offence itself and the seriousness of it. In order to assess the seriousness of the offence the court must assess your client's culpability within the offence and the harm he has caused by the commission of it. There are four levels of culpability starting at 1 in terms of seriousness:

1. Intention
2. Recklessness
3. Knowledge
4. Negligence

Harm can be towards an individual victim, the community or to society at large. Culpability and harm must be placed in the context of the aggravating and mitigating features of the offence. You must also consider any statutory aggravating features in assessing the seriousness of the offence, including whether:

1. This offence was committed whilst on bail?
2. He has any relevant previous convictions? and/or
3. This offence was racially/religiously aggravated or motivated by victim's presumed or actual disability or sexuality?

Whilst the youth court is not bound by the adult offence specific guidelines it can be guided by them to the limited extent of identifying any aggravating and mitigating features that relate to the offence. Look at the relevant adult guideline to enable you to address the court on any additional offence related mitigating features or indeed to identify any aggravating features of it. It is also worth bearing in mind what the starting point sentence for an adult offender convicted of the same offence would be, so that you can tailor your mitigation down from the starting point bearing in mind that a youth should not be dealt with more severely than an adult. You must however consider this is in the context of the SGC Overarching Principles – Sentencing Youths which takes precedence over any other guideline and the court is bound by it. Where a specific offence youth guideline exists i.e. for Robbery you must refer to that guideline in your preparation and mitigation but be aware that the starting point is based on a 17 year old and therefore if your client is 16 or under and not at risk of custody, you should ask the court to reduce the starting point based on the youth guideline. If your client is at risk of custody and custody is unavoidable, also look at the adult guidelines and apply the appropriate reduction (see below for clients at risk of custody).

YOUR CLIENT'S RISK OF FURTHER OFFENDING AND RISK OF FURTHER HARM/HIS VULNERABILITY

Consider your client's risk of further offending and risk of further harm by him caused by the commission of further offending. This is very important for youths. The principle aim of youth justice is to prevent further offending so whilst punishment is of course relevant and must be proportionate to the offence, it must be in the context of reducing the risk of re-offending bearing in mind the welfare of your client. Once you have obtained a copy of the pre-sentence report (or spoken to a representative from the YOT following a verbal report), assess whether your client is vulnerable and look at the risk assessment contained within it to ascertain whether your client is of low, medium or high risk of re-offending and his assessed level of risk of future harm (this is called the ASSET tool). These are all relevant factors to consider within your mitigation and will impact on the type, level and intensity of the sentence imposed by the justices. If your client is already subject to an order, speak to the YOT and find out how he is responding to it. If for example, he is subject to an order which is in its infancy then you have an argument that it has not yet had the chance to take effect and therefore the court does not necessarily need to make it more onerous in order to reduce the risk of further offending. In that case you would hope to persuade to persuade the magistrates to revoke the current order and impose a new one in precisely the same terms as the old one. Conversely if your client has been subject to it for some time and despite that, is still committing further offences, the risk of further offences on the face of it is higher and more intensive supervision/intervention *may* be appropriate.

HIS PREVIOUS CONVICTIONS AND RESPONSE TO PREVIOUS ORDERS

Consider next your client's antecedent history and his response to any previous court orders. If your client is under 15, consider whether on the basis of his previous convictions he is a persistent offender, which is whether he has been convicted of or received a reprimand/final warning/conditional caution for three imprisonable offences in the preceding 12 months. Consider whether he is eligible for a conditional discharge or a referral order and if on paper he is not, whether any exceptional circumstances exist which could allow the court to exercise their discretion to impose one. Just because your client was dealt with in a certain way for his last offence does not automatically mean that the court will have to deal with him more severely on this occasion.

HIS PERSONAL MITIGATION

Consider next your client's personal mitigation. Establish whether he has any learning difficulties, mental health difficulties, substance misuse issues and his family circumstances. If there is a specific sentence that you are trying to persuade the court to impose, his personal mitigation can be an effective way of doing so.

However, when making submissions regarding the defendant's personal mitigation, in particular difficult family circumstances, try to avoid making the mitigation sounding like a sob story. District Judges are likely to remind you of the thousands of young people who have less than ideal family situations who do not resort to anti-social behaviour and petty crime.

CREDIT FOR GUILTY PLEA (IF APPLICABLE)

Consider as always the appropriate level of reduction for a guilty plea if applicable and any ancillary orders that the court could impose.

CLIENT AT RISK OF CUSTODY

If, taking into account all of the above, you feel your client is at risk of custody remember that there are prescribed lengths of DTO – 4, 6, 8, 10, 12, 18 or 24 months. Unless the court is ordering consecutive DTOs it cannot make a DTO of any other length. Remember also in your submissions that custody should only be used as a measure of last resort. Where you think your client is at real risk of receiving a DTO a good argument against its imposition is to ask the magistrates to instead consider a YRO with Intensive Supervision or fostering (if available in your area). This is a direct alternative to custody and is only available if the custody threshold is passed. If the magistrates are not persuaded by this submission, they must give reasons as to why not. Youth benches are reluctant to send all but the most serious or persistent offenders into custody so the custody threshold is higher for youths than for adults. If the court in dealing with an adult for the same offence would impose a custodial sentence of less than four months then a DTO should not be imposed. Where there are no youth specific guidelines for the offence, depending on the age and maturity of your client, consider your submissions on length of sentence.

The Sentencing Council Guidelines – Overarching Principles – Sentencing Youths gives the following guidance at page 24, para 11.16:

- **Where the offender is aged 15, 16 or 17,** the court will need to consider the maturity of the offender as well as chronological age. Where there is no offence specific guideline, it may be appropriate, depending on maturity, to consider a starting point from <u>half to three quarters of that which would have been identified for an adult offender</u>.

  The closer an offender was to age 18 when the offence was committed and the greater maturity of the offender or sophistication of the offence, the closer the starting point is likely to be to that appropriate for an adult. Some offenders will be extremely mature, more so than some offenders who are over 18, whilst others will be significantly less mature.

  For younger offenders, greater flexibility will be required to reflect the potentially wide range of culpability.

  Where an offence shows considerable planning or sophistication, a court may need to adjust the approach upwards.

  Where the offender is particularly immature, the court may need to adjust the approach downwards.

- **Where the offender is 14 or less,** sentence should normally be imposed in a youth court ... sentence will normally be shorter than for an offender ages 15–17 convicted of the same offence.

To give an example of how this works in practice:

ABH. Offence involves a kick to the victim whilst on the ground causing minimal injury.	
Defendant is 16, but very immature and mixes with friends of 13 and 14.	
Starting point:	26 weeks custody
Reduction of 50% due to immaturity	(–13 weeks)
Appropriate length of sentence	**13 weeks**
(Therefore DTO not an available sentence)	
NB: reduction in sentence for guilty plea is calculated once the appropriate starting point has been established.	
Appropriate starting point	13 weeks
Credit for early guilty plea	4.3 weeks
Sentence	8.7 weeks

To use the same circumstances as above but a maturity appropriate 16 year old:

Starting point	26 weeks
Reduction of 25% for age	(–6.5 weeks)
Appropriate length of sentence	19.5 weeks
Appropriate DTO	4 months
But if pleaded guilty first opp.	
Credit for early guilty plea	(–6.5 weeks)
Appropriate length of sentence	13 weeks
Therefore DTO not available	

If your client has been remanded in custody for the offence (or subject to a qualifying curfew) you must remember to ask the court to take this into account when determining the appropriate sentence. Unlike adult offenders the court cannot reduce the sentence to reflect the days spent in custody once the period of imprisonment has been determined.

Youths are likely to agree to any suggested sentence that will avoid a custodial sentence but always remember your responsibility of not allowing any sentence to be imposed that is plainly unworkable. Be bold enough to make this submission to the court when you have to.

ADVISING YOUR CLIENT ON SENTENCE

As for adults be realistic with your client about what sentence he is likely to receive and this in the cases of youths is easier said than done. To have to advise a frightened child and his distraught parents that he is likely to be receive a DTO is an unpleasant part of the profession but one you must come to terms with. Try to be sensitive to age and immaturity, even more so if there are real concerns about the defendant's ability to cope in a custodial environment.

When faced with the prospect of an immediate custodial term, the showy bravado displayed by your client to his group of waiting friends on his arrival at court will disappear and you will be left with a crying, terrified child. So, take all the time that is needed to explain and advise on every aspect of the hearing, the likely outcome and what happens after he has been sentenced. His parents may require further explanation regarding visiting and conditions in Young Offenders Institutions so take the time to explain the details to them. A little reassurance from a lawyer can sometimes go a long way.

As with any pre-hearing advice, but in particular with youths, never finish the conference until you are satisfied that the defendant and his family understand the implications of any sentence.

In terms of the information that you will need from your client (or additionally from a parent or guardian), take instructions on the following where applicable:

1. The offence including the circumstances of it and why he committed it
2. His attitude to his offence
3. His age
4. His family circumstances including any problems within it
5. If he is in care, the background to that and how many different placements he has lived in
6. His educational background
7. Whether he has any learning difficulties and is so, details of any help that he is receiving regarding this
8. Whether he has any behavioural difficulties and if so, details of any intervention regarding it by external agencies, i.e. a child psychologist
9. Whether he has any mental health problems and if so, details of any intervention regarding it by external agencies
10. Whether he has any substance misuse issues
11. Any extracurricular activities he takes part in
12. His ambitions for the future
13. His antecedent history
14. The reasons if any for any previous breaches of court orders
15. If he is currently subject to an order, obtain details about how often he is attending supervision etc and how well he is engaging
16. His ability to comply with the proposed sentence
17. Any other information that may be relevant to the specific circumstances of your client

Remember to warn your client that the magistrates or District Judge will address him directly and help him by giving him some guidance about how he should respond. Children and young people find speaking in public very difficult and in the environment of a courtroom his nerves and anxiety will get worse so if you fear a certain reaction, whether that to be surliness, a nervous laughter or complete silence, speak to the defendant about what is expected. If you have real concerns that he will not cope with any dialogue with the bench, do not be afraid to raise those concerns with the justices in a bid to draw the sting from any perceived disrespect shown by the defendant to the court.

Finally if your client is aged 17, remember to complete a means form with him.

THE COURT HEARING

Whilst the provisions relating to the youth sentence are very different to that which relate to adults, the hearing itself is very similar and you are therefore recommended to read earlier chapters in that respect. The Criminal Procedure

218

rules apply which means that the expectation is that if your client is pleading guilty, most cases should be concluded in the same day.

Unless the court is dealing with, a mandatory referral order i.e. the first one for an imprisonable offence, a financial penalty or a conditional discharge the starting point is that a pre-sentence report (whether verbal or written) will be required by the YOT before the court decides upon sentence. The exception to this is where a recent pre-sentence report is available or the YOT is able to do a verbal update to the court about your client's compliance with his current order and make their sentence recommendation based on that.

As with adults, you must address the court in mitigation before a pre-sentence report is ordered in terms of the nature and type of report that is appropriate. Unless a DTO is a real prospect always remember to ask the magistrates to rule out custody.

The main difference is that as part of the sentencing exercise the magistrates will talk directly to your client and their parent and guardian and this will take place after your mitigation and before the justices retire to consider their decision.

APPENDIX 1 FIRST COURT ATTENDANCE RECORD

Client's name:	F/E:				
File number:	Pros:				
Date:	Clerk:				
Court:	DJ/Lay bench:				
Prep:	Waiting:				
Travel: Miles: Parking:	Attendance:				
	Client	CPS	Clerk	Bail	Wit
Hearing:	Hearing code:				

OFFENCES PLEA MOT	APPLICATIONS

CLIENT ATT Y/N

Legal aid granted y/n

ATTENDANCE ON PROS/LEGAL AID/CLERK

_____

_____

_____

_____

ATTENDANCE CLIENT

What you have advised client re charge(s)/what prosecution have to prove?

_____

_____

_____

_____

What are client's instructions?

_____

_____

_____

_____

What is your advice to client on strength/weakness of evidence?

_____

_____

_____

_____

What is your advice to client on plea? G/NG

In ALL CASES confirm you have advised re credit for a guilty plea? Y

What is client's decision on plea?

Have you checked pre-cons with client? Y/NA

Have you advised re bad character if applicable? If so, what?

_____

_____

_____

_____

What have you advised re mode of trial if applicable?

_____

_____

_____

_____

What is client's decision re mode of trial if applicable?

_____

If not guilty have you advised client trial may proceed in absence? Y/N

If client admitted offence but disputes prosecution facts, have you advised re Newton hearing/basis of plea? Y/N

If summary trial – have you completed the case management form? Y/N

What have you advised re likely sentence if convicted?

_____

_____

_____

IS THE MATTER EITHER WAY AND HAVE THE MAGISTRATES ACCEPTED JURISDICTION? Y/N

IF MAGS DECLINE JURISDICTION HAVE YOU COMPLETED FORM LAC1 FOR SIGNATURE BY THE LEGAL ADVISER? Y/N

OUTCOME

_____

_____

_____

_____

_____

NEXT DATE: _____ COURT: _____
TIME: _____

NEED CLIENT ATTEND Y/N

BAIL CONDITIONS/OTHER COMMENTS

_____

_____

_____

ACTION:

(1) Diary noted re next court date?

(2) Appointment offered to client? Y/N

(3) Letter written to client confirming above events?

(4) Authority to write to third party, e.g. expert/parent?

(5) Any other...list below:

APPENDIX 2   YOUTH COURT – FIRST HEARING ATTENDANCE RECORD

Client's name:	F/E:
File number:	Pros:
Date:	Clerk:
Court:	DJ/Lay bench:
Prep:	Waiting:
Travel: Miles: Parking:	Attendance:

Client	CPS	Clerk	Bail	Wit

Hearing:	Hearing code:

OFFENCES PLEA MOT	APPLICATIONS

CLIENT ATT Y/N

Legal aid granted y/n

ATTENDANCE ON PROS/LEGAL AID/CLERK/YOT/PARENT OR GUARDIAN

_____

_____

_____

_____

ATTENDANCE CLIENT

What you have advised client re charge(s)/what prosecution have to prove?

_____

_____

_____

_____

What are client's instructions?

_____

_____

_____

_____

What is your advice to client on strength/weakness of evidence?

_____

_____

_____

_____

What is your advice to client on plea? G/NG

In ALL CASES confirm you have advised re credit for a guilty plea? Y

What is client's decision on plea?

Have you checked pre-cons with client? Y/NA

Have you advised re bad character if applicable? If so, what?

_____

_____

_____

_____

Is the offence a grave crime or a specified offence? Y/N

If Y what have you advised client about venue?

_____

_____

_____

If not guilty have you advised client trial may proceed in absence? Y/N

If client admitted offence but disputes prosecution facts, have you advised re Newton hearing/basis of plea? Y/N

If youth court trial – have you completed the case management form? Y/N

What have you advised re likely sentence if convicted?

_____

_____

_____

IF MAGS DECLINE JURISDICTION HAVE YOU COMPLETED FORM LAC1 FOR SIGNATURE BY THE LEGAL ADVISER? Y/N

OUTCOME

_____

_____

_____

_____

_____

NEXT DATE: _____ COURT: _____
TIME: _____

NEED CLIENT ATTEND Y/N

BAIL CONDITIONS/OTHER COMMENTS

_____

_____

_____

ACTION:

(6)   Diary noted re next court date?

(7)   Appointment offered to client? Y/N

(8)   Letter written to client confirming above events?

(9)   Authority to write to third party, e.g. expert/parent?

(10)   Any other...list below:

APPENDIX 3   ADULT SENTENCING HEARING COURT ATTENDANCE RECORD

Client's name:	F/E:				
File number:	Pros:				
Date:	Clerk:				
Court:	DJ/Lay bench:				
Prep:	Waiting:				
Travel: Miles: Parking:	Attendance:				
	Client	CPS	Clerk	Bail	Wit
Hearing:	Hearing code:				

CLIENT ATT Y/N

PREPARATION

1. Have you considered Magistrates' Court sentencing guidelines/SC guidelines? Y/N
2. Any relevant case law? Y/N
3. Is it a specified offence? Y/N
4. Aggravating features of the offence:
5. Mitigating features of the offence:
6. Personal mitigating features:
7. Is client good character? Y/N
8. If not good character, length of time between this and other offending?
9. Length of time between offence and sentence?
10. Is employment at risk depending on sentence imposed? Do you have evidence? Y/N
11. Have you advised about likely sentence? Y/N
12. Has your client completed a means form? Y/N
13. Is compensation an issue? (have pros provided proof?) Y/N
14. Is fine or discharge appropriate? Y/N (remind magistrates sentencers must consider all of the disposals available within or below the threshold at the time of sentence and reject them before reaching the provisional

decision to make community sentence and that even where the threshold for a community sentence has been passed, a fine or discharge may still be appropriate i.e. if inexpedient to impose any further penalty)

15. Is a community order appropriate? Y/N
16. Is offence seriousness likely to require a low, medium or high range?
17. What type of community order is likely to be most suitable for the offender AND commensurate with the seriousness of the offence? If two or more requirements, are they compatible?
18. Is client in custody? Y/N
19. If so, work out how long client has spent on remand and ask for days to count.
20. Is a deferred sentence appropriate? Y/N
21. If custody threshold is passed, can it be suspended? Y/N

ATTENDANCE ON PROS/PROBATION/LEGAL ADVISER

_____

_____

_____

_____

ATTENDANCE ON CLIENT

Have you checked his previous convictions with him?

If applicable, what if any community orders is he willing/able to comply with?

_____

_____

_____

_____

_____

_____

_____

WHAT IS YOUR ADVICE TO CLIENT ON LIKELY SENTENCE/ ANCILLARY ORDERS

_____

_____

_____

_____

HEARING

_____

_____

_____

_____

_____

_____

_____

_____

_____

_____

APPEAL?

What advice have you given on appeal? What are client's views on appeal?

Confirm you have advised client 21 days to appeal.

_____

_____

ACTION:

1 Outcome letter to client including advice on appeal

2 File for billing/back to instructing solicitor

3 Notice of appeal if appealing

APPENDIX 4   GLOSSARY OF TERMS FREQUENTLY USED BY LAWYERS

ABE – Achieving best evidence

ADI/AI – Advanced information

AG-REF – If this is at the beginning of an authority, it refers to an appeal by the Crown against an unduly lenient sentence

ANPR – Automated number plate recognition.

ASBO – Anti social behaviour order

ATV – Application to vacate

Beaks – Magistrates

Bilking – To leave without paying, generally only used in reference to non-payment of petrol.

Carve – The defendant pleads guilty on the day of trial to one or some of the charges he faces as an acceptable disposal to the case

Chair of the bench (chair) – Only relates to lay magistrates and is the magistrate who sits in the centre and who speaks on behalf of the bench.

Clerk – Legal adviser

Concurrent sentence – Both sentences will run at the same time

Consecutive sentence – Two sentences that run one after the other

CPN – Community psychiatric nurse

CPO – Case progression officer

CPR – Criminal Procedure Rules.

Crack – The case does not proceed to trial due to the defendant pleading guilty on the first day of trial

CRASBO – Criminal anti-social behaviour order

DCS – Defence case statement

DJ – District Judge

DPP – Director of Public Prosecutions

DWP – Department of Work and Pensions

EBTI – Evidential breath test instrument

Either way offence – A case that can be dealt with by either the Magistrates' Court or the Crown Court.

Exceptional hardship – Application to reduce the length of disqualification from driving or to not disqualify at all used in totting cases.

FME – Forensic medical examiner

Going down – Going to prison.

Going up the road/upstairs – The case is going to the Crown Court.

Grave crime – Refers to Youths and is a crime that in the case of an adult has a maximum sentence of 14 years or more

Half time submission – Submission of no case to answer during a trial

HMRC – Her majesties' revenue and customs

IDPC – Initial details of the prosecution case (more commonly known as advanced information)

Indictable only – Can only be dealt with by the Crown Court. For example, rape.

IOJ – Interests of justice

JR – Judicial review

LJA – Local justice area

LSC – Legal services commission

M.O – Modus operandi. The way someone commits a crime.

NCT – National courts team

Newton Hearing – Trial within a guilty plea to establish extent of guilt

NFA – No fixed abode OR no further action

OIC – Officer in the case

On his toes – On the run

On his feet – Used to describe an advocate who is making submissions

OTD – Other than dwelling

PCMH – Plea and case management hearing

Potted – Sent to prison

Pre-cons – Previous convictions

Previous – Previous convictions

Prima facie – On the face of it

Produced – Client being produced from custody

PSR – Pre-sentence report

PTR – Pre-trial review

PWI/PWIT – Possession with intent to supply

Read out committal – Contested committal hearing

RIC – Remanded in custody

Runner – A defence that has a chance of succeeding

S6(1) committal – Contested committal hearing

S6(2) committal – Defendant consents to his case being committed to the crown Court

SC – Sentencing Council

Section 9 – Agreed statement to be read to the court (if in relation to CJA 1988)

Section 10 – Agreed admissions between prosecution and defence (if in relation to CJA 1967)

Section 36 – Direction prohibiting defendant cross-examining named witnesses (if in relation to YJCEA 1999)

Section 38 – Direction appointing a solicitor to conduct the cross examination (if in relation to YJCEA 1999)

Section 39 – Direction prohibiting details of a child witness being published by the press

Section 76 – Application to exclude a confession (PACE 1984)

Section 78 – Application to exclude evidence (PACE 1984)

Sending – Case sent to the Crown Court for trial

SGC – Sentence Guidelines Council

SMS – Substance misuse service

SOCA – Serious Organised Crime Agency

SOCO – Scenes of crimes officer

SOPO – Sexual offences prevention order

Special reasons – Application not to endorse the driving licence with details of the offence

SSO – Suspended sentence order

Stipe/stipendiary – Previous title for the office of District Judge

Summary only offence – Can only be dealt with by the Magistrates' Court. For example, common assault. In some instances a summary offence can be added to an indictment.

TDA – Taking and driving away (also See TWOC)

Three striker – Refers to third dwelling burglary or drug trafficking offence (includes PWI) being indictable only.

Totter – A defendant who has accrued more than 12 penalty points within a three year period

TWOC – Taking without consent

Voir Dire – Trial within a trial (usually to determine a discreet issue, such as admissibility of evidence)

Wingers – The magistrate/s who sits to the left or the right of the chair.

YOI – Young offenders institute

YOS/YOT – Youth offending service/youth offending team

YRO – Youth rehabilitation order

3545487R00139

Printed in Great Britain
by Amazon.co.uk, Ltd.,
Marston Gate.